THE 'OLD OLIGARCH':

THE *CONSTITUTION OF THE ATHENIANS*

ARIS & PHILLIPS CLASSICAL TEXTS

THE OLD OLIGARCH

The Constitution of the Athenians

Attributed to Xenophon

Edited with an introduction, translation and commentary by

J. L. Marr & P. J. Rhodes

Aris & Phillips is an imprint of Oxbow Books

First published in the United Kingdom in 2008. Reprinted 2014, 2015 by
OXBOW BOOKS
10 Hythe Bridge Street, Oxford OX1 2EW

and in the United States by
OXBOW BOOKS
908 Darby Road, Havertown, PA 19083

© The authors J. L. Marr & P. J. Rhodes

Paperback Edition: ISBN 978-0-85668-781-5

A CIP record for this book is available from the British Library

For a complete list of Aris & Phillips titles, please contact:

UNITED KINGDOM
Oxbow Books
Telephone (01865) 241249
Fax (01865) 794449
Email: oxbow@oxbowbooks.com
www.oxbowbooks.com

UNITED STATES OF AMERICA
Oxbow Books
Telephone (800) 791-9354
Fax (610) 853-9146
Email: queries@casemateacademic.com
www.casemateacademic.com/oxbow

Oxbow Books is part of the Casemate Group

Printed and bound by CPI Group (UK) Ltd, Croydon, CR0 4YY

In memory
of our friend
PETER DEROW

CONTENTS

PREFACE

Work on this edition was begun by John Marr. He showed drafts to P. J. R., and after his retirement from the University of Exeter in 2004 he invited P. J. R. to join him in finishing it. We have discussed the work on various occasions, by meeting and by correspondence, and this final version was produced by P. J. R. in the light of and as the agreed result of our discussions. We accept joint responsibility for the Greek text and the English translation and for the various opinions and interpretations offered in the book.

We thank Dr. Kelly Joss and the University of St. Andrews for permission to make use of the thesis cited on p. 76; and P. J. R. thanks Prof. Robin Osborne for showing him in advance of publication a draft of his revised *LACTOR* edition of the Old Oligarch. Above all we thank Aris & Phillips for originally agreeing to publish this book, and Oxbow Books as successors to Aris & Phillips for waiting patiently and for publishing it now.

Two works of particular relevance have been published since our material was sent to the publisher. V. J. Gray (ed.), *Xenophon on Government* (CUP, 2007), contains the Greek text of and commentary on the *Constitution of the Athenians*, together with Xenophon's *Hiero* and *Constitution of the Lacedaemonians*: her interests are more literary than historical, and she inclines to a date before the Peloponnesian War for the treatise. A. Keen and N. Sekunda, 'Xenophon the Rhetor' in N. Sekunda (ed.), *Corolla Cosmo Rodewald* (Foundation for the Development of Gdańsk University, 2007), 25–38, rely on the assignment of the treatise in some manuscripts to 'Xenophon the Rhetor', take him to be an otherwise unknown Xenophon who associated with Socrates, and suggest that he wrote it soon after the battle of Delium (424 B.C.) as a captive in Boeotia. We stand by the opinions expressed in this book.

Exeter   J. L. M.
Durham   P. J. R.

REFERENCES

Abbreviations for ancient authors and their works (though for most works we give the title more fully), and for some standard modern works, follow the usage of the third edition of the *Oxford Classical Dictionary*; by analogy with the *OCD*'s ML we use RO to denote P. J. Rhodes and R. Osborne, *Greek Historical Inscriptions, 404–323 B.C.* (OUP, 2003). Abbreviations for periodicals follow the usage of *L'Année Philologique* with the usual anglophone modification (using *AJP* etc. where *L'Année Philologique* uses *AJPh* etc.). Works listed in the Select Bibliography on pp. 33–4 are cited by author's name only, with date added when necessary to distinguish between two works by the same author.

INTRODUCTION

1. The name 'Old Oligarch'

This expression does not occur in the text, and it is not used by any ancient writers or critics. In modern scholarship it is used mainly by English-language scholars. It is more rarely employed by continental scholars, who commonly refer to the author as 'Pseudo-Xenophon' (*e.g.* de Romilly). This designation is based on two considerations:

(*a*) in the surviving manuscripts this work is always placed among the works of Xenophon, and we know that it was so grouped in antiquity; but

(*b*) the authorship was disputed by some ancient scholars (see section 4, below), and it is now thought by nearly all modern critics not to be a genuine work of Xenophon.

The expression 'Old Oligarch' seems to have first occurred in print in Gilbert Murray's *A History of Ancient Greek Literature* of 1897 (London: Heinemann; pp. 167–9). The expression is put in inverted commas at its first occurrence, which perhaps suggests that the sobriquet was current in the academic conversation of Murray's day, but had not previously appeared in scholarly print. Whatever the expression's date of origin, the adjective 'old' in the designation was almost certainly not intended to characterise the age of the author. It may have had a scholarly function, with reference to the date of the author's treatise, *i.e.*, he is an 'old' oligarch in the sense that he is fairly certainly writing before oligarchy was ever established in practice as a form of government in Athens (briefly replacing democracy in 411–410, and again in 404–403). However, it is more likely that 'old' has an emotional force, characterising and emphasising the author's apparent extremity of viewpoint (*cf.* 'old Tory', 'old Bolshie' – 'old Labour' does not yet quite have the same connotation!).

The expression 'Old Oligarch' is a neat and handy one, especially since the author, if he is not Xenophon, is unknown. Hence its widespread current use, at least amongst English-language scholars (so, *e.g.*, Gomme, Fuks, Hornblower, cited in our Select Bibliography). Efforts to put a stop to the usage would be a waste of time. But the sobriquet is misleading, on two counts:

(*a*) the author is almost certainly a young man (perhaps very young)
  – see section 4, below, on the authorship of the treatise.

(*b*) though he is opposed to the Athenian democracy by instinct and
  background, his arguments are not those of a conventional oligarch.
  On the contrary, throughout the treatise he imagines himself to
  be arguing against those who hold conventional anti-democratic
  views, and whose criticisms of the democracy he regards as naïve
  and misplaced (see section 5, below, on the audience, and section
  6, on the nature of the author's argument).

For convenience we have chosen (following Gomme) to refer to the author
as 'X'. This simply denotes unknown identity; it is not an abbreviation for
'Xenophon'. On balance, we tend to agree with the now standard view that
Xenophon was not the author of this work. The arguments for this position,
however, need to be examined, since they are by no means as self-evident
or conclusive as some scholars assume (*e.g.* Frisch, 41; Bowersock [1968],
461; Moore, 19). See section 4, below.

2. The title of the work

The title *Constitution of the Athenians* (*Athenaion Politeia*) is also
misleading, if by that one is led to think of an objective, or supposedly
objective, constitutional history and comprehensive institutional survey
of Athens (such as we have in the Aristotelian *Athenaion Politeia,* a work
written in the 330s and revised in the 320s). The coincidence of title does
nothing to dispel confusion on this point. Probably the title given in the
manuscripts to X's work has simply been taken from the first five words of
the opening sentence, almost certainly by a later commentator rather than
by the author himself. Whether the work originally had any formal title is
doubtful.

What we actually have is a short work, just three chapters or fifty-three
sections in length, of a markedly argumentative character (hence a 'treatise'),
in which there is no pretence of objectivity. The author forcefully propounds
an unusual, not to say paradoxical, case. This is that, though he himself is
opposed to democracy as a political constitution and ideology, the criticisms
which are frequently made against the Athenian democracy by its opponents
elsewhere in the Greek world are naïve and misplaced. For X the Athenian
democracy has a carefully thought-out set of policies and practices, which

are all designed to buttress the system, and to further the interests of those who run it, *i.e.* the *demos* (for X this means the lower classes, and particularly the urban lower classes: see section 7, below). What is more, in X's view, the system works well, it is extremely successful in doing what it sets out to do.

It is evident from the most cursory reading of the work that, despite the implication of the title, X is not a constitutional historian. In fact his work contains almost nothing in the way of historical or institutional details, *i.e.* dates, names, facts. On the contrary, he seems to go out of his way to avoid such material, preferring instead to generalise and theorise at every turn. One effect of the extremely high degree of generalisation and marked absence of factual detail is to make it difficult for scholars to date the work on the basis of internal indications (see section 3, below, on the date).

This feature also distinguishes X's work from other argumentative political pamphlets of the late fifth and fourth centuries, such as [Andoc.] IV. *Against Alcibiades* and, probably, the 'Theramenes papyrus', P. Michigan 5982, which seems to contain part of a defence of the controversial Theramenes written early in the fourth century by an author who knew Lysias XII. *Eratosthenes* and XIII. *Agoratus* (publication by R. Merkelbach and H. C. Youtie, 'Ein Michigan-Papyrus über Theramenes', *ZPE* 2 [1968], 161–9; see the discussions of A. Henrichs, 'Zur Interpretation des Michigan-Papyrus über Theramenes', *ZPE* 3 [1969], 101–8, A. Andrewes, 'Lysias and the Theramenes Papyrus', *ZPE* 6 [1970], 35–8). These are essentially literary exercises, which, while not contemporary with the situations and issues which they deal with, contain (unlike X's treatise) much specific factual and personal detail. Apparently more similar to X's work was another pamphlet critical of Athens' democracy (which perhaps provides the earliest attested instance of the noun *demagogos*), of the late fifth century, of which a fragment survives in *P. Heid.* 182 (discussed by M. Gigante, 'Un nuovo frammento politico', *Maia* 9 [1957], 68–74).

3. The date of the work

There is no external evidence for the date of this work. It is not quoted or even referred to by any extant writer before Diogenes Laertius, of the early third century A.D. As we shall see (section 4, below), the Alexandrian scholars mostly assigned it to Xenophon's authorship, but they do not seem to have had any view as to whether it was an early, middle or late work of Xenophon. In attempting to date it, therefore, we are wholly reliant on internal indications. The treatise makes virtually no explicit reference to clearly identifed events or individuals. All we can do is to use the internal material to try to establish (*a*) the *terminus post quem*, the date after which the work must have been written, and (*b*) the *terminus ante quem*, the date before which it must have been written. If these chronological parameters can be established, then we can at least identify the period within which the work was composed.

The objective of (*a*) is to identify datable events or actions which are being referred to, or alluded to, by the author. The treatise must obviously be later than the date of such events. However, this is not such a straightforward procedure as it sounds. The problem is that X's treatise is composed almost entirely of generalised and theoretical assertions. There is a striking absence of factual detail. Very few historical events, and no historical individuals, are mentioned in it (see p. 27, below). Nevertheless, on occasions, a strong case, if not a conclusive one, can he made that this or that generalisation is based on a particular attested historical event, that there is a kernel of known fact which underlies it. If that event can be securely dated, then it follows that the treatise must have been written after that date.

The object of (*b*) is to identify datable historical events which contradict the author's thesis. The inference then is that he could not have written this or that passage after such and such an event had occurred. The treatise must therefore be earlier than the date of these events. But this is a less reliable approach than the former one. X is not an objective historian or impartial political commentator. He has, *e.g.*, a demonstrable fondness for gross exaggeration and forced contrasts, and the highly subjective and tendentious character of the work is evident throughout. We must not assume that he could not, or did not, proffer any generalised assertions or theories on political, economic, or strategic matters, unless they were fully supported by all the facts at his disposal. Thus, if a datable event or activity seems to falsify his hypothesis at any point, we cannot conclude *ipso facto* that the treatise must have been written before that event or activity. Even less are we entitled to infer that, on the unique occasion when he does refer directly to some identifiable historical events to illustrate his point (at 3.11: see commentary *ad loc.*), the fact that he does not mention certain other events of a similar type proves that the treatise must have been written before the date of these other events.

There are a number of passages in the treatise which have been thought to carry implications for the question of its date. The most important and most often discussed of these are 1.15, 2.1, 2,4, 5, 13, 14–16, 17, 18, 3.2, 5, 10, 11. These passages and their dating implications are considered and analysed in detail in the commentary.

Dates proposed have ranged widely, from the 440's (particularly because there is nothing later than 443 among the allusions in 3.11: *e.g.* Bowersock) to the fourth century: see our survey of proposed datings on p. 31–2. However, despite the dangers in arguments about the *terminus ante quem* which we mention above, nearly all scholars have judged the work to be earlier than the first overthrow of the democracy, in 411, and indeed before the replacement of the Delian League's tribute with a harbour tax, in 413 (2.1, 3.2, 5, contr. Thuc. VII. 28.4). More specifically, the cumulative weight of evidence provided by the above (and other) passages points, in our view and in the view of many scholars, overwhelmingly to a date for X's treatise between 431 and 424. Almost certainly the treatise belongs to the period 425–424, after the Athenian capture of Pylos in 425 (Thuc. IV. 2–6, 8–23, 26–41), which is surely alluded to in 2.13, and perhaps after the performance of Aristophanes' *Knights* in early 424 (see 2.18 and pp. 131–5, below), but very probably before Brasidas' overland march to Thrace in summer 424 (IV. 75–83), an event which strikingly disproves what is said in 2.5, and the battle of Delium in autumn 424 (IV. 89–101), when the Athenians were caught unprepared and did fight and lose a hoplite battle against the enemy (*cf.* 2.1). The fighting at Megara (IV. 66–74) which immediately preceded Brasidas' march could be alluded to in 2.15, but there were earlier episodes which could lie behind that passage, such as the Theban attack on Plataea in 431 (Thuc. II. 2–6). Similarly, the reference in 2.17 to the *demos'* denial of responsibility 'if anything bad results from the *demos'* policies' could allude to the reaction in 424 after Athens' generals in Sicily acquiesced in a treaty and agreed to withdraw (Thuc. IV. 58–65), but again X could have earlier episodes in mind.

There seems to be an underlying assumption in much of chapter 2 of the treatise that the Athenians are currently at war, and successfully so, and it is possible to see several allusions to the Peloponnesian War as it was fought between 431 and 424, whereas we see nothing which requires a later date and some statements which it is hard to think were made or could be made after 424 (2.5, 14–16). Similarities of expression between Thucydides and X, we believe, show not that either was aware of the other, but only that both were products of the same intellectual background in late-fifth-century Athens (see 1.19–20, 2.2, 14–16 and notes).

The unqualified success which Athens is currently enjoying thanks to its naval power, and the mood of self-confidence and optimism which that success is engendering in the Athenian lower classes (who provide the manpower and know-how for the navy), is the underlying contemporary reality behind all the arguments, assertions, and theories in X's treatise. He does not like the phenomenon, but he understands it, respects it, perhaps even in a grudging way admires it. Exactly this situation, one of virtually total military success, and certainly boundless public optimism, is the one depicted by Thucydides as prevailing in Athens in the early summer of 424 (IV. 65.4). This was the high point of Athenian success during the Archidamian War. Subsequently things went significantly, though not disastrously, awry. Thucydides' words are worth quoting:

> *Such was the effect on the Athenians of their present good fortune that they thought that nothing could go wrong for them; that the possible and the more difficult were equally attainable, whether the forces they employed were large or rather inadequate. It was their surprising success in most areas which caused this state of mind, forming a strong basis for their hopes.*

One important consequence of our suggested date for the treatise (indeed, of any date before 420) is that this work becomes the earliest surviving example of a literary text in Attic prose, and the earliest prose critique of Athenian democracy. Hence interesting comparisons can be made with critical passages in the contemporary political comedies of Aristophanes, *Acharnians*, *Knights* and *Wasps* (Osborne, 10, has some useful comments on this aspect of the treatise). We can also compare it with some passages in two contemporary tragedies of Euripides, *Suppliants* and *Electra* (*cf*. pp. 23–4, 25–6, below).

4. The authorship of the work

Writing in the early third century A.D., Diogenes Laertius (II. 57) supplies a full list of the works of Xenophon, starting with the *Anabasis*. At the end of the list, after the *Agesilaus*, he refers to a '*Constitution of the Athenians and Lacedaemonians*, which Demetrius of Magnesia says is not by Xenophon' (Ἀθηναίων καὶ Λακεδαιμονίων Πολιτείαν – ἥν φησιν οὐκ εἶναι Ξενοφῶντος ὁ Μάγνης Δημήτριος). It would appear then that Demetrius (a writer of the first century B.C.) denied Xenophon's authorship of a work, which the singular ἥν and the use and position of the connecting words (first καὶ, then just ἥν) in this reference indicate was regarded in antiquity as a single book, just like the *Agesilaus*. The two *Constitutions,* short pieces of just 15 (Sparta) and 3 (Athens) chapters respectively, were thought of as constituting a single book, with, probably, the Lacedaemonian coming first and the Athenian second, despite Diogenes' order (see note on 1.1), since that is the order in which they appear in all the surviving manuscripts, where the *Constitution of the Athenians* follows immediately after the *Constitution of the Lacedaemonians*.

Furthermore, the implication of Diogenes' comment is that the *Constitution of the Athenians* was generally regarded in the first century B.C. as being by Xenophon (no doubt this tradition was established by the Alexandrian scholars of the third century B.C.), and that, although this was disputed by Demetrius (or rather, although he denied Xenophon's authorship of what was then viewed as a single combined book), his challenge was not regarded by scholars as decisive. This interpretation is confirmed by the fact that grammarians of the period (and subsequently) quote from the *Constitution of the Athenians*, and refer to its author as Xenophon. Pollux (second century A.D.) quotes 2.10 (Poll. VII. 167 and IX. 43), Stobaeus (fifth century A.D.) quotes 1.14 and 2.20 (Stob. XLIII. 50, 51).

Modern scholars rightly regard the two *Constitutions* as separate works, and they almost unanimously follow Demetrius in denying Xenophon's authorship of the *Constitution of the Athenians*, though not in denying his authorship of the *Constitution of the Lacedaemonians*, which is now generally thought to be a genuine work of Xenophon (*e.g.* by Bowersock [1968], Ollier; Chrimes is an exception).

This prevailing view is based on two main grounds, style and chronology; but beneath these arguments one suspects there lurks another reason, which is much less often made explicit. Most scholars do not *want* Xenophon to be the author of the *Constitution of the Athenians*. The mature Xenophon of the early fourth century was a fine soldier and military commander, and a cultured and respectable country gentleman. As an author, though not an original thinker, he was an accomplished purveyor of easy-to-read narrative and popular philosophy. X, by contrast, is stylistically awkward, intellectually muddled, politically extreme, and morally unprincipled. How then could Xenophon be X, or X be Xenophon? Xenophon does not dazzle modern critics, but his general worthiness is seldom questioned. X, on the other hand, puzzles and intrigues, but he has few, if any, admirers. His sobriquet, the 'Old Oligarch', is not, and was not, meant to be, an affectionate or flattering one (see section 1, above, on the name).

In actual fact, there is nothing in what little we know of Xenophon's early life down to 401, *i.e.* his political associations and his family background and connexions, which would make it obviously impossible for him during that period to have been the author of such a partisan treatise. On the contrary, it is clear that Xenophon was a knight (*hippeus*), a member of the wealthy élite who in war formed the Athenian cavalry, and in that capacity he served with the forces of the Spartan-backed Thirty, led by the oligarchic fanatic Critias (see note on 1.9), throughout their civil war against the democrats in 404 and 403 (see, *e.g.*, Anderson, 47–60 – a remarkable example of a whitewashing narrative, in which, although the facts about what the knights did during the civil war are admitted, a series of excuses and claims about the 'shame' which Xenophon 'must have felt' is propounded, without any basis of evidence).

Because of the uncertainty about his date of birth (below), we do not know when Xenophon formally began service as a knight, though it would naturally be at the age of 18 (Dexileos died in battle as a cavalryman in 394/3 at the age of twenty: RO 7. *B*). It should be noted that, even in the 420's, there were doubts about the constitutional loyalty of the Athenian knights, and strong public suspicions of their 'laconising' affectations (*cf.* Ar. *Knights* 580, 1121, *Wasps* 466, 475–6, *Birds* 1281–2); and that, correspondingly, an admiration of all things Spartan was a characteristic of Xenophon throughout most of his life. The fact that the author of the treatise seems to envisage his immediate 'audience', the opponents he is arguing with, as primarily Spartan (see section 5, below, on the author and his audience) would certainly be entirely consistent with a Xenophontic authorship of the work. However much scholars do not want Xenophon to be X, it cannot be ruled out on grounds of political standpoint.

Arguments about authorship based on stylistic criteria should always be treated with caution. Certainly the style of the treatise is rough, with many obscurities of meaning and harsh ellipses, the structural arrangement is weak, the connection of thought between sections often unclear, and the vocabulary is limited and repetitive. These are not features of most of the other works attributed to, and accepted as genuinely by, Xenophon, a writer whose smooth simplicity of style, clarity of expression, and wide and varied vocabulary, are justifiably admired characteristics.

However, we must be careful to compare like with like. All the other works attributed to Xenophon which we possess were written in the first half of the fourth century, when Xenophon was a mature man (see later on

Xenophon's date of birth), who had developed a mature prose style. We would naturally expect them to share many stylistic features in common, as they do. But this treatise is a much earlier composition, certainly written many years before anything else we have which is attributed to Xenophon (see section 3, above, on the date). If it had been written by Xenophon as a very young man, we should not, and ought not to, expect it to display the mature stylistic qualities which are demonstrated in these much later productions.

That being said, it may be instructive to take a closer look at the *Constitution of the Lacedaemonians* (text and translation can be found in the Loeb volume of Xenophon's *Scripta Minora*, 136–89). When was this work written? E. C. Marchant in the Introduction to the volume (1925; retained in the 1968 revision), p. xxii, argued that chapter 14 was a later addition, written in the early 370s, but that the rest of the work belongs to an earlier period, the 380s or even possibly the 390's. Chrimes, rejecting Xenophon's authorship, argued that the whole work including chapter 14 was written in the mid 390s (17–22). Recently N. Humble has defended chapter 14 as an integral part of the work and has argued that it cannot be dated more precisely than 394–371 ('The Author, Date and Purpose of Chapter 14 of the *Lakedaimoniôn Politeia*', in Tuplin, 215–28). In any case it seems clear that it is one of the earliest, if not the earliest, of Xenophon's extant works. It appears for the most part to be the work of a confident writer, employing a practised, periodic style. But it is not as smooth-flowing and lucid as Xenophon's subsequent works. The order and arrangement of topics is not perfect. After the first, coherent, section (chs. 1–10), the topics thereafter have seemed to many to be tacked on as a series of appendixes (see Marchant, xxi–xxii, but contrast the defence of the work's coherence by Humble). This less than satisfactory structural arrangement is reminiscent, albeit to a lesser extent, of the poor arrangement and obscure connexionsof thought between topics which characterise the *Constitution of the Athenians*.

There are some other noticeable stylistic features which the two works have in common, viz. (*a*) self-reference; (*b*) generalised 'you' or 'one'; (*c*) programmatic statements and summaries; (*d*) the imagined interlocutor. In Xenophon's *Constitution of the Lacedaemonians* self-reference occurs at 1.1, 2.1, 8, 12, 5.9, 8.1, 5, 9.6, 10.1, 13.8, 14.1; generalised 'you' or 'one' at 1.10, 2.10, 3.5, 5.9, 9.1, 11.1, 12.7, 13.5, 14.1; programmatic statements and summaries at 1.3, 14, 2.1, 14, 5.1, 11.1, 12.1, 13.1, 15.1; and the imagined interlocutor at 2.8 and 14.1.

These stylistic traits are all common features in X's treatise. For self-reference in X see Frisch, 88–9; there are 28 examples. Generalised 'you' or 'one' occurs at 1.8–9, 10, 11 (twice), 3.3, 13. Programmatic statements and summaries occur at 1.1, 2, 3.1, 8–9. For the imagined interlocutor in X see section 5 and Appendix 1, below. There are at least twenty examples in the treatise.

It is thus apparent that in fact the two works do have a range of stylistic features in common. These similarities, reinforcing the apparent similarity of theme, were surely recognised by ancient scholars, and probably explain why they coupled the two *Constitutions* into a single work, with Xenophon as its author. On the criterion of style, although the differences between the two works are still considerable, it is certainly not inconceivable that the author of the *Constitution of the Lacedaemonians* was also, as a young man, many years earlier, the author of the *Constitution of the Athenians.*

The second main grounds on which scholars deny Xenophon's authorship of the treatise are chronological. The case here is stronger, though not totally conclusive. It is argued that, given a date for the treatise in the mid 420's (which we should accept: see section 3, above), Xenophon cannot have written it, since at that date he was a mere child. But Xenophon's dates are not clear-cut. Although most scholars tend to follow the view of Anderson (10), that Xenophon was born 'a little after 430', E. Badian, 'Xenophon the Athenian', in Tuplin, 33–53 esp. 38–40, stresses how insecure the evidence is.

For Xenophon's birth date Diogenes Laertius (II. 55) gives no evidence. He says merely that Xenophon 'was at his peak' (ἤκμαζε) in the fourth year of the ninety-fourth Olympiad, *i.e.* 401/0. Anderson (9) takes this as a reference to 'his most famous exploit', *i.e.* the march of the 10,000 in support of Cyrus, which took place in 401, and which Diogenes proceeds to mention in his next sentence (Xenophon uses the verb of himself, in a different sense, in *Anabasis* III. 1.25). In Anderson's view this comment has no value for determining the date of Xenophon's birth. He argues that Xenophon was about 30 in 401, on the basis of his well-attested friendship with one Proxenus of Thebes, who had persuaded Xenophon to join the expedition (*Anabasis* III. 1. 4–10) Proxenus was one of a number of generals killed by the Persians, as a result of treachery on the part of the satrap Tissaphernes (*Anabasis* II. 5.31–6.1). Xenophon says that, at the time of his death, Proxenus was 'about 30' (*Anabasis* II. 6.20), *i.e.* he was born about 431. Anderson (9) argues that Xenophon 'seems to have been rather younger than his friend Proxenus.' In support of this conclusion he adduces *Anabasis* III. 1.14, a passage in which

Xenophon describes how he finally decided to offer himself as the army's commander, after the deaths of Proxenus and the other leaders. For a while he had hesitated, thinking that he might not be considered old enough (*cf.* also III. 1.25, cited above). But this is not a conclusive argument. Proxenus seems to have been a special case. The other four generals killed with him were older (two were 35, one was 50, the other was somewhere in between). Xenophon's doubts about himself may have been based on his comparative lack of experience of command (before then he had no official position in the expeditionary force, *cf.* III. 1.4), as much as his actual age.

Diogenes (II. 56) does tell us the date of Xenophon's death: 'according to Stesiclides of Athens, he died in the first year of the 105th Olympiad, in the archonship of Callidemides', *i.e.* 360/59. In fact this is certainly wrong, since a reference to Tisiphonus of Pherae shows him to be alive later than that (*Hellenica* VI. 4.37). His *Ways and Means* (*Poroi*) was probably written after Athens' Social War of 356–355, and his death occurred probably in the late 350's (Anderson, 193, 198, dates it 'after 356'). But Diogenes adds the further detail, that 'he died at Corinth, as is stated by Demetrius of Magnesia, obviously by then at a well-advanced age (τέθνηκε δ' ἐν Κορίνθῳ, ὥς φησι Δημήτριος ὁ Μάγνης, ἤδη δηλαδὴ γηραιὸς ἱκανῶς).' To call attention in this way to Xenophon's old age at the time of his death suggests that Diogenes, or, more likely, his source Demetrius, from whom the added comment probably comes, thought of him as being more than, say, seventy years old.

The verb ἀκμάζειν, 'to be at one's peak (*akme*)', is sometimes used with reference to the subject's fortieth year (the scheme used by the chronographer Apollodorus, of the second century B.C.), and, though the context suggests that Diogenes himself is not using it in that sense at II. 55, it is possible that that was how the word was used by his ultimate source for the 401/0 references (for Diogenes' dependence on sources in his use of ἀκμάζειν *cf.* II. 59). But we do not know how reliable that source was.

What other indications are there? Strabo, writing in the late first century B.C., says that Socrates rescued Xenophon when he had fallen off his horse at the battle of Delium in 424 (403 / IX. 1.7); the story is also narrated by Diogenes in his life of Socrates (II. 22–3). If true, this would certainly put Xenophon's date of birth in the 440's, but the story is probably historically worthless, merely a confusion of Xenophon with Alcibiades, who, in the original version of the story, is said to have protected the retreating Socrates at Delium (Pl. *Symposium* 221a, Plut. *Alcibiades* 7.4). We do not know the basis for the claim in [Lucian], *Makrobioi* 21, that Xenophon lived to be over ninety; or, pointing in the other direction, for Athenaeus' claim (V. 216d) that Xenophon was too young to have participated in the *Symposium* of which he wrote, for which the dramatic date is *c.* 422/1.

A more interesting divergent detail is found in the early third century A.D. writer, Philostratus (*Lives of the Sophists* I. 12), to the effect that Xenophon was a prisoner of war in Boeotia, but got himself released on bail, so that he could attend the lectures of Prodicus. If true, it would imply that Xenophon was born some time before 430, since by far the most likely time for the capture to have happened is 412, when the Boeotians seized the Athenian frontier post at Oropus, together with its garrison (Thuc. VIII. 60.1), and Xenophon is unlikely to have been sent on active service in an exposed front-line position at the tender age of eighteen. But again we do not know how reliable Philostratus is in this story.

We conclude that Xenophon could have been born somewhat before 430, but that the insecure evidence does not justify confidence in his being born in 440 or earlier. A precocious person might conceivably have written a pamphlet of this kind in his mid teens: all the indications are that the author of the treatise *was* a young man (*cf.* section 5, below); and Alcibiades seems to have been one of Socrates' pupils when he was a teenager (*cf.* Plat. *Protagoras* 309a–b, with a dramatic date in the 430's). But how likely is it that Xenophon would have kept this youthful essay, when he produced none of his other published works until several decades later, after he had left Athens first to go on Cyrus' military campaign in Asia and after that to go into exile in the Peloponnese?

We do not know what grounds the Alexandrian scholars of the third century B.C. had for assigning the work to Xenophon. There are absolutely no internal indications of authorship. They must have had what they thought was acceptable evidence, but that may have been no more than a perceived similarity between the *Constitution of the Lacedaemonians* which was not that of Aristotle's school and the *Constitution of the Athenians* which also was not that of Aristotle's school.

All things considered, it seems that, if our date for the *Constitution of the Athenians* is right, Xenophontic authorship is highly unlikely, though the opinions expressed are opinions which the young Xenophon could certainly have held and there are some stylistic affinities with his *Constitution of the Lacedaemonians*.

5. The author and his immediate audience

Throughout his work X envisages himself as engaging directly in a sort of running argument with a group of critics, opponents, interlocutors. The views of these postulated opponents are constantly anticipated, referred to, or cited, and on each occasion X proceeds at once to answer the imagined objection. This occurs on some twenty or more occasions throughout the short work. Without a full appreciation of this pervasive thematic and structural feature, X's treatise simply cannot be properly understood, let alone used as a historical source (for details see Appendix 1).

The author's opponents seem to be envisaged as actually present (*cf.* 3.1, 6) as he argues his case, and this 'agonal' setting, with X apparently trying to convince an immediate 'audience', gives his work a certain liveliness and spontaneity, whatever one might think about its style and argumentation. But who are these opponents (sometimes referred to in the singular, sometimes in the plural) supposed to be? They are not democrats. None of the string of arguments anticipated, referred to, or quoted by X is pro-democratic. On the contrary, his opponents are, just like himself, hostile to contemporary Athenian democracy. What then is the nature of the disagreement between X and his 'opponents'? Their criticisms are essentially criticisms of particular (and to them obnoxious) features and practices, of the democratic constitution. X does not deny these practices exist; he accepts that they do, and for the most part he shares his opponents' antipathy to them in themselves. But he argues that all the particular features objected to by his opponents are essential elements of the democratic constitution as a whole. They are deliberately there, since they all serve the purpose of strengthening that constitution, and they cannot be changed, or rectified, or removed, without undermining and destroying that constitution as a whole (*cf.* 3.8). In X's view the Athenian constitution can certainly be improved (by changing or removing some or all of these objectionable features), but in that case it will become something which is no longer a democracy (see section 6, below, on the argument).

X himself is an Athenian. Mattingly thinks otherwise, but this seems certain (note the decisive first person plurals at 1.12, 2.11–12). But where do his opponents come from? It seems clear that they are not envisaged as being themselves Athenian. There are several passages where X strongly implies that his imagined interlocutors, his immediate audience, in contrast to himself, do not understand all the details of how things work at Athens, or are used to practices which are different from those of Athens, and there is a very clear indication in the introductory, programmatic section that his 'opponents' are envisaged as other, *i.e.* non-Athenian, Greeks ('the rest of the Greeks think that they act mistakenly': 1.1).

Although these assumed foreign interlocutors are oligarchs in the sense that they are presented as objecting to many features of the Athenian democracy, they are not necessarily to be thought of as simply oligarchs of wealth (*i.e.* men who believed that power should be exclusively in the hands of a small number of the richest citizens). A number of passages in the treatise (*e.g.* 1.8–9, 10, 11–12, 2.17–18, 3.11–12; see commentary *ad locc.*) suggest that X thinks of them primarily as Spartans, who naturally do not like the present Athenian constitution, democracy in its most radical form, and would prefer something much more restricted, but not necessarily a narrow oligarchy of wealth. After all, Sparta itself was not an oligarchy of wealth, and the *demos* of Spartiate citizens was in some areas the sovereign body of state.

But where are we to understand the 'debate' between X and his interlocutors as taking place? Where is X at the time of writing? It has sometimes been suggested that he is in exile (this is the view of, *e.g.*, Frisch, 92–9; *cf.* D. M. Lewis, *CR* n.s.19 [1969], 46). Much has been made of X's use of the word αὐτόθι ('in the place') to refer to Athens. It is indeed true that X always uses the word αὐτόθι rather than the more explicit ἐνθάδε ('here') to refer to Athens (seven times: at 1.2, 10 [twice], 11, 13, 3.1, 6). But neither does X use the word ἐκεῖ ('there' as opposed to 'here') to refer to Athens, though that is what we might expect if author and audience were in fact somewhere else.

The word αὐτόθι does not mean simply 'there'. Like αὐτοῦ, it adds emphasis and calls attention ('right here', 'just there'), and it is often used of some thing or place that has already been mentioned. So its use would be quite appropriate in a theoretical, academic composition concerned with the politics of a particular state, even if the work were actually being composed and delivered within that state. In our opinion, this is precisely the kind of composition that this work is (see later in this section). In fact, on five occasions (1.10 [twice], 11, 13, 3.1) αὐτόθι is used in the imagined objections of a supposed non-Athenian interlocutor (see section 5, below) rather than when X is speaking for himself. In exactly the same way X frequently (see Appendix 5) uses the expression Ἀθήνησι ('at Athens'), and Athens is referred to as 'the *polis*' (occurring first at 1.2), simply by virtue of the fact that it is the main subject of X's thesis, as is made clear in 1.1.

Apart from the (invalid) argument based on the frequent use of αὐτόθι, the only passage in the work which might lend support to the view that it was composed by someone in exile is 2.20. In this passage the interpretation of the word οἰκεῖν is crucial. The context shows that here it cannot mean simply 'inhabit' but means 'be politically active in' (see commentary *ad loc.*), and therefore need not imply that the author is outside Athens.

There is in fact no good reason to doubt that the work was written in Athens, by an Athenian. But it is not a speech or a pamphlet designed to have any practical effect in the real, public, world of Athenian politics. It would not cut any ice on the hustings or in the lawcourts, since it is far too theoretical and generalised. It reads much more like an academic composition, a lecture or paper, a classroom orator's exercise (see note on ἀποδείξω, 'I shall demonstrate', on p. 61 and compare ἐπέδειξα, 'I have explained', at 3.1), on a topic which has been set for X by his teacher or tutor: 'Your next assignment is to write and deliver a paper defending the Athenian democratic constitution against the sort of objections you would expect to be levelled against it by the Spartans and their allies, but [and here is the sophist's twist] defend it not on the basis of democratic ideology, but by applying the political theory you have just learned, that *all governments, whatever their complexion, govern by pursuing policies which will benefit themselves*' (see section 6, below, on the argument). In this interpretation we are influenced by the suggestion of Forrest (1975, 43–5) that X's treatise might have been a response to a treatise written from that Spartan viewpoint – but by another student of the sophists in Athens rather than an actual Spartan.

What can we say about X's age? Despite the sobriquet 'Old Oligarch', he is surely not old, but young, perhaps very young. The immaturity of his style, the obscurity and incoherence of parts of the argumentation, the abrupt transitions from topic to topic, all betray a pupil who still has much to learn from his tutor in terms of rhetorical skills and intellectual analysis. Add to that the combative tone, the frequent self-assertion, the constant close verbal repetition, the fondness for exaggeration and forced contrasts, the obsessive generalisation – all these are characteristic indications of youthful authorship.

Finally, can we conclude that X really was an oligarch, or was he just assuming the role for the purpose of the exercise he had been set? That question cannot be definitively answered. In response to the view of David Stockton, who challenges the traditional sobriquet (*The Classical Athenian Democracy*

[OUP, 1997], 169), one can only record a strong impression that, beneath the superior tone towards conventional anti-democratic critics and the sophisticated pose of moral relativism (see section 6, below), there is a genuinely-felt class hatred, which reveals itself very clearly in class terminology at, *e.g.*, 1.5, 9, 2.17, 20 (see sections 7 and 8, below, for more details). X seems steeped in instinctive, old-fashioned class prejudice, taken presumably from the circle of his family and their friends, though he is only at an early stage of giving it an intellectual and rhetorical underpinning. Whether X continued to maintain these prejudices when he grew up, and was in a position to engage with, and have an effect on, the real world, is another matter. Others of his generation certainly did, and their moment came after the disastrous defeat in Sicily in 413. One of the principal interests of X's treatise is the light it sheds on the adolescent views and formative thinking of certain upper-class Athenians, who were later to involve themselves in actively undermining and overthrowing the democratic constitution (in 411 and 404). In the mid 420s such people were a small minority of political no-hopers (see section 7, below), but everything changed after 413. We speculate in the note on 2.20 that X may have been a pupil of the orator and sophist, Antiphon, a man who took a leading role in the oligarchic revolution of 411.

6. The author's argument: the self-interest theory

A division of constitutions into three kinds – monarchy = the rule of one, oligarchy = the rule of a few and democracy = the rule of the many – is first found in Pindar, *Pythian Odes* 2.87–8 (of 477–467), and by the later fifth century it had become standard in Greek political thought. It is the basis of the constitutional debate (implausibly attributed to the Persians in the 520s) recorded by Herodotus (III. 80–2). There was fierce argument as to which was the best (*e.g.* this passage in Hdt., Eur. *Suppliants* 403–55, Thuc. VI. 39), and it became common to make a distinction between 'good' and 'bad' versions of each of the three kinds: the good rulers ruled according to the laws and in the interests of all, the bad ruled in defiance of the laws and in the interests of themselves. This distinction is well established in the fourth century (*e.g.* Pl. *Statesman* 291d–292a, Arist. *Politics* III. 1279a–b), but the germ of it can be seen in Herodotus, writing in the 440s–420s (see III. 82).

However, not everyone accepted this conventional moral evaluation. The sophists, the intellectuals and teachers who were active in Greece in the late fifth century, were fond of the contrast between *physis* ('nature') and *nomos* (a word often used to denote 'law', but in this context 'convention'): some things are as they are by nature, and therefore could not be otherwise, but others are as they are merely by convention, human decision, and could have been decided differently (*e.g.* Antiphon 87ᴮ 4 DK). One possible application of this contrast was to the form of government, and it could be argued that there is no 'natural' right way of governing a state, but by 'convention' different states are governed in different ways, and by 'nature' different groups of men will aim for a particular form of government that promotes their own particular group interests, and they cannot be blamed for doing so (see for instance Lysias XXV. *Defence Against a Charge of Subverting the Democracy*, esp. 7–13; also Thrasymachus in Plato's *Republic* (I. 336b–354b, especially 338c–339a, 343c) and Callicles in his *Gorgias* (481b–527e, especially 483b–484c, 488b, 490a, 491c–d). It is against this background that we should see X's analysis of the nature of Athenian democracy: he is heavily influenced by this theory of self-interest.

As we have seen, most of the structure of the treatise consists of a series of imagined criticisms of Athenian democracy by others, which X replies to, point by point. His replies, however, are not a defence of the system, based on the ideology of democracy, such as, *e.g.*, Pericles might have given. Time and again X accepts that the criticism is accurate, that the objectionable practice does indeed occur. But he maintains that all the practices referred to are essential elements of the system as a whole, which is carefully and deliberately designed to further the self-interest of the Athenian *demos*, and which is extremely successful and effective in doing so. It delivers the goods perfectly, doing exactly what it is supposed to do. Any changes therefore, such as reform or removal of any of the features discussed, will have the effect of weakening the system as a whole, undermining its cohesion and effectiveness, thus fatally damaging it. A 'reformed' democracy, as implied by the views of his opponents, is thus, according to X, unworkable: it is a contradiction in terms (*cf.* 3.8–9).

Thus X's argument is not based on traditional aristocratic or oligarchic ideology, but, while taking for granted the aristocratic / oligarchic view that democracy is a bad form of government, he replies that, although it is bad in principle, it is appropriate to and effective in Athens because it is a system through which the ruling *demos* successfully pursues its own self-interest.

It is not that X disagrees with his assumed interlocutors' disapproval of the various features of the democratic constitution which are discussed. He, too, disapproves of these features, just as he disapproves of the system as a whole (1.1, 3.1). The difference is that, in X's opinion, his interlocutors' viewpoint is naïve and shallow. This, incidentally, is a prime indication of sophistic influence on X. It seems to have been characteristic of some of the early sophists to dismiss opposing views, especially traditional ones, as naïve and simple-minded – a trait caricatured in Ar. *Clouds* (of 423), in the portrayal first of Socrates, and then of Pheidippides, and their arrogant and condescending treatment of Strepsiades (note especially lines 814–76, 1321–1475).

His own analysis is, in his opinion, much more profound and realistic. It is based on an alleged universally applicable theory of self-interest (*cf.* above). Each social group, or rather each class (X's picture of Athenian society is profoundly class-based: see section 7, below) will naturally and inevitably look to its own self-interest. If it is in power, if it rules (as the *demos* rules at Athens), it will naturally pursue policies and practices which are designed to further its own economic and political self-interest. For X this is a universal law of human nature and society, which one just has to accept (*cf.* 2.20). The *oligoi*, his own class (see section 7, below), would do exactly the same thing if they were in power. If they ruled, they would 'enslave' the *demos* (1.9). This is not a traditional aristocratic / oligarchic view: that view can be seen, *e.g.*, in the argument attributed to Megabyxus in Herodotus' Persian debate (III. 81), that 'the best men will naturally produce the best policy' (*i.e.* the best for the state as a whole). Thus, through his replies to the imagined criticisms, X not only explains, but to some extent justifies, the way in which the contemporary Athenian democracy functions (*cf.* 1.2, 2.20).

The upshot of all this is that, in X's view, the democratic constitution cannot be 'reformed' (as his interlocutors naïvely suppose it can be) by the removal or moderation of the various practices they object to. The whole system is carefully and deliberately organised to be what it is, in every particular. Any changes in any particular will have the effect of weakening the system as a whole, indeed of undermining it fatally. Piecemeal reform of the democracy is simply not an option. That conviction underlies everything X says in his treatise.

For a modern version of the view that Athens' democracy was indeed dominated by the *demos* see J. Ober, *Mass and Elite in Democratic Athens* (Princeton UP, 1989), who argues (approvingly) that the *demos* prescribed the rules and the élite politicians had to perform in accordance with those rules.

7. *The two-fold class division: the* demos *versus the* oligoi

In X's treatise the word *demos* occurs over forty times, almost always as a political term in the restricted sense of 'the lower class' (see Appendix 2 for details). For X 'democracy' is always rule by the poor (majority) over the rich (minority), in their own self-interest (which X interprets primarily, though not exclusively, as economic self-interest). Various qualities and characteristics are ascribed by him to the *demos*. All are reprehensible, and, by contrast, their opposites are ascribed to his own class – the *oligoi* (see Appendix 3 for details).

This restricted and partisan sense of *demos* is the one which is standard in the fourth-century political theorists, Plato and Aristotle, but it goes back well before that. In an interesting passage of his *Life of Pericles* (11.3), Plutarch tells us that it was during the political rivalry between Pericles and Thucydides son of Melesias, *i.e.* in the 440s, that an open political division between the Athenian citizens developed, and it was at this time that the two groups came to be called respectively the *demos* and the *oligoi* (the 'few').

Plutarch does not name his source for what he says here. It may be that it was indeed in the 440s that the word *oligoi* acquired specific political connotations: 'the class of the rich few'. But there is no evidence that this Thucydides, any more than his predecessor, relative and political role model, Cimon ([Arist.] *Ath. Pol.* 28.2), was an oligarch, in the sense that he wanted to see the democratic constitution abolished in favour of rule by a small group, 'the few': on the difference between the aristocrats of the mid fifth century and the oligarchs of the late fifth century see P. J. Rhodes, 'Oligarchs in Athens', in R. Brock and S. Hodkinson (eds), *Alternatives to Athens* (OUP, 2000), 119–36 at 126–31. As for the word *demos*, *pace* Plutarch, even in the time of Homer it could be used to denote the lower orders, as against their leaders and betters (*e.g. Iliad* II. 198), and it was used in exactly this way by the Athenian reformer Solon in the early sixth century (*cf.*, *e.g.*, frs. 5 and 6 West, quoted in [Arist.] *Ath. Pol.* 12.1–2).

Whatever the history of the terms, it is clear that, by the time X wrote his treatise, one aspect of the political and military polarisation of the Greek world between Athens and Sparta was the identification of Athens as democratic and a champion of democracy and of Sparta as oligarchic (in its own, idiosyncratic way) and a champion of oligarchy; and it seems that some wealthy Athenians were using these two terms in a contrasting, highly politicised way, applying them to what they saw, or affected to see, as a fundamental, bi-polar division *within* the citizen body, with their class, the *oligoi*, in fundamental and irreconcilable opposition to the *demos*, the lower orders, and *vice-versa* (*cf.* the use of the terms by the historian Thucydides, *e.g.* in his account of the civil war in Corcyra: notice *demos* >< *oligoi* in III. 74.1–2). In reality, what these disaffected upper-class men disliked, could not stomach, was the fact that they did not have the unfettered freedom to do whatever they wished politically, something which they regarded as their birthright, but instead, like any other Athenian, they had to appeal to, and gain the support of, a majority of the whole citizen body, through a vote in the assembly.

However, this attitude was almost certainly not characteristic of the Athenian upper classes generally (see above). Of course there was a wealthy social élite in late fifth century Athens. It would have been remarkable if there had not been. But the evidence suggests that, at least down to 413 and the disaster in Sicily, the vast majority of such men were loyal to the democratic constitution, were content to operate within its limits, indeed were able to enjoy very successful political careers by utilising the possibilities it afforded. This was demonstrated by, *e.g.*, Cimon, Pericles, Nicias, and even the historian Thucydides. X is simply wrong in his assumption that all, or nearly all (*cf.* 2.19–20), such men were inherently oligarchs, fiercely opposed to the democratic system.

However, X's treatise is evidence that, when he was writing (probably the mid 420s: see section 3, above, on the date) there was in Athens a hard core of anti-democratic irreconcilables. Their political opportunity was to come after the disaster in Sicily in 413. But their stark 'analysis' of contemporary Athenian politics and society was not just oversimplified; it was essentially flawed. It just did not correspond to contemporary reality, a fact which we can see if we examine a little more closely what X actually means when he uses the word *demos*.

We must bear in mind that this restricted sense of the word *demos* was not the only sense that the word could bear in the later fifth century. Earlier Solon, who used *demos* in its restricted sense elsewhere (*cf.* above), had probably used it to refer to the whole citizen body in fr. 36.2 West, quoted in [Arist.] *Ath. Pol.* 12.4. The debate which Herodotus locates in Persia in the 520s (*cf.* above) more probably reflects later-fifth-century Greek views and debate. An opponent of democracy, Megabyxus, does use the word *demos* in its restricted sense and pejoratively (III. 81) = 'the poor, ignorant, masses.' On the other hand, the pro-democracy Otanes claims in effect (though not using the word: III. 80.6) that the *demos* is actually the whole people (ἐν γὰρ τῷ πολλῷ ἔνι τὰ πάντα, translated in the Penguin Herodotus as 'for the state and the people are synonymous terms'). This inclusive and universal sense of *demos* is also the one in which the word is used by Pericles in the Funeral Oration in 430 (Thuc. II. 34–46; note especially II. 37.1), and by the Syracusan democrat Athenagoras in 415 (Thuc. VI. 39.1). The word was also used 'officially' in this sense in Athens in the fifth century and later, as we can see from the standard formula found on large numbers of inscribed decrees, viz. 'It was resolved by the *boule* (council) and by the *demos*' (*i.e.* the citizen body as a whole, through a majority vote in the assembly). For the vast majority of Athenians in this period *demos* meant the whole people, the entire citizen body, and *demokratia* was a system of government based on the principle of a universal franchise, one man, one vote, with policy being determined by majority decisions after open debate. They would simply not have accepted X's assumption that *demos* meant the lower classes only.

Let us return to X. Throughout his treatise he divides the citizen body of Athens into two opposing classes, his own class and the *demos*. But who exactly are the *demos* for X? They are not just those citizens who are not rich. X may not have thought it through consistently, but sometimes, at any rate, his *demos* does not include the hoplites (*cf.* 1.2), *i.e.* (probably) the *zeugitai*, the third lowest of the four property classes attributed to Solon ([Arist.] *Ath. Pol.* 7.3–4, Plutarch *Solon* 18.1–2). It must therefore be limited to the lowest of the four, the *thetes*, the poorest class (interestingly, X never uses this word). And not necessarily even all of them, since it does not appear to include any of the farmers either (*cf.* 2.14), some of whom almost certainly did not qualify as hoplites. The *demos* must therefore simply be the urban poor. However, perhaps because he does not always remember to draw the line here, X takes it for granted that they are in a numerical majority over all other groups (*cf.* 1.4). That is why they can maintain in existence the democratic constitution they favour.

But does this implied thesis, that the urban poor of Athens were the largest single element of the citizen population, correspond to the known facts? No, it does not. It is directly contradicted by the authoritative evidence of Thucydides, who twice states explicitly (II. 14, 16) that in 431 the majority of the Athenian citizens were living in the countryside of Attica, *i.e.*, by strong implication, they were peasant-farmers. This is supported by a comment of Dionysius of Halicarnassus, with reference to a speech delivered by Lysias in 403 (*Essay on Lysias* 32). At that time there had been a proposal that the restored democracy should be one in which only those Athenians who possessed land should have voting rights. Lysias wrote this speech (whose beginning, quoted by Dionysius, is number XXXIV in the Lysianic corpus) for someone who wished to oppose the proposal, and it was in fact defeated. Only that quoted beginning now survives, but Dionysius, who had all of it, tells us in his summary that the proposal, if carried, would have disfranchised 'almost 5000 Athenians'. Given the context, which plays up the threat, we can safely assume that this is a maximum figure. How many adult male citizens were there at the time? Estimates vary; in 431 at the beginning of the war there were perhaps as many as 60,000. These numbers had been much reduced through war and disease by 403, but at a minimum there must still have been some 20,000 in 403, and many think about 30,000. In other words, at most only 25% of the citizen body were landless men. This evidence for Athens in 403 thus supports the statements of Thucydides with reference to Athens in 431. The notion that Athenian politics during the period of democracy were dominated by a landless urban proletariat is a fantasy, whether it is propounded by ancient or by modern writers.

It is thus apparent that X's basic assumptions in his treatise are flawed. Not only does he use the word *demos* in a restricted and pejorative sense, which was not the sense in which it was commonly used by his contemporaries, but he implicitly contradicts himself in his picture of who the *demos* were. On the one hand he assumes throughout that the Athenian *demos* are a majority, who are able, given one man one vote, to maintain themselves in power over the *oligoi*; on the other hand his prejudices present them as merely the urban poor, who, the evidence shows, were not in fact a majority of the citizen population in the later fifth century. On the contrary, they were a small minority.

Most of the farmers of Attica were not part of the wealthy social élite, *i.e.* X's own class, the *oligoi*. In time of war they served mainly as hoplites, the heavy infantry; and it was not the hoplites but the *hippeis*, the cavalrymen, who were the military manifestation of the Athenian upper classes (see, *e.g.*, Ar. *Knights* 242–54). But X cannot afford to accept that any of the farmers of Attica can be members of the *demos* (taking that word in the restricted sense in which he uses it), because that would make it much harder for him to give the word the highly pejorative connotations which he wishes it to have. Yet only if he were to include the farmers in what he regards as the *demos* would he be justified in his constant assumption that the *demos* are the majority of the citizens.

X's rigidly schematic, twofold division of the Athenian citizen body is unlikely to have been an original piece of analysis on his part. It is much more likely that it was a currently fashionable doctrine in the social and intellectual circles in which he moved. Given the nature of late-fifth-century Athenian society, this notion is also unlikely to have been something that was kept secret or private. The Athens of this period was a startlingly open society (a feature for which it is too rarely given much credit), and doubtless this thesis, like a myriad others, went into the melting pot of contemporary public discussion.

In that context, it is interesting that what seems to be a direct and deliberate counter-argument is found in a play of Euripides, the *Suppliants*, a work which is now usually dated to the late 420s, *i.e.* very shortly after X's treatise (see section 3, above) (see the edition of C. Collard [Groningen: Bouma, 1975], i. 10–11; A. M. Bowie in C. B. R. Pelling, ed., *Greek Tragedy and the Historian* [OUP, 1997], 45–56). In the *Suppliants* Theseus, the Athenian king, adopts a distinctly pro-democratic line (rather surprising for a ruler of the legendary period) in an argument (403–55) with an anti-democratic Theban herald, whose terminology (*e.g.* lines 417–25) is very reminiscent of that used by X in his treatise. A little earlier in the play (238–45) Theseus himself propounds a division of the Athenian citizen body (like X), but he divides them into *three*, not two, classes. The rich (ὄλβιοι, 'blessed'), *i.e.* X's class, are dismissed in two lines as 'useless (ἀνωφελεῖς) and always lusting for more'. The poor (οὐχ ἔχοντες καὶ σπανίζοντες βίου, 'having nothing and lacking livelihood') are criticised also, as dangerous, envious, and easily deceived by 'the speeches of worthless champions' (γλώσσαις πονηρῶν προστατῶν φηλούμενοι). However, there is a 'middle' class ([ἐ]ν μέσῳ, 'in the middle'), which for Theseus is thoroughly admirable. This class preserves the city and 'protects the good order which the state has set up' (κόσμον φυλάσσουσ᾽ ὅντιν᾽ ἂν τάξῃ πόλις), *i.e.* it is the backbone of their society.

In other words, for 'Theseus' (and presumably, Euripides), as against X, the *demos* which includes men other than the poor (406–8) is not monolithic, and most of its members are in fact worthy and patriotic citizens. There are admittedly some disgruntled poor citizens, misled by extremists, but, correspondingly, the whole class of the rich, the self-styled *chrestoi* ('valuable': see section 8, below) are the precise opposite of what they claim to be: they are actually useless (as well as being insatiably greedy)!

The coincidence of date, and the anachronistic political content of the

Suppliants, make it difficult to believe there was no intended connection here with contemporary debate, or that 'Theseus' is not deliberately given arguments by Euripides which directly address and take issue with the simplistic and misguided thesis of bi-polar class division on which X's treatise is based.

For the use of *demos* and its cognates, and for the characteristics ascribed to the *demos* and to the *oligoi* in X's treatise, see Appendixes 2 and 3.

8. Class designations and class labels

X uses a variety of terms (usually through a combination of the definite article, singular or plural, and an adjective, to produce a generic noun) to describe or label the two opposing political classes (viz. the *demos* and his own class, the *oligoi*) into which he divides the entire Athenian citizen body (see section 7, above), frequently making a contrast between them.

Sometimes these terms are purely descriptive (type A: *cf.* Appendix 4), *e.g.* 'the rich' (οἱ πλούσιοι) and 'the poor', (οἱ πένητες). But frequently they also contain an evaluative element, either socially (type B) or morally (type C1). Thus δυνάμενος ('able', 'influential') and ὄχλος ('mob') are socially evaluative, and οἱ βελτίους ('the better classes'), and οἱ χείρους ('the inferior classes') are morally evaluative terms. These expressions are frequently placed by X in direct contrast with one another, either singly or often in combinations (*cf.*, *e.g.*, 1.2, 4–5). This is a favourite way for X to indulge his fondness for forced contrasts in his treatise (see sections 6 and 7, above).

Needless to say, those terms indicating a positive evaluation, approval, are always used of his own class, the *oligoi*, and those with a negative evaluation are always used of the *demos*. His most frequent contrast is that between οἱ χρηστοί ('the valuable / good') and οἱ πονηροί ('the worthless / bad'). These two terms are particularly interesting because they contain within themselves both social and moral connotations (type C2), and are, consequently, particularly difficult to translate with a one-word English equivalent which can both function as a political label and preserve the social and moral connotations of the Greek word. We have translated them uniformly as 'the valuable' and 'the worthless', though we are conscious that these English terms do not do complete justice to the nuances of the Greek expressions.

All societies which have social hierarchies (*i.e.* almost all historical societies) have developed terminology of this sort, words which combine a descriptive and an evaluative element, and which can function as social class labels amenable to the prejudices of the dominant class. Thus, from English history, 'the upper classes' and 'the lower classes' are examples of type B terminology, and 'the nobles / nobility' and 'the commons / commoners' are examples of type C.

The use of such loaded terminology has the effect of reinforcing the prejudices and confirming the privileged position of the dominant class, whether public-school-educated English 'gentlemen' or Greek aristocrats of the archaic and classical periods. Such language was used by Greeks from Homer onwards, and in this conceptual area, at least, X is no different from a traditional Greek aristocrat, with views typical of his class. But it is noticeable that in his short treatise he employs a strikingly large and varied number of such terms, and he expects his interlocutors (see section 5, above) to accept as natural his routine employment of this terminology (thereby, surely, indicating a genuinely-held, innate, class prejudice on his part, *i.e.* he really is an oligarch. Indeed, his (to us) excessive, almost obsessive, use of this terminology perhaps suggests a value system under pressure. One characteristic reaction to growing public criticism of a traditional social value system is for its adherents aggressively to repeat its loaded terminology.

Of course, these type C words need not be employed only as class labels. They may be used to indicate straightforward moral evaluation. X sometimes uses these terms, either the adjectives or nouns formed from them, in this non-political way, thus providing himself with a simple, though disingenuous, method by which he can confirm the superiority of his class and the rightness of his views (*e.g.* at 2.19). It becomes difficult to maintain that a χρηστός (= 'socially useful man') can be anything other than χρηστός (= 'valuable, good'), or a πονηρός (= 'toiling, troubled man') anything other than πονηρός (= 'worthless, bad'), and virtually inconceivable that the socially ἀγαθός / βελτίων / ἄριστος man should not be morally good, or the socially κακός / χείρων / κάκιστος should not be morally bad.

Even so, in the ferment of ideas that characterised Athens in the later fifth century these assumptions did not go unchallenged, as we can see, perhaps most strikingly, from another play of Euripides, the *Electra*. This play has sometimes been dated to 413, on the basis of a passage at the end of the play where the Dioscuri, Castor and Polydeuces, say they are going 'to the Sicilian sea, to save ships' (1347–53). This has been taken to be a reference to the famous Sicilian campaign of 415–413, and specifically to the second, reinforcing expedition sent out by the Athenians in 413

(J. D. Denniston in his OUP edition of 1939, pp. xxxiii–xxxix, agreed with that as a generally accepted view). That interpretation was challenged by G. Zuntz (*The Political Plays of Euripides* [Manchester UP, 1955], 64–71), who dated the play to the late 420s; and more recently B. M. W. Knox in the *Cambridge History of Classical Literature*, i (CUP, 1985), 316, includes it among the plays to be dated to the decade 427–417. It is also worth noting that there was an Athenian fleet in Sicilian waters in the period 427–424, and a date either in that period, or when Zuntz suggests, would put the *Electra* chronologically very close to X's treatise (on our dating of it). One of the important themes of this play is the character of Electra's husband, an unnamed peasant (*autourgos*), to whom she had been given in marriage by Clytemnestra, to humiliate her and neutralise her influence. This man is presented throughout the play as a thoroughly admirable character, whose nobility of character is soon recognised by her brother, Orestes; and this leads Orestes, in a famous passage, to muse on what really constitutes a good man (367–85). He attacks traditional views, saying that Electra's peasant husband, despite being of humble origins, and merely 'one of the masses' (ἐν τοῖς . . . πολλοῖς), has turned out to be ἄριστος (382), *i.e.* a man of excellence, one who possesses *arete*. He then very abruptly changes to the second person plural, and rhetorically denounces 'you fools, full of empty theories, who need to learn to judge a man's nobility by his dealings with others and his character' (383–5). This sudden generalising apostrophe is very striking, and it is certainly tempting to see this speech as a direct riposte by Euripides to the traditional aristocratic class terminology employed in the arguments and publications of men such as X, and their arrogant but hollow socio-ethical claims (hence 'empty theorisers'), just as Theseus' social analysis in the *Suppliants* seems to be a direct authorial reply to their simplistic two-fold class division of the citizen body into *oligoi* (good) and *demos* (bad): see section 7, above.

In Appendix 4 we give a list of all the class labels of this sort which appear in X's treatise, together with references to their occurrences in the text.

9. Other stylistic features

The vocabulary of X's treatise is rather limited in range, but some words and expressions feature prominently, and were obviously favoured by him. We identify here his most favoured words and expressions (other than those discussed in sections 7 and 8), and we give a list with references in Appendix 5. It is to be noted that X frequently refers to himself in the first person; he frequently uses words of knowing, deciding and choosing; he frequently uses words of necessity and of possibility. These are all typical of the 'new education' which was being introduced into Athens by the sophists (*cf.* pp. 16–17, above), and which is fiercely satirised in Aristophanes' *Clouds* (of 423).

Close verbal repetition is a very marked stylistic feature of X's work. Again and again we find the same word, or cognate forms of that word, used two, three or more times within the space of a few sentences, often never to be used again. It would not be unfair to describe 'short-term' verbal repetition as the most distinctive feature of X's prose style. Such immaturity of verbal style again suggests youthful authorship, though we must bear in mind that literary prose-writing was still in its infancy when X wrote his treatise (*cf.* section 3, above). The survey in Appendix 6 (not by any means exhaustive) will illustrate the pervasive nature of this feature.

Generalisation is another all-pervasive feature of X's work. Although the treatise purports to offer a political evaluation of one particular state's constitution, *i.e.*, the Athenian democracy and its main characteristics, there is a marked absence (certainly in chapters 1 and 2) of specific, factual, detail: X seems to go out of his way to avoid this sort of material. The survey in Appendix 7 will give some indication of the prominence of this feature. Whatever else he is, X is an obsessive generaliser. Of course, generalisation makes it much easier for X to get away with the two most marked features of his overall argument, exaggeration and simplistic contrasts (see sections 7 and 8, above).

10. Structure

The division of the treatise into chapters (three) and sections (twenty, twenty and thirteen respectively) is due not to X or even to later ancient scholars but to modern editors (the division of Xenophon's longer works into books is ancient, but the earliest edition in which we have found the now-standard chapters and sections is that of E. Wells [Oxford: Sheldonian Theatre, 1690–1703]). The division into three chapters can be misleading, if it suggests that X thought of the first twenty sections of the treatise as having a particular thematic identity, which made them distinct from the next twenty sections, and similarly as between these and the final thirteen sections. For X, 2.1

followed on directly after 1.20, and 3.1 similarly so after 2.20. There are some indications of intended authorial division, *e.g.* in the middle of 3.1 and at the end of 3.9, but they do not correspond to the divisions which we have now.

The arrangement of material throughout the treatise, and the connexion of thought between successive passages, have given rise to much scholarly debate. The transitions often seem very abrupt and the links unclear. Sometimes the connexion is based on a purely verbal, not thematic, link (see, *e.g.*, 1.10 and commentary *ad loc.*), and sometimes there is no discernible link at all. The final four sections (3.10–13) comprise two further points tacked on to the end of the work, despite the fact that the treatise has apparently come to a summarised conclusion at 3.9 (see commentary *ad loc.*). It is clear that the author is lacking in skills in this area, and his poor technical control over composition and transition may be seen as one of many indications of youthful authorship (see section 4, above).

The text

The four principal surviving manuscripts are:

A	(Vaticanus 1950)	15th century
B	(Vaticanus 1335)	late 14th century or early 15th century
C	(Mutinensis 145)	15th century
M	(Marcianus 511)	14th century

The other manuscripts are all derivative from M (see Kalinka; *cf.* Bowersock [1966], 39–40).

The relationship of ABCM is as follows (see Bowersock [1966], 40–4, [1968], 466–9). ABC have a common origin (α) which M does not share. A and B are independent of each other: there was at least one manuscript (β) intermediate between α and AB. In only one instance does C have the obviously right reading against ABM (at 3.1: ἐπειδὴ δ' C: ἐπειδήπερ ABM), and that is an easy conjecture. The variants in C, taken together, show signs of a consistent effort to improve, correct, or complete this difficult text, and it seems that a pedantic interpolator has been at work, but C also has blatant errors which suggest that the intended corrections were not made for the first time in C: hence γ, intermediate between α and C. C is virtually useless except on the rare occasions where it agrees with M against AB (*e.g.* at 3.8: ὀλιγίστας CM, ὀλιγούσας AB). Bowersock assumes an archetype in minuscule script (Ω) for ABCM in which a copyist made the original misreadings of an uncial text (at 2.9, ΚΤΑΣΘΑΙ for the correct ΙΣΤΑΣΘΑΙ; 3.3, ΕΠΕΔΙΔΟΣΑΝ for the correct ΕΤΙ ΕΔΙΔΟΣΑΝ). His *stemma*, in which Greek letters denote postulated manuscripts no longer surviving, is therefore:

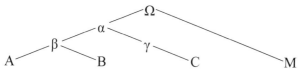

Although all the surviving manuscripts are comparatively late, quotations in Pollux' *Onomasticon* (late 2nd century A.D.) of 2.10 (Poll. *Onom.* VII. 167, IX. 43), and in Stobaeus' *Florilegium* (late 5th century A.D.) of 1.14 (Stob. *Flor.* XLIII. 50) and 2.20 (Stob. *Flor.* XLIII. 51) confirm the manuscript tradition we now have: *e.g.* at 1.14 Stobaeus confirms the apparently awkward reading ἰσχυροὶ. It thus seems that the scholars of antiquity read the text of X's work in very much the same form as we do now. Its difficulties and problems do not derive from poor manuscript transcription.

In this edition we provide a critical *apparatus* which is highly selective, but which includes information at all points where our text differs from that of Bowersock 1968. The variant readings are discussed in the commentary *ad locc.*

DATES ASSIGNED TO THE
CONSTITUTION OF THE ATHENIANS

Our preferred dating, 425–424 (between Athens' success at Pylos and Brasidas' journey through Thessaly to the north-east), was first championed by W. Roscher, reviewing A. Fuchs, *Quaestiones de Libris Xenophonteis de Republica Lacedaemoniorum et de Republica Atheniensium*, (*GGA* 1841 [i], 409–24 + 425–9). He argued from 2.18 that X's work must be earlier than Aristophanes' *Knights*, produced early in 424; A. Kirchhoff, 'Über die Abfassungszeit der Schrift vom Staate der Athener' (*Abh. Berlin* 1878, 1–25), accepted Roscher's other arguments but not the argument from 2.18, and dated the work to the first half of 424. We think it possible but not certain that 2.18 was actually written shortly after *Knights* and with *Knights* in mind (see pp. 131–5, below).

440s	Bowersock (because no later allusions in 3.11)
c. 440–432	F. Jacoby, *Atthis* (OUP, 1949), 292 n. 13 (certainly before Peloponnesian War; author outside Athens)
before 432	Frisch
before 431	de Romilly
431	M. L. Lang, 'Cleon as the Anti-Pericles', *CP* 67 (1972), 159–69 (work of Cleon, answered in Pericles' funeral oration)
after 431 certain and 424 most likely	de Ste. Croix
431–424	L. Canfora, *Studi sull'A.P. pseudosenofontea* (Turin: Accademia delle Scientie, 1980) (author an Athenian in exile but not in Sparta – in fact Critias, as suggested on the basis of 3.6 compared with Poll. VIII. 25 by A. Boeckh, *Die Staatshaushaltung der Athener*[2] [Berlin: Reimer, 1851], 423–7 n. *e*, and others)
431–413	Osborne
425–424	Moore
424	Forrest
421–418	C. Leduc, *La Constitution d'Athènes attribuée à Xénophon* (Ann. Litt. Univ. Besançon. Paris: Les Belles Lettres, 1976) (product of optimistic Athens after Peace of Nicias)

415	Gomme
414	Mattingly (author not an Athenian but a citizen of one of the allied states)
410–406/5	M. J. Fontana, *L' Athenaion Politeia dal V secolo a. C.* (Palermo: Cappugi, 1968) (reflects polarisation of oligarchs and democrats after failure of oligarchic revolutions of 411)
405 early summer	J. D. Smart, 'The Athenian Empire' (review article), *Phoen.* 31 (1977), 245–57 at 250 with n. 12 (sees allusions to events from 413 down to the liberation of slaves to fight at Arginusae in 406)
after 411 and probably well into C4	F. Roscalla, 'περὶ δὲ τῆς ᾿Αθηναίων πολιτείας . . .', *QUCC* 79 = 2nd series 50 (1995 no. 2), 105–30 (introduction reflects fourth-century praise and anti-praise of constitutions)
after 400	Hornblower (exercise written as if in late fifth century but by an author who had read Thucydides)

SELECT BIBLIOGRAPHY

Items listed here are cited in this book by author's name and, where necessary, date.

On Xenophon

Anderson, J. K. *Xenophon*. London: Duckworth / New York: Scribner, 1974.

Chrimes, K. M. T. *The Respublica Lacedaemoniorum Ascribed to Xenophon*. Manchester UP, 1948.

Ollier, F. *Xénophon, La République des Lacédémoniens*. Lyon: Bosc, 1934.

Tuplin, C. (ed.), *Xenophon and His World*. (*Historia* Einzelschriften 172.) Stuttgart: Steiner, 2004.

On the Constitution of the Athenians

Bowersock, G. W. 'Pseudo-Xenophon.' [text] *HSCP* 71 (1966), 33–55.

Bowersock, G. W. *Constitution of the Athenians*, in reissue of Xenophon, vol. vii. *Scripta Minora* [text and translation] (Loeb. London: Heinemann / Harvard UP, 1968), 459–507 and 515.

de Ste. Croix, G. E. M. *The Origins of the Peloponnesian War* (London: Duckworth / Cornell UP, 1972), 307–10 app. 6.

Forrest, W. G. 'The Date of the Pseudo-Xenophontic *Athenaion Politeia.*' *Klio* 52 (1970), 107–16.

Forrest, W. G. 'An Athenian Generation Gap.' *YCS* 24 (1975), 37–52.

Fränkel, H. 'Notes on the Closing Sections of Pseudo-Xenophon's *Constitution of the Athenians.*' *AJP* 68 (1947), 309–12.

Frisch, H. *The Constitution of the Athenians*. [text, translation, commentary] Copenhagen: Gyldendal, 1942.

Fuks, A. 'The Old Oligarch.' *Scripta Hierosolymitana* 1 (1954), 21–35.

Gomme, A. W. 'The Old Oligarch.' *HSCP* Supp. 1 (1940), 211–45, = his *More Essays in Greek History and Literature* (Oxford: Blackwell, 1962), 38–69.

Hornblower, S. 'The *Old Oligarch* (Pseudo-Xenophon's *Athenaion Politeia*) and Thucydides: A Fourth-Century Date for the *Old Oligarch*?' in P. Flensted-Jensen *et al.* (eds), *Polis and Politics: Studies in Ancient Greek History Presented to Mogens Herman Hansen* (Copenhagen: Museum Tusculanum Press, 2000), 363–84.

Kalinka, E. *Die pseudo-Xenophontische* Athenaion Politeia: *Einleitung, Übersetzung, Erklärung.* [text, German translation, commentary] Leipzig and Berlin: Teubner, 1913.

Marr, J. L. 'Making Sense of the Old Oligarch.' *Hermathena* 160 (1996), 37–43.

Marr, J. L. 'Notes on the Pseudo-Xenophontic *Athenaion Politeia.' C&M* 34 (1983), 45–53.

Mattingly, H. B. 'The Date and Purpose of the Pseudo-Xenophontic *Constitution of the Athenians.' CQ* n.s. 47 (1997), 352–7.

Moore, J. M. *Aristotle and Xenophon on Democracy and Oligarchy.* [translation and commentary] (London: Chatto and Windus / University of California Press, 1975; 2nd ed., 1983), 19–61.

Osborne, R. *The Old Oligarch: Pseudo-Xenophon's Constitution of the Athenians,* 2nd ed. (*LACTOR* 2) [translation and notes] London Association of Classical Teachers, 2004.

O'Sullivan, J. N. 'Notes on the "Old Oligarch".' *LCM* 3 (1978), 193–5.

Romilly, J. de. 'Le Pseudo-Xénophon et Thucydide.' *RP* 36 (1962), 225–41.

Sutton, D. F. *A Concordance to the Anonymous Constitution of Athens.* Chicago: Bolchazy–Carducci, 1981.

Also cited by author's name

Rhodes, P. J. *A Commentary on the Aristotelian Athenaion Politeia.* (OUP, 1981; reissued with addenda 1993).

ΑΘΗΝΑΙΩΝ ΠΟΛΙΤΕΙΑ

THE CONSTITUTION OF THE ATHENIANS

1

(1) περὶ δὲ τῆς Ἀθηναίων πολιτείας, ὅτι μὲν εἵλοντο τοῦτον τὸν τρόπον τῆς πολιτείας οὐκ ἐπαινῶ διὰ τόδε, ὅτι ταῦθ' ἑλόμενοι εἵλοντο τοὺς πονηροὺς ἄμεινον πράττειν ἢ τοὺς χρηστούς· διὰ μὲν οὖν τοῦτο οὐκ ἐπαινῶ. ἐπεὶ δὲ ταῦτα ἔδοξεν οὕτως αὐτοῖς, ὡς εὖ διασῴζονται τὴν πολιτείαν καὶ τἆλλα διαπράττονται ἃ δοκοῦσιν ἁμαρτάνειν τοῖς ἄλλοις Ἕλλησι, τοῦτ' ἀποδείξω.

(2) πρῶτον μὲν οὖν τοῦτο ἐρῶ, ὅτι δίκαιοι αὐτόθι καὶ οἱ πένητες καὶ ὁ δῆμος πλέον ἔχειν τῶν γενναίων καὶ τῶν πλουσίων διὰ τόδε, ὅτι ὁ δῆμός ἐστιν ὁ ἐλαύνων τὰς ναῦς καὶ ὁ τὴν δύναμιν περιτιθεὶς τῇ πόλει, καὶ οἱ κυβερνῆται καὶ οἱ κελευσταὶ καὶ οἱ πεντηκόνταρχοι καὶ οἱ πρῳρᾶται καὶ οἱ ναυπηγοί – οὗτοί εἰσιν οἱ τὴν δύναμιν περιτιθέντες τῇ πόλει πολὺ μᾶλλον ἢ οἱ ὁπλῖται καὶ οἱ γενναῖοι καὶ οἱ χρηστοί. ἐπειδὴ οὖν ταῦτα οὕτως ἔχει, δοκεῖ δίκαιον εἶναι πᾶσι τῶν ἀρχῶν μετεῖναι ἔν τε τῷ κλήρῳ καὶ τῇ χειροτονίᾳ καὶ λέγειν ἐξεῖναι τῷ βουλομένῳ τῶν πολιτῶν. (3) ἔπειτα ὁπόσαι μὲν σωτηρίαν φέρουσι τῶν ἀρχῶν χρησταὶ οὖσαι καὶ μὴ χρησταὶ κίνδυνον τῷ δήμῳ ἅπαντι, τούτων μὲν τῶν ἀρχῶν οὐδὲν δεῖται ὁ δῆμος μετεῖναι (οὔτε τῶν στρατηγῶν κλήρῳ οἴονται σφίσι χρῆναι μετεῖναι οὔτε τῶν ἱππαρχιῶν)· γιγνώσκει γὰρ ὁ δῆμος ὅτι πλείω ὠφελεῖται ἐν τῷ μὴ αὐτὸς ἄρχειν ταύτας τὰς ἀρχάς, ἀλλ' ἐὰν τοὺς δυνατωτάτους ἄρχειν. ὁπόσαι δ' εἰσὶν ἀρχαὶ μισθοφορίας ἕνεκα καὶ ὠφελίας εἰς τὸν οἶκον, ταύτας ζητεῖ ὁ δῆμος ἄρχειν.

(4) ἔπειτα δέ, ὃ ἔνιοι θαυμάζουσιν, ὅτι πανταχοῦ πλέον νέμουσι τοῖς πονηροῖς καὶ πένησι καὶ δημοτικοῖς ἢ τοῖς χρηστοῖς, ἐν αὐτῷ τούτῳ φανοῦνται τὴν δημοκρατίαν διασῴζοντες. οἱ μὲν γὰρ πένητες καὶ οἱ δημοτικοὶ καὶ οἱ χείρους εὖ πράττοντες καὶ πολλοὶ οἱ τοιοῦτοι γιγνόμενοι τὴν δημοκρατίαν αὔξουσιν· ἐὰν δὲ εὖ πράττωσιν οἱ πλούσιοι καὶ οἱ χρηστοί, ἰσχυρὸν τὸ ἐναντίον σφίσιν αὐτοῖς καθιστᾶσιν οἱ δημοτικοί. (5) ἔστι δὲ πάσῃ γῇ τὸ βέλτιστον ἐναντίον τῇ δημοκρατίᾳ. ἐν γὰρ τοῖς βελτίστοις ἔνι ἀκολασία τε ὀλιγίστη καὶ ἀδικία, ἀκρίβεια δὲ πλείστη εἰς τὰ χρηστά, ἐν δὲ τῷ δήμῳ ἀμαθία τε πλείστη καὶ ἀταξία καὶ πονηρία· ἥ τε γὰρ πενία αὐτοὺς μᾶλλον

(1) But with regard to the Athenians' constitution, I do not approve of the fact that they have chosen to have this type of constitution, for the following reason, that in making their choice they have chosen that the worthless men should do better than the valuable. That is the reason why I do not approve of it. However, given that they have decided that things should be as they are, I shall demonstrate how effectively they preserve their constitution and also transact their other public business, in those respects in which the rest of the Greeks think that they act mistakenly.

(2) First of all, I will say this, that the poor and the *demos* are justified there in having more than the well-born and the rich, because of the fact that it is the *demos* who operate the ships and who confer its strength on the city; the steersmen, the boatswains, the lieutenants, the look-outs and the naval engineers – these are the people who confer its strength on the city, much more so than the hoplites and the well-born and the valuable. Since this is the case, it seems right that everyone should share in the holding of public office, both the allotted and the elective offices, and that any citizen who wishes should be allowed to have his say. (3) In fact, there are offices which bring safety to the whole *demos* when well conducted, but danger when not well conducted, and the *demos* do not want to have any share in these (for example they do not think they should have an allotted share in the generalships or the cavalry commands). For the *demos* know that they gain more benefit by not holding such offices themselves and, instead, leaving them for the most able to hold. But as for those offices which involve receipt of pay and domestic benefit, these are the ones which the *demos* are eager to hold.

(4) Next, a thing which some people are surprised at, namely the fact that in every area they assign more to the worthless and the poor and the common people than they do to the valuable; but it will become clear that it is precisely through this practice that they preserve their democracy. For the poor and the common people and the inferior classes will increase the strength of the democracy by doing well and by increasing the numbers of themselves and their like. If, however, the rich and the valuable do well, the common people make the opposition to themselves strong. (5) Throughout the world the best element is opposed to democracy. For within the best men there is the least amount of licentiousness and injustice, and the most scrupulousness over what is valuable; whereas within the *demos* there is the greatest ignorance, indiscipline and worthlessness. For poverty tends to lead

ἄγει ἐπὶ τὰ αἰσχρά, καὶ ἡ ἀπαιδευσία καὶ ἡ ἀμαθία δι᾿ ἔνδειαν χρημάτων <ἔνι> ἐνίοις τῶν ἀνθρώπων. (6) εἴποι δ᾿ ἄν τις ὡς ἐχρῆν αὐτοὺς μὴ ἐᾶν λέγειν πάντας ἐξῆς μηδὲ βουλεύειν, ἀλλὰ τοὺς δεξιωτάτους καὶ ἄνδρας ἀρίστους. οἱ δὲ καὶ ἐν τούτῳ ἄριστα βουλεύονται ἐῶντες καὶ τοὺς πονηροὺς λέγειν. εἰ μὲν γὰρ οἱ χρηστοὶ ἔλεγον καὶ ἐβούλευον, τοῖς ὁμοίοις σφίσιν αὐτοῖς ἦν ἀγαθά, τοῖς δὲ δημοτικοῖς οὐκ ἀγαθά· νῦν δὲ λέγων ὁ βουλόμενος ἀναστὰς ἄνθρωπος πονηρὸς ἐξευρίσκει τὸ ἀγαθὸν αὐτῷ τε καὶ τοῖς ὁμοίοις αὐτῷ. (7) εἴποι τις ἄν, "τί ἂν οὖν γνοίη ἀγαθὸν αὐτῷ ἢ τῷ δήμῳ τοιοῦτος ἄνθρωπος;" οἱ δὲ γιγνώσκουσιν ὅτι ἡ τούτου ἀμαθία καὶ πονηρία καὶ εὔνοια μᾶλλον λυσιτελεῖ ἢ ἡ τοῦ χρηστοῦ ἀρετὴ καὶ σοφία καὶ κακόνοια. (8) εἴη μὲν οὖν ἂν πόλις οὐκ ἀπὸ τοιούτων διαιτημάτων ἡ βελτίστη, ἀλλ᾿ ἡ δημοκρατία μάλιστ᾿ ἂν σῴζοιτο οὕτως. ὁ γὰρ δῆμος βούλεται οὐκ, εὐνομουμένης τῆς πόλεως, αὐτὸς δουλεύειν, ἀλλ᾿ ἐλεύθερος εἶναι καὶ ἄρχειν, τῆς δὲ κακονομίας αὐτῷ ὀλίγον μέλει. ὁ γὰρ σὺ νομίζεις οὐκ εὐνομεῖσθαι, αὐτὸς ἀπὸ τούτου ἰσχύει ὁ δῆμος καὶ ἐλεύθερός ἐστιν. (9) εἰ δ᾿ εὐνομίαν ζητεῖς, πρῶτα μὲν ὄψει τοὺς δεξιωτάτους αὐτοῖς τοὺς νόμους τιθέντας· ἔπειτα κολάσουσιν οἱ χρηστοὶ τοὺς πονηροὺς καὶ βουλεύσουσιν οἱ χρηστοὶ περὶ τῆς πόλεως καὶ οὐκ ἐάσουσι μαινομένους ἀνθρώπους βουλεύειν οὐδὲ λέγειν οὐδὲ ἐκκλησιάζειν. ἀπὸ τούτων τοίνυν τῶν ἀγαθῶν τάχιστ᾿ ἂν ὁ δῆμος εἰς δουλείαν καταπέσοι. (10) "τῶν δούλων δ᾿ αὖ καὶ τῶν μετοίκων πλείστη ἐστὶν Ἀθήνησιν ἀκολασία, καὶ οὔτε πατάξαι ἔξεστιν αὐτόθι οὔτε ὑπεκστήσεταί σοι ὁ δοῦλος." οὗ δ᾿ ἕνεκέν ἐστι τοῦτο ἐπιχώριον, ἐγὼ φράσω· εἰ νόμος ἦν τὸν δοῦλον ὑπὸ τοῦ ἐλευθέρου τύπτεσθαι ἢ τὸν μέτοικον ἢ τὸν ἀπελεύθερον, πολλάκις ἂν οἰηθεὶς εἶναι τὸν Ἀθηναῖον δοῦλον ἐπάταξεν ἄν· ἐσθῆτά τε γὰρ οὐδὲν βελτίων ὁ δῆμος αὐτόθι ἢ οἱ δοῦλοι καὶ οἱ μέτοικοι, καὶ τὰ εἴδη οὐδὲν βελτίους εἰσίν. (11) εἰ δέ τις καὶ τοῦτο θαυμάζει, ὅτι ἐῶσι τοὺς δούλους τρυφᾶν αὐτόθι καὶ μεγαλοπρεπῶς διαιτᾶσθαι ἐνίους, καὶ τοῦτο γνώμῃ

1.5   <ἔνι> Christian, Bowerstock

1.6   ἐξῆς ABCM: ἐξ ἴσης Bergk, Bowersock
       οἱ δὲ Marchant: οἳ δὲ Kalinka, Bowersock
       ἐβούλευον Morus: ἐβουλεύοντο ABCM, Bowersock

1.7   οἱ δὲ Marchant: οἳ δὲ Kalinka, Bowersock

1.9   αὐτοῖς ABCM, Bowersock: αὑτοῖς Müller-Strübing

them into shameful behaviour, and in the case of some people their lack of education and their ignorance is the result of their lack of money.

(6) Someone might say that they ought not to allow everyone in turn the right to speak or to serve on the council, but only the cleverest and the best men. However, on this point too, their policy, of allowing even the worthless to speak, is in their best interests. For if only the valuable were to speak and be members of the council, it would be good for the likes of themselves, but not good for the common people. As things are, any worthless person who wishes can stand up in the assembly and procure what is good for himself and those like him. (7) Someone might say, 'How could such a person recognise what is good for himself and the *demos*?' But they know that this man's ignorance and worthlessness and good will are more advantageous to them than are the excellence and wisdom and ill will of the valuable man. (8) It is true that a state would not be the best on the basis of such practices, but the fact is that the democracy would most securely preserve itself by these means. For the *demos* do not wish the state to be governed well while they themselves are slaves, but rather to be free and to rule, and so they are not concerned about bad government. The *demos* actually derive their strength and their freedom precisely from what you consider not to be good government. (9) If you are looking for good government, you will find that, first, the cleverest men draw up the laws for them. After that, the valuable men will punish the worthless ones; they will be the ones who make policy for the state, and they will not allow wild persons to be members of the council or to speak or to attend meetings of the assembly. So, as a result of these good measures, the *demos* would very quickly be reduced to slavery.

(10) 'But again the slaves and the metics at Athens enjoy extreme licence, and it is not possible to strike them there, nor will a slave step aside for you.' Well, I shall tell you the reason why this is their local practice. If it were legal for the slave or the metic or the freedman to be beaten by a free-born citizen, he would often strike an Athenian by mistake, thinking that he was a slave. For the *demos* there are no better dressed than the slaves and the metics, nor are they any better in their appearance. (11) If anyone is also surprised at the fact that they allow the slaves to live luxuriously there and, some of them,

φανεῖεν ἂν ποιοῦντες· ὅπου γὰρ ναυτικὴ δύναμίς ἐστιν, ἀπὸ χρημάτων ἀνάγκη τοῖς ἀνδραπόδοις δουλεύειν, ἵνα λαμβάνωμεν ἃς πράττει τὰς ἀποφοράς, καὶ ἐλευθέρους ἀφεῖναι. ἐν δὲ τῇ Λακεδαίμονι ὁ ἐμὸς δοῦλος σ' ἐδεδοίκει.'' ἐὰν δὲ δεδίῃ ὁ σὸς δοῦλος ἐμέ, κινδυνεύσει καὶ τὰ χρήματα διδόναι τὰ ἑαυτοῦ ὥστε μὴ κινδυνεύειν περὶ ἑαυτοῦ. ὅπου δ' εἰσὶ πλούσιοι δοῦλοι, οὐκέτι ἐνταῦθα λυσιτελεῖ τὸν ἐμὸν δοῦλον σὲ δεδιέναι. (12) διὰ τοῦτ' οὖν ἰσηγορίαν καὶ τοῖς δούλοις πρὸς τοὺς ἐλευθέρους ἐποιήσαμεν, καὶ τοῖς μετοίκοις πρὸς τοὺς ἀστούς, διότι δεῖται ἡ πόλις μετοίκων διά τε τὸ πλῆθος τῶν τεχνῶν καὶ διὰ τὸ ναυτικόν· διὰ τοῦτο οὖν καὶ τοῖς μετοίκοις εἰκότως τὴν ἰσηγορίαν ἐποιήσαμεν.

(13) τοὺς δὲ γυμναζομένους αὐτόθι καὶ τὴν μουσικὴν ἐπιτηδεύοντας καταλέλυκεν ὁ δῆμος, <οὐ> νομίζων τοῦτο οὐ καλὸν εἶναι, γνοὺς <δὲ> ὅτι οὐ δυνατὸς ταῦτά ἐστιν ἐπιτηδεύειν. ἐν ταῖς χορηγίαις αὖ καὶ γυμνασιαρχίαις καὶ τριηραρχίαις γιγνώσκουσιν ὅτι χορηγοῦσι μὲν οἱ πλούσιοι, χορηγεῖται δὲ ὁ δῆμος, καὶ γυμνασιαρχοῦσι οἱ πλούσιοι, ὁ δὲ δῆμος τριηραρχεῖται καὶ γυμνασιαρχεῖται. ἀξιοῖ οὖν ἀργύριον λαμβάνειν ὁ δῆμος καὶ ᾄδων καὶ τρέχων καὶ ὀρχούμενος καὶ πλέων ἐν ταῖς ναυσίν, ἵνα αὐτός τε ἔχῃ καὶ οἱ πλούσιοι πενέστεροι γίγνωνται. [ἔν τε τοῖς δικαστηρίοις οὐ τοῦ δικαίου αὐτοῖς μᾶλλον μέλει ἢ τοῦ αὑτοῖς συμφόρου.]

(14) περὶ δὲ τῶν συμμάχων – ὅτι ἐκπλέοντες συκοφαντοῦσιν, ὡς δοκοῦσι, καὶ μισοῦσι τοὺς χρηστούς, γιγνώσκοντες ὅτι μισεῖσθαι μὲν ἀνάγκη τὸν ἄρχοντα ὑπὸ τοῦ ἀρχομένου, εἰ δὲ ἰσχύσουσιν οἱ πλούσιοι καὶ ἰσχυροὶ ἐν ταῖς πόλεσιν, ὀλίγιστον χρόνον ἡ ἀρχὴ ἔσται τοῦ δήμου τοῦ Ἀθήνησι, διὰ ταῦτα οὖν τοὺς μὲν χρηστοὺς ἀτιμοῦσι καὶ χρήματα ἀφαιροῦνται καὶ ἐξελαύνονται καὶ ἀποκτείνουσι, τοὺς δὲ πονηροὺς αὔξουσιν. οἱ δὲ χρηστοὶ Ἀθηναίων τοὺς χρηστοὺς ἐν ταῖς συμμαχίσι πόλεσι σῴζουσι, γιγνώσκοντες ὅτι σφίσιν ἀγαθόν ἐστι τοὺς βελτίστους σῴζειν ἀεὶ ἐν ταῖς πόλεσιν. (15) εἴποι δέ τις ἂν ἰσχύς ἐστιν αὕτη Ἀθηναίων, ἐὰν οἱ σύμμαχοι δυνατοὶ ὦσι

1.11 λαμβάνωμεν ἃς πράττει Leonclavius: λαμβάνων μὲν πράττῃ τὰς ABCM; obelised Bowersock
ὅπου δ' εἰσὶ ... σὲ δεδιέναι after περὶ ἑαυτοῦ Marr: after ἐλευθέρους ἀφιέναι ABCM, Bowersock

1.13 <οὐ> νομίζων ... γνοὺς <δὲ> Orelli: obelised Bowersock
δυνατὸς C: δυνατὰ ABM, Bowersock
οὖν M: γοῦν ABC, Bowersock
ἔν τε τοῖς ... αὑτοῖς συμφόρου out of place here, perhaps displaced from 1. 16 after ἐπὶ δίκας Ἀθήναζε Marr

1.14 ἰσχυροὶ ABCM, Stobaeus: χρηστοὶ Heinrich, Bowersock

in a grand style, it will become clear that they do this too with good reason. For where there is a naval power, economic reasons make it necessary for us to be slaves to our slaves in order that we may take their earnings, and to manumit them. 'But in Lacedaemon my slave fears you.' Yes, but if your slave fears me, there will be a risk that he will also offer me his money so as not to be in physical danger. And in a state where there are rich slaves it is no longer to my benefit as a master there that my slave should fear you. (12) This then is the reason why we have established equality of free speech as between slaves and free men; and also as between metics and citizens, since the city needs metics because of the great number of their skills and the requirements of the fleet. So that is why we have, naturally, established equality of free speech for the metics too.

(13) The *demos* have made it unfashionable for individuals to engage in athletic exercise and musical activities there, not because they think this is a bad thing, but because they know that they cannot afford to engage in these activities. Correspondingly, in the case of public choral performances and athletic competitions and trireme provisions they know that the rich provide the choruses while the *demos* take part in them, and that the rich provide the athletic competitions while the *demos* take part in trireme service and athletic competitions. Thus the *demos* think they have a right to receive money for singing and running and dancing and sailing in the ships, so as to get wealth for themselves and to make the rich poorer. [And in the lawcourts they are concerned less with justice than with their own advantage.]

(14) But with regard to their allies, and the claim that they sail out there and bring malicious charges against, and hate, the valuable among them – it is because they know that the ruler is necessarily hated by the ruled, and that, if the rich and strong come into power in the allied states, the empire of the Athenian *demos* will only last for a very short time. That is the reason why they take away the political rights of the valuable, and confiscate their property, and exile and kill them, and, correspondingly, promote the interests of the worthless. But the valuable men at Athens try to protect the valuable men within the allied states, since they realise that it is good for themselves always to protect the best men in the allied states. (15) Someone might say that the Athenians' strength lies in leaving the allied states with the ability to

χρήματα εἰσφέρειν· τοῖς δὲ δημοτικοῖς δοκεῖ μεῖζον ἀγαθὸν εἶναι τὰ τῶν συμμάχων χρήματα ἕνα ἕκαστον Ἀθηναίων ἔχειν, ἐκείνους δὲ ὅσον ζῆν, καὶ ἐργάζεσθαι ἀδυνάτους ὄντας ἐπιβουλεύειν.

(16) δοκεῖ δὲ ὁ δῆμος ὁ Ἀθηναίων καὶ ἐν τῷδε κακῶς βουλεύεσθαι, ὅτι τοὺς συμμάχους ἀναγκάζουσι πλεῖν ἐπὶ δίκας Ἀθήναζε. οἱ δὲ ἀντιλογίζονται ὅσα ἐν τούτῳ ἔνι ἀγαθὰ τῷ δήμῳ τῷ Ἀθηναίων. πρῶτον μὲν ἀπὸ τῶν πρυτανείων τὸν μισθὸν δι' ἐνιαυτοῦ λαμβάνειν. εἶτ' οἴκοι καθήμενοι ἄνευ νεῶν ἔκπλου διοικοῦσι τὰς πόλεις τὰς συμμαχίδας, καὶ τοὺς μὲν τοῦ δήμου σῴζουσι, τοὺς δ' ἐναντίους ἀπολλύουσιν ἐν τοῖς δικαστηρίοις· εἰ δὲ οἴκοι εἶχον ἕκαστοι τὰς δίκας, ἅτε ἀχθόμενοι τοῖς Ἀθηναίοις τούτους ἂν σφῶν αὐτῶν ἀπώλλυσαν οἵτινες φίλοι μάλιστα ἦσαν Ἀθηναίων τῷ δήμῳ. (17) πρὸς δὲ τούτοις ὁ δῆμος τῶν Ἀθηναίων τάδε κερδαίνει τῶν δικῶν Ἀθήνησιν οὐσῶν τοῖς συμμάχοις· πρῶτον μὲν γὰρ ἡ ἑκατοστὴ τῇ πόλει πλείων ἢ ἐν Πειραιεῖ· ἔπειτα, εἴ τῳ συνοικία ἐστίν, ἄμεινον πράττει· ἔπειτα εἴ τῳ ζεῦγός ἐστιν ἢ ἀνδράποδον μισθοφοροῦν· ἔπειτα οἱ κήρυκες ἄμεινον πράττουσι διὰ τὰς ἐπιδημίας τὰς τῶν συμμάχων. (18) πρὸς δὲ τούτοις, εἰ μὲν μὴ ἐπὶ δίκας ᾖσαν οἱ σύμμαχοι, τοὺς ἐκπλέοντας Ἀθηναίων ἐτίμων ἂν μόνους, τούς τε στρατηγοὺς καὶ τοὺς τριηράρχους καὶ πρέσβεις. νῦν δ' ἠνάγκασται τὸν δῆμον κολακεύειν τὸν Ἀθηναίων εἷς ἕκαστος τῶν συμμάχων, γιγνώσκων ὅτι δεῖ μὲν ἀφικόμενον Ἀθήναζε δίκην δοῦναι καὶ λαβεῖν οὐκ ἐν ἄλλοις τισὶν ἀλλ' ἐν τῷ δήμῳ, ὅς ἐστι δὴ νόμος Ἀθήνησι· καὶ ἀντιβολῆσαι ἀναγκάζεται ἐν τοῖς δικαστηρίοις καὶ εἰσιόντος τοῦ ἐπιλαμβάνεσθαι τῆς χειρός. διὰ τοῦτο οὖν οἱ σύμμαχοι δοῦλοι τοῦ δήμου τῶν Ἀθηναίων καθεστᾶσι μᾶλλον. (19) πρὸς δὲ τούτοις διὰ τὴν κτῆσιν τὴν ἐν τοῖς ὑπερορίοις καὶ διὰ τὰς ἀρχὰς τὰς εἰς τὴν ὑπερορίαν λελήθασι μανθάνοντες ἐλαύνειν τῇ κώπῃ αὐτοί τε καὶ οἱ ἀκόλουθοι· ἀνάγκη γὰρ ἄνθρωπον πολλάκις πλέοντα κώπην λαβεῖν καὶ αὐτὸν καὶ τὸν οἰκέτην, καὶ ὀνόματα μαθεῖν τὰ ἐν τῇ ναυτικῇ· (20) καὶ κυβερνῆται ἀγαθοὶ γίγνονται δι' ἐμπειρίαν τε τῶν πλόων καὶ διὰ μελέτην· ἐμελέτησαν δὲ οἱ μὲν πλοῖον κυβερνῶντες, οἱ δὲ ὁλκάδα, οἱ δ' ἐντεῦθεν ἐπὶ τριήρεσι κατέστησαν. οἱ δὲ πολλοὶ ἐλαύνειν εὐθέως οἷοί τε εἰσβάντες εἰς ναῦς ἅτε ἐν παντὶ τῷ βίῳ προμεμελετηκότες.

1.16   οἱ δὲ Marchant: οἳ δὲ Kalinka, Bowersock
1.17   πράττει Schneider: πράττειν ABC, Bowersock
1.20   οἱ μὲν . . . οἱ δὲ . . . οἱ δ' Marchant: οἳ μὲν . . . οἳ δὲ . . . οἳ δ' Kalinka, Bowersock

keep making payments of money. However, the common people think that it is more of a good thing that each and every Athenian should individually own the resources of their allies, and that they, the allies, should have only what is enough to survive on, and should continue to cultivate the land, but without being able to plot revolt.

(16) On this point, too, it is thought that the Athenian *demos* act ill-advisedly, namely, that they compel the allies to sail to Athens for lawsuits. But they list on the other side of the balance sheet all the advantages for the Athenian *demos* which there are in this requirement. First, that from the legal deposits they receive their jury pay throughout the year. Secondly, they manage the affairs of the allied states by just sitting at home, with no need of naval expeditions; by using their lawcourts they protect the supporters of the *demos* and ruin their opponents. If the allied states each conducted their trials locally, they would, because of their resentment against the Athenians, have ruined those of their number who were the principal friends of the Athenian *demos*. (17) In addition, the Athenian *demos* profit in the following ways from the fact that trials involving their allies are held in Athens. First, the one per cent tax in the Piraeus brings in more for the state. Secondly, if anyone has a lodging house, he does better. So does anyone who has a carriage or a slave for hire. Thirdly, the auctioneers do better from the visits of the allies. (18) In addition to this, if the allies did not go to Athens for lawsuits, they would honour only those Athenians who sailed out to their country, namely the generals and the trierarchs and ambassadors. As it is, each and every one of the allies has been compelled to flatter the Athenian *demos*, in the realisation that it is necessary for any litigant who comes to Athens to appear as a defendant or as a prosecutor before none other than the *demos*; this indeed is the law at Athens. And inside the courts he is compelled to beseech, and to grasp the hand of, anyone who enters. Consequently, because of this, the allies have become, rather, the slaves of the Athenian *demos*.

(19) Furthermore, because of the land they have acquired in overseas territories, and the offices which take them abroad, they have learned to row without noticing it, both they themselves and their slaves. For it is inevitable that a person who often has to travel by sea should take up an oar, both himself and his slave, and should learn the naval terminology. (20) They become good steersmen also, through experience gained in their voyaging and through practice. Some have had practice in steering a boat, others in steering a cargo ship, and from there some have passed on to triremes. So the many are able to operate their ships immediately they board them, since they have been practising in advance for the whole of their lives.

2

(1) τὸ δὲ ὁπλιτικὸν αὐτοῖς, ὃ ἥκιστα δοκεῖ εὖ ἔχειν Ἀθήνησιν, οὕτω καθέστηκεν καὶ τῶν μὲν πολεμίων ἥττους τε σφᾶς αὐτοὺς ἡγοῦνται εἶναι καὶ ὀλείζους, τῶν δὲ συμμάχων οἳ φέρουσι τὸν φόρον καὶ κατὰ γῆν κρείττους, καὶ νομίζουσι τὸ ὁπλιτικὸν ἀρκεῖν εἰ τῶν συμμάχων κρείττονές εἰσι. (2) πρὸς δὲ καὶ κατὰ τύχην τι αὐτοῖς τοιοῦτον καθέστηκε. τοῖς μὲν κατὰ γῆν ἀρχομένοις οἷόν τ᾽ ἐστιν ἐκ μικρῶν πόλεων συνοικισθέντας ἀθρόους μάχεσθαι. τοῖς δὲ κατὰ θάλατταν ἀρχομένοις, ὅσοι νησιῶταί εἰσιν, οὐχ οἷόν τε συνάρασθαι εἰς τὸ αὐτὸ τὰς πόλεις· ἡ γὰρ θάλαττα ἐν τῷ μέσῳ, οἱ δὲ κρατοῦντες θαλασσοκράτορές εἰσιν. εἰ δ᾽ οἷόν τε καὶ λαθεῖν συνελθοῦσιν εἰς ταὐτὸ τοῖς νησιώταις εἰς μίαν νῆσον, ἀπολοῦνται λιμῷ. (3) ὁπόσαι δ᾽ ἐν τῇ ἠπείρῳ εἰσὶ πόλεις ὑπὸ τῶν Ἀθηναίων ἀρχόμεναι, αἱ μὲν μεγάλαι διὰ δέος ἄρχονται, αἱ δὲ μικραὶ πάνυ διὰ χρείαν. οὐ γάρ ἐστι πόλις οὐδεμία ἥτις οὐ δεῖται εἰσάγεσθαί τι ἢ ἐξάγεσθαι· ταῦτα τοίνυν οὐκ ἔσται αὐτῇ, ἐὰν μὴ ὑπήκοος ᾖ τῶν ἀρχόντων τῆς θαλάττης. (4) ἔπειτα δὲ τοῖς ἄρχουσι τῆς θαλάττης οἷόν τ᾽ ἐστὶ ποιεῖν ἅπερ τοῖς τῆς γῆς ἐνίοτε, τέμνειν τὴν γῆν τῶν κρειττόνων· παραπλεῖν γὰρ ἔξεστιν ὅπου ἂν μηδεὶς ᾖ πολέμιος ἢ ὅπου ἂν ὀλίγοι, ἐὰν δὲ προσίωσιν ἀναβάντα ἀποπλεῖν· καὶ τοῦτο ποιῶν ἧττον ἀπορεῖ ἢ ὁ πεζῇ παραβοηθῶν. (5) ἔπειτα δὲ τοῖς μὲν κατὰ θάλατταν ἄρχουσιν οἷόν τε ἀποπλεῦσαι ἀπὸ τῆς σφετέρας αὐτῶν ὁπόσον βουλεῖ πλοῦν, τοῖς δὲ κατὰ γῆν οὐχ οἷόν τε ἀπὸ τῆς σφετέρας αὐτῶν ἀπελθεῖν πολλῶν ἡμερῶν ὁδόν· βραδεῖαί τε γὰρ αἱ πορεῖαι καὶ σῖτον οὐχ οἷόν τε ἔχειν πολλοῦ χρόνου πεζῇ ἰόντα. καὶ τὸν μὲν πεζῇ ἰόντα δεῖ διὰ φιλίας ἰέναι ἢ νικᾶν μαχόμενον, τὸν δὲ πλέοντα, οὗ μὲν ἂν ᾖ κρείττων, ἔξεστιν ἀποβῆναι, οὗ δ᾽ ἂν μὴ ᾖ, μὴ ἀποβῆναι ταύτῃ τῆς γῆς, ἀλλὰ παραπλεῦσαι ἕως ἂν ἐπὶ φιλίαν χώραν ἀφίκηται ἢ ἐπὶ ἥττους αὑτοῦ. (6) ἔπειτα νόσους τῶν καρπῶν, αἳ ἐκ Διός εἰσιν, οἱ μὲν κατὰ γῆν κράτιστοι χαλεπῶς φέρουσιν, οἱ δὲ κατὰ θάλατταν ῥᾳδίως· οὐ γὰρ ἅμα πᾶσα γῆ νοσεῖ, ὥστε ἐκ τῆς εὐθενούσης ἀφικνεῖται τοῖς τῆς θαλάττης ἄρχουσιν.

2.1 ὀλείζους Wilamowitz, Bowersock: μείζους ABCM
     κρείττους Marr: κράτιστοί εἰσι ABCM, Bowersock
2.4 παραβοηθῶν ABCM, Bowersock: παραποήσων Kalinka
2.5 ἔξεστιν ἀποβῆναι, οὗ δ᾽ ἂν μὴ ᾖ, μὴ ἀποβῆναι Kalinka: γῆς οὗ δ᾽ ἂν μὴ ᾖ, μὴ ἀποβῆναι C; οὗ δ᾽ ἂν μὴ ᾖ, μὴ ἀποβῆναι omitted ABM; lacuna after ἔξεστιν ἀποβῆναι Bowersock
     ταύτῃ Hermann: ταύτης ABM, Bowersock; ἐνταῦθα C
2.6 εὐθενούσης Dindorf, Bowersock: εὐθηνούσης ABCM
     lacuna before ἀφικνεῖται suspected Marr

(1) As for their hoplite force and the view that this is not at all an Athenian strong point, the fact is that they have set it up to be as it is; they hold that, although they are in themselves weaker and fewer than their enemies, they are stronger even on land than their tribute-paying allies, and they think that their hoplite force is quite sufficient for them as long as they remain stronger than these allies.

(2) Furthermore, they also enjoy the following natural advantage: those who are subjects on land are able to unite their small cities and fight all together, but those who are subjects at sea, as many as are islanders, are unable to unite their cities into a single unit. For the sea lies between them, and their masters are rulers of the sea. Even if the islanders do manage, without being noticed, to join together on one single island, they will die of starvation. (3) As for those states subject to Athens' rule which are situated on the mainland, the big ones are kept in subjection through fear, the small ones very much so through need. For there is no state which does not need to import or export something, and these activities will not be open to it, unless it is compliant with the rulers of the sea.

(4) Then again, the rulers of the sea have the ability to do what the rulers of the land have the ability to do only sometimes, namely, ravage the territory of the more powerful. For it is possible for them to sail along the coast and put in wherever there is no enemy, or where there are only a few, and then, if the enemy forces attack, to re-embark and sail away. The power which does this has less of a problem than the one which responds with its infantry. (5) Moreover, the rulers of the sea have the ability to sail as far as you like away from their own country, whereas the rulers of the land do not have the ability to undertake a journey of many days away from their country. For progress is slow, and he who travels on foot cannot carry provisions sufficient for a long period. It is necessary for the one who goes on foot to travel through territory which is friendly, or else to fight to win his way through, whereas it is possible for the seafarer to disembark wherever he is stronger, and, wherever he is not the stronger, not to disembark at this point of the land, but to sail along the coast until he comes to friendly territory, or to the territory of those weaker than himself. (6) Further, with regard to crop diseases which are the result of bad weather, even the strongest land power is badly affected by them, but the sea power can bear them easily. For the whole earth is not diseased at one and the same time, and so imports from an area which is flourishing reach the rulers of the sea.

(7) εἰ δὲ δεῖ καὶ σμικροτέρων μνησθῆναι, διὰ τὴν ἀρχὴν τῆς θαλάττης πρῶτον μὲν τρόπους εὐωχιῶν ἐξηῦρον ἐπιμισγόμενοι ἄλλῃ ἄλλοις· ὅ τι ἐν Σικελίᾳ ἡδὺ ἢ ἐν Ἰταλίᾳ ἢ ἐν Κύπρῳ ἢ ἐν Αἰγύπτῳ ἢ ἐν Λυδίᾳ ἢ ἐν τῷ Πόντῳ ἢ ἐν Πελοποννήσῳ ἢ ἄλλοθί που, ταῦτα πάντα εἰς ἓν ἠθροίσθη διὰ τὴν ἀρχὴν τῆς θαλάττης. (8) ἔπειτα φωνὴν πᾶσαν ἀκούοντες ἐξελέξαντο τοῦτο μὲν ἐκ τῆς, τοῦτο δὲ ἐκ τῆς· καὶ οἱ μὲν Ἕλληνες ἰδίᾳ μᾶλλον καὶ φωνῇ καὶ διαίτῃ καὶ σχήματι χρῶνται, Ἀθηναῖοι δὲ κεκραμένῃ ἐξ ἁπάντων τῶν Ἑλλήνων καὶ βαρβάρων. (9) θυσίας δὲ καὶ ἱερὰ καὶ ἑορτὰς καὶ τεμένη – γνοὺς ὁ δῆμος ὅτι οὐχ οἷόν τέ ἐστιν ἑκάστῳ τῶν πενήτων θύειν καὶ εὐωχεῖσθαι καὶ ἵστασθαι ἱερὰ καὶ πόλιν οἰκεῖν καλὴν καὶ μεγάλην, ἐξηῦρεν ὅτῳ τρόπῳ ἔσται ταῦτα. θύουσιν οὖν δημοσίᾳ μὲν ἡ πόλις ἱερεῖα πολλά· ἔστι δὲ ὁ δῆμος ὁ εὐωχούμενος καὶ διαλαγχάνων τὰ ἱερεῖα. (10) καὶ γυμνάσια καὶ λουτρὰ καὶ ἀποδυτήρια τοῖς μὲν πλουσίοις ἐστὶν ἰδίᾳ ἐνίοις, ὁ δὲ δῆμος αὐτὸς αὑτῷ οἰκοδομεῖται ἰδίᾳ παλαίστρας πολλάς, ἀποδυτήρια, λουτρῶνας· καὶ πλείω τούτων ἀπολαύει ὁ ὄχλος ἢ οἱ ὀλίγοι καὶ οἱ εὐδαίμονες.

(11) τὸν δὲ <ναυτικὸν> πλοῦτον μόνοι οἷοί τ' εἰσὶν ἔχειν τῶν Ἑλλήνων καὶ τῶν βαρβάρων. εἰ γάρ τις πόλις πλουτεῖ ξύλοις ναυπηγησίμοις, ποῖ διαθήσεται, ἐὰν μὴ πείσῃ τὸν ἄρχοντα τῆς θαλάττης; τί δ' εἴ τις σιδήρῳ ἢ χαλκῷ ἢ λίνῳ πλουτεῖ πόλις, ποῖ διαθήσεται, ἐὰν μὴ πείσῃ τὸν ἄρχοντα τῆς θαλάττης; ἐξ αὐτῶν μέντοι τούτων καὶ δὴ νῆές μοί εἰσι, παρὰ μὲν τοῦ ξύλα, παρὰ δὲ τοῦ σίδηρος, παρὰ δὲ τοῦ χαλκός, παρὰ δὲ τοῦ λίνον, παρὰ δὲ τοῦ κηρός. (12) πρὸς δὲ τούτοις ἄλλοσε ἄγειν οὐκ ἐάσουσιν οἵτινες ἀντίπαλοι ἡμῖν εἰσιν, ἢ οὐ χρήσονται τῇ θαλάττῃ. καὶ ἐγὼ μὲν οὐδὲν ποιῶν ἐκ τῆς γῆς πάντα ταῦτα ἔχω διὰ τὴν θάλατταν, ἄλλη δ' οὐδεμία πόλις δύο τούτων ἔχει· οὐδ' ἔστι τῇ αὐτῇ ξύλα καὶ λίνον, ἀλλ' ὅπου λίνον ἐστὶ πλεῖστον λεία χώρα καὶ ἄξυλος· οὐδὲ χαλκὸς καὶ σίδηρος ἐκ τῆς αὐτῆς πόλεως οὐδὲ τἆλλα δύο ἢ τρία μιᾷ πόλει, ἀλλὰ τὸ μὲν τῇ, τὸ δὲ τῇ.

2.9–10 perhaps displaced from after 1. 13 πενέστεροι γίγνωνται Marr

2.9 ἵστασθαι Kirchhoff, Bowersock: κτᾶσθαι ABCM; perhaps καθίστασθαι Brock & Heath

2.10 οἰκοδομεῖται ἰδίᾳ ABCM, Bowersock: ἰδίᾳ possibly to be deleted Marr

2.11 τὸν δὲ <ναυτικὸν> πλοῦτον Marr: τὸν δ' ἐ<κ πλοῦ> πλοῦτον Frisch; no insertion Bowersock
τὸν ἄρχοντα (1) M: τοὺς ἄρχοντας ABC, Bowersock
τὸν ἄρχοντα (2) ABCM: τοὺς ἄρχοντας Kirchhoff, Bowersock

2.12 οἵτινες ACM: εἴ τινες B; οἳ τινες Renehan, Bowersock; οὔ τινες O'Sullivan
οὐδ' ἔστι Marchant: οὐδ' ἐστὶ Kalinka, Bowersock

(7) If one should also mention lesser matters, first, it is through their rule of the sea that they have mixed with other peoples in other places, and so discovered varieties of luxury foods. Whatever the delicacy in Sicily or Italy or Cyprus or Egypt or Lydia or Pontus or the Peloponnese or anywhere else, all these delicacies have been gathered together in the one place, simply because of their rule of the sea. (8) Secondly, through hearing every sort of language, they have acquired for themselves this word from one language, that from another. The other Greeks stick rather to their individual language and diet and dress, whereas the Athenians employ a mixture, which comes from all the Greeks and non-Greeks.

(9) As for sacrifices and sanctuaries and feasts and precincts, the *demos* realise that each individual of the poor does not have the ability to sacrifice and provide a feast and set up sanctuaries and create a beautiful and great city to live in, and so they have found a way by which all these things can be acquired. Hence it is the state which at public expense sacrifices many victims, but it is the *demos* who enjoy the feasts, and to whom the victims are allocated. (10) The rich, some of them, have their own private gymnasia, baths and changing rooms; but the *demos* are getting built for themselves many exercise areas, changing rooms and baths of their own, and from these the mob derive more enjoyment than do the few and the well-to-do.

(11) They alone of Greeks and non-Greeks are able to possess naval wealth. For if some city is rich in timber for shipbuilding, where will it dispose of it, if it does not have the consent of the ruler of the sea? What if a city is rich in iron or copper or flax? Where will it dispose of it, if it does not have the consent of the ruler of the sea? And yet it is from these very materials that I get my ships, taking timber from one place, iron from another, copper from another, flax from another, and wax from another. (12) Furthermore, they will prevent any of our rivals from transporting these materials as a cargo to any other place, with the threat that, otherwise, they will be stopped from using the sea at all. Thus, despite producing nothing from my land, I possess all these materials because of the sea. Yet no other city has two of these things. Timber and flax are not found in the same city; rather, where there is an abundance of flax, the land is flat and timberless. Copper and iron do not come from the same city either, nor is there any other combination of two or three of the materials to be found in any one city, but, rather, there is just one in this place, another in that.

(13) ἔτι δὲ πρὸς τούτοις παρὰ πᾶσαν ἤπειρόν ἐστιν ἢ ἀκτὴ προέχουσα ἢ νῆσος προκειμένη ἢ στενόπορόν τι· ὥστε ἔξεστιν ἐνταῦθα ἐφορμοῦσι τοῖς τῆς θαλάττης ἄρχουσι λωβᾶσθαι τοὺς τὴν ἤπειρον οἰκοῦντας. (14) ἑνὸς δὲ ἐνδεεῖς εἰσιν· εἰ γὰρ νῆσον οἰκοῦντες θαλασσοκράτορες ἦσαν Ἀθηναῖοι, ὑπῆρχεν ἂν αὐτοῖς ποιεῖν μὲν κακῶς εἰ ἠβούλοντο, πάσχειν δὲ μηδέν, ἕως τῆς θαλάττης ἦρχον, μηδὲ τμηθῆναι τὴν ἑαυτῶν γῆν μηδὲ προσδέχεσθαι τοὺς πολεμίους. νῦν δὲ οἱ γεωργοῦντες καὶ οἱ πλούσιοι Ἀθηναίων ὑπέρχονται τοὺς πολεμίους μᾶλλον, ὁ δὲ δῆμος, ἅτε εὖ εἰδὼς ὅτι οὐδὲν τῶν σφῶν ἐμπρήσουσιν οὐδὲ τεμοῦσιν, ἀδεῶς ζῇ καὶ οὐχ ὑπερχόμενος αὐτούς. (15) πρὸς δὲ τούτοις καὶ ἑτέρου δέους ἀπηλλαγμένοι ἂν ἦσαν εἰ νῆσον ᾤκουν, μηδέποτε προδοθῆναι τὴν πόλιν ὑπ' ὀλίγων μηδὲ πύλας ἀνοιχθῆναι μηδὲ πολεμίους ἐπεισπεσεῖν· πῶς γὰρ νῆσον οἰκούντων ταυτ' ἂν ἐγίγνετο; μηδ' αὖ στασιάσαι τῷ δήμῳ μηδένα εἰ νῆσον ᾤκουν· νῦν μὲν γάρ, εἰ στασιάσαιεν, ἐλπίδα ἂν ἔχοντες ἐν τοῖς πολεμίοις στασιάσειαν ὡς κατὰ γῆν ἐπαξόμενοι. εἰ δὲ νῆσον ᾤκουν, καὶ ταῦτα ἂν ἀδεῶς εἶχεν αὐτοῖς. (16) ἐπειδὴ οὖν ἐξ ἀρχῆς οὐκ ἔτυχον οἰκήσαντες νῆσον, νῦν τάδε ποιοῦσι· τὴν μὲν οὐσίαν ταῖς νήσοις παρατίθενται πιστεύοντες τῇ ἀρχῇ τῇ κατὰ θάλατταν, τὴν δὲ Ἀττικὴν γῆν περιορῶσι τεμνομένην, γιγνώσκοντες ὅτι εἰ αὐτὴν ἐλεήσουσιν ἑτέρων ἀγαθῶν μειζόνων στερήσονται. (17) ἔτι δὲ συμμαχίας καὶ τοὺς ὅρκους ταῖς μὲν ὀλιγαρχουμέναις πόλεσιν ἀνάγκη ἐμπεδοῦν· ἢν δὲ μὴ ἐμμενῶσι ταῖς συνθήκαις ἢ ὑπό του ἀδικῇ, <τὰ> ὀνόματα γραπτὰ τῶν ὀλίγων οἳ συνέθεντο. ἅσσα δ' ἂν ὁ δῆμος συνθῆται ἔξεστιν αὐτῷ, ἑνὶ ἀνατιθέντι τὴν αἰτίαν τῷ λέγοντι καὶ τῷ ἐπιψηφίσαντι ἀρνεῖσθαι τοῖς ἄλλοις ὅτι "οὐ παρῆν οὐδὲ ἀρέσκει ἐμοί γε" ἃ συγκείμενα πυνθάνονται ἐν πλήρει τῷ δήμῳ. καὶ εἰ μὴ δόξαι εἶναι ταῦτα, προφάσεις μυρίας ἐξηύρηκε τοῦ μὴ ποιεῖν ὅσα ἂν μὴ βούλωνται. καὶ ἂν μέν τι κακὸν ἀναβαίνῃ ἀπὸ ὧν ὁ δῆμος ἐβούλευσεν, αἰτιᾶται ὁ δῆμος ὡς ὀλίγοι ἄνθρωποι αὐτῷ ἀντιπράττοντες διέφθειραν· ἐὰν δέ τι ἀγαθόν, σφίσιν αὐτοῖς τὴν αἰτίαν ἀνατιθέασι.

2.17 ὑπό του ἀδικῇ Frisch, Bowersock: ὑφ' ὅτου ἀδικεῖ ABCM
     <τὰ> ὀνόματα γραπτὰ Marr: ὀνόματα ἀπὸ ABCM, Bowersock; ὀνόματα ἅπτὰ <τὰ>
     Frisch
     ἐμοί γε Kirchhoff: οἵ γε AM, Bowersock; εἴ γε BC
     ἃ συγκείμενα πυνθάνονται Müller: τὰ συγκείμενα πυνθάνονται ABCM; πυνθάνονται
     obelised Bowersock

(13) Furthermore, every mainland coast has either a projecting headland, or an offshore island, or some narrow strait; with the result that it is possible for the rulers of the sea to make a landing there, and to devastate the inhabitants of the mainland.

(14) But there is one thing which they lack. If the Athenians were thalassocrats who lived on an island, it would be possible for them to inflict damage, if they so wished, but, as long as they ruled the sea, not to suffer any, not to have their land ravaged and not to have to face the enemy's invasions. As it is, the farmers and the rich among the Athenians truckle to the enemy, rather, whereas the *demos*, since they know well that the enemy will not burn or cut down anything of theirs, live without fear, and without truckling to them. (15) Moreover, if they lived on an island, they would be free of another fear as well, namely that the city would ever be betrayed, or the gates opened, by oligarchs, or the enemy burst in. For how could these things happen if they lived on an island? Nor would they have to fear that anyone might rebel against the democracy, if they lived on an island. As it is, if there were a civil war, the rebels would have hopes of getting support from the enemy, by bringing them in by land. But if they lived on an island, this too would not be a cause of concern for them. (16) So now, because from the start they have not had the natural good fortune to have lived on an island, they do the following things. Trusting in their command of the sea, they place their possessions on the islands, and allow the land of Attica to be ravaged, since they realise that, if they show concern for it, they will lose other, greater, benefits.

(17) Further, with regard to alliances and the oaths, it is necessary for oligarchically-governed cities to stand by them. If they do not abide by the agreements, or if you are wronged by anyone, the names of the small number of men who made the agreement are written down. By contrast, it is possible for the *demos* to disown whatever agreements it makes, by referring the responsibility to the one man who proposed the motion and the one who put it to the vote, and for the rest to say, by way of denial, that 'I was not present, nor do I approve' of the things which they are told were agreed in a full assembly-meeting. And if it does not suit them that these agreements should come into force, they have discovered innumerable excuses for not doing what they do not want to do. Indeed, if anything bad results from the *demos*' policies, the *demos* blame a small group of men, working against them, for ruining their plans. But if anything good results, they assign the credit to themselves.

(18) κωμῳδεῖν δ' αὖ καὶ κακῶς λέγειν τὸν μὲν δῆμον οὐκ ἐῶσιν, ἵνα μὴ αὐτοὶ ἀκούωσι κακῶς· ἰδίᾳ δὲ κελεύουσιν, εἴ τίς τινα βούλεται, εὖ εἰδότες ὅτι οὐχὶ τοῦ δήμου ἐστὶν οὐδὲ τοῦ πλήθους ὁ κωμῳδούμενος ὡς ἐπὶ τὸ πολύ, ἀλλ' ἢ πλούσιος ἢ γενναῖος ἢ δυνάμενος, ὀλίγοι δέ τινες τῶν πενήτων καὶ τῶν δημοτικῶν κωμῳδοῦνται καὶ οὐδ' οὗτοι ἐὰν μὴ διὰ πολυπραγμοσύνην καὶ διὰ τὸ ζητεῖν πλέον τι ἔχειν τοῦ δήμου, ὥστε οὐδὲ τοὺς τοιούτους ἄχθονται κωμῳδουμένους.

(19) φημὶ οὖν ἔγωγε τὸν δῆμον τὸν Ἀθήνησι γιγνώσκειν οἵτινες χρηστοί εἰσι τῶν πολιτῶν καὶ οἵτινες πονηροί, γιγνώσκοντες δὲ τοὺς μὲν σφίσιν αὐτοῖς ἐπιτηδείους καὶ συμφόρους φιλοῦσι, κἂν πονηροὶ ὦσι, τοὺς δὲ χρηστοὺς μισοῦσι μᾶλλον· οὐ γὰρ νομίζουσι τὴν ἀρετὴν αὐτοῖς πρὸς τῷ σφετέρῳ ἀγαθῷ πεφυκέναι, ἀλλ' ἐπὶ τῷ κακῷ. καὶ τοὐναντίον γε τούτου ἔνιοι ὄντες ὡς ἀληθῶς τοῦ δήμου, τὴν φύσιν οὐ δημοτικοί εἰσι. (20) δημοκρατίαν δ' ἐγὼ μὲν αὐτῷ τῷ δήμῳ συγγιγνώσκω· αὐτὸν μὲν γὰρ εὖ ποιεῖν παντὶ συγγνώμη ἐστίν. ὅστις δὲ μὴ ὢν τοῦ δήμου εἵλετο ἐν δημοκρατουμένῃ πόλει οἰκεῖν μᾶλλον ἢ ἐν ὀλιγαρχουμένῃ, ἀδικεῖν παρεσκευάσατο καὶ ἔγνω ὅτι μᾶλλον οἷόν τε διαλαθεῖν κακῷ ὄντι ἐν δημοκρατουμένῃ πόλει μᾶλλον ἢ ἐν ὀλιγαρχουμένῃ.

(18) Again, when it comes to comic mockery and abuse, they do not allow this to be directed against the *demos*, in order that they may not have to hear themselves being abused. But in the case of individuals, they encourage anyone who wishes to attack anyone else, since they are well aware that the person mocked is not, for the most part, from the *demos* or the masses, but one of the rich or well born or influential. Only a few of the poor and the common people are mocked, and in these cases only because of their meddlesomeness and their attempts to gain some advantage over the *demos*. Hence they are not upset at seeing such people, also, mocked in comedy.

(19) It is my personal opinion that the *demos* at Athens know which citizens are valuable and which are worthless, but that, despite this knowledge, they cherish those who are convenient and useful to themselves, even if they are worthless; as for the valuable ones, they hate them rather. For the *demos* do not think that the innate excellence of such men will be used to bring about their good, but, rather, to bring about their harm. Conversely, there are some men who actually take the side of the people, even though they are not by nature commoners. (20) Now I forgive the *demos* themselves for their democracy. For one has to forgive anyone for looking after himself. But whoever is not a member of the *demos*, and yet has chosen to have a political life in a democratic city rather than an oligarchic one, has deliberately set himself to act unjustly, and has realised that it is easier for a man who is wicked to escape notice in a democratically governed city than it is in an oligarchic one.

(1) καὶ περὶ τῆς Ἀθηναίων πολιτείας τὸν μὲν τρόπον οὐκ ἐπαινῶ· ἐπειδὴ δ᾽ ἔδοξεν αὐτοῖς δημοκρατεῖσθαι, εὖ μοι δοκοῦσι διασῴζεσθαι τὴν δημοκρατίαν τούτῳ τῷ τρόπῳ χρώμενοι ᾧ ἐγὼ ἐπέδειξα. ἔτι δὲ καὶ τάδε τινὰς ὁρῶ μεμφομένους Ἀθηναίους, ὅτι ἐνίοτε οὐκ ἔστιν αὐτόθι χρηματίσαι τῇ βουλῇ οὐδὲ τῷ δήμῳ ἐνιαυτὸν καθημένῳ ἀνθρώπῳ. καὶ τοῦτο Ἀθήνησι γίγνεται οὐδὲν δι᾽ ἄλλο ἢ διὰ τὸ πλῆθος τῶν πραγμάτων· οὐχ οἷοί τε πάντας ἀποπέμπειν εἰσὶ χρηματίσαντες. (2) πῶς γὰρ ἂν καὶ οἷοί τε εἶεν, οὕστινας πρῶτον μὲν δεῖ ἑορτάσαι ἑορτὰς ὅσας οὐδεμία τῶν Ἑλληνίδων πόλεων (ἐν δὲ ταύταις ἧττόν τινα δυνατόν ἐστι διαπράττεσθαι τῶν τῆς πόλεως), ἔπειτα δὲ δίκας καὶ γραφὰς καὶ εὐθύνας ἐκδικάζειν ὅσας οὐδ᾽ οἱ σύμπαντες ἄνθρωποι ἐκδικάζουσι, τὴν δὲ βουλὴν βουλεύεσθαι πολλὰ μὲν περὶ τοῦ πολέμου, πολλὰ δὲ περὶ πόρου χρημάτων, πολλὰ δὲ περὶ νόμων θέσεως, πολλὰ δὲ περὶ τῶν κατὰ πόλιν ἀεὶ γιγνομένων, πολλὰ δὲ καὶ τοῖς συμμάχοις, καὶ φόρον δέξασθαι καὶ νεωρίων ἐπιμεληθῆναι καὶ ἱερῶν; ἆρα δή τι θαυμαστόν ἐστιν εἰ τοσούτων ὑπαρχόντων πραγμάτων μὴ οἷοί τ᾽ εἰσὶ πᾶσιν ἀνθρώποις χρηματίσαι; (3) λέγουσι δέ τινας· "ἢν τις ἀργύριον ἔχων προσίῃ πρὸς βουλὴν ἢ δῆμον, χρηματιεῖται." ἐγὼ δὲ τούτοις ὁμολογήσαιμ᾽ ἂν ἀπὸ χρημάτων πολλὰ διαπράττεσθαι Ἀθήνησι, καὶ ἔτι ἂν πλείω διαπράττεσθαι εἰ πλείους ἔτι ἐδίδοσαν ἀργύριον. τοῦτο μέντοι εὖ οἶδα, διότι πᾶσι διαπρᾶξαι ἡ πόλις τῶν δεομένων οὐχ ἱκανή, οὐδ᾽ εἰ ὁποσονοῦν χρυσίον καὶ ἀργύριον διδοίη τις αὐτοῖς. (4) δεῖ δὲ καὶ τάδε διαδικάζειν, εἴ τις τὴν ναῦν μὴ ἐπισκευάζει ἢ κατοικοδομεῖ τι δημόσιον. πρὸς δὲ τούτοις χορηγοῖς διαδικάσαι εἰς Διονύσια καὶ Θαργήλια καὶ Παναθήναια καὶ Προμήθια καὶ Ἡφαίστια ὅσα ἔτη. καὶ τριήραρχοι καθίστανται τετρακόσιοι ἑκάστου ἐνιαυτοῦ, καὶ τούτων τοῖς βουλομένοις διαδικάσαι ὅσα ἔτη. πρὸς δὲ τούτοις ἀρχὰς δοκιμάσαι καὶ διαδικάσαι καὶ ὀρφανοὺς δοκιμάσαι καὶ φύλακας δεσμωτῶν καταστῆσαι.

3.1   ἐπειδὴ δ᾽ C: ἐπειδήπερ ABM, Bowersock
       καὶ τοῦτο ABCM, Bowersock: perhaps τοῦτο <δ᾽> Marr
       ἢ διὰ . . . πραγμάτων· οὐχ οἷοί O'Sullivan: ἢ <διότι> διὰ . . . πραγμάτων οὐχ οἷοί
       Kirchhoff, Bowersock
3.2   τοῖς συμμάχοις ABCM, Bowersock: <περὶ τῶν ἐν> τοῖς συμμάχοις Schneider
3.3   ἔτι ἐδίδοσαν Cobet, Bowersock: ἐπεδίδοσαν ABCM
3.4   τετρακόσιοι ABCM: perhaps τριακόσιοι Bowersock

(1) With regard to the Athenians' constitution, I do not approve of its form. But, since they have decided to have a democratic constitution, I think that they preserve their democracy effectively by adopting the practices which I have explained.

A further point. I see that some people blame the Athenians because it is sometimes not possible for the council or the assembly to do business with a person there, even though he sits waiting for a whole year. This happens at Athens because of nothing other than the large amount of public business: they are not able to do business with everyone before sending them away. (2) How would they be able to do so, when, first of all, they have to hold more festivals than any of the Greek states (and during these there is even less possibility that any of the state's business can be transacted); secondly, they have to conduct private and public lawsuits and examinations of officials in greater numbers than the whole of mankind; and then the council has to deliberate a great deal about the war, a great deal about provision of finances, a great deal about the framing of legislation, a great deal about day-to-day domestic matters, a great deal also with regard to the allies, and it has to take receipt of tribute and look after the dockyards and sanctuaries. So is it at all surprising that, when they have so much existing business, they are not able to deal with all mankind? (3) But some people say, 'If anyone approaches the council or assembly with money, he will get his business dealt with then.' I would agree with them that many things get accomplished at Athens with money, and still more would be accomplished if more people offered money. But there is one thing that I am quite sure of, namely, that the state is simply not capable of dealing with every petitioner, not even if one were to offer them any amount of gold and silver.

(4) They also have to judge in the following cases, namely, if a man does not repair his ship, or builds something on public land. In addition to this, they have to adjudicate every year over the appointment of *choregoi* at the Dionysia, Thargelia, Panathenaea, Promethia and Hephaestia. Each year four hundred trierarchs are appointed, and every year they have to settle disputes over the appointments in the cases of any who wish it. In addition to this, they have to approve and judge officials, and to approve orphans

(5) ταῦτα μὲν οὖν ὅσα ἔτη. διὰ χρόνου <δὲ> διαδικάσαι δεῖ ἀστρατείας καὶ ἐάν τι ἄλλο ἐξαπιναῖον ἀδίκημα γίγνηται, ἐάν τε ὑβρίζωσί τινες ἄηθες ὕβρισμα, ἐάν τε ἀσεβήσωσι. πολλὰ ἔτι πάνυ παραλείπω. τὸ δὲ μέγιστον εἴρηται πλὴν αἱ τάξεις τοῦ φόρου· τοῦτο δὲ γίγνεται ὡς τὰ πολλὰ δι' ἔτους πέμπτου. (6) φέρε δὴ τοίνυν, ταῦτα οὐκ οἴεσθαι <χρὴ> χρῆναι διαδικάζειν ἅπαντα; εἰπάτω γάρ τις ὅ τι οὐ χρῆν αὐτόθι διαδικάζεσθαι. εἰ δ' αὖ ὁμολογεῖν δεῖ ἅπαντα χρῆναι διαδικάζειν, ἀνάγκη δι' ἐνιαυτοῦ, ὡς οὐδὲ νῦν δι' ἐνιαυτοῦ δικάζοντες ὑπάρχουσιν ὥστε παύειν τοὺς ἀδικοῦντας ὑπὸ τοῦ πλήθους τῶν ἀνθρώπων. (7) φέρε δή, ἀλλὰ φήσει τις χρῆναι δικάζειν μέν, ἐλάττους δὲ δικάζειν. ἀνάγκη τοίνυν, ἐὰν μὴ ὀλίγα ποιῶνται δικαστήρια, ὀλίγοι ἐν ἑκάστῳ ἔσονται τῷ δικαστηρίῳ, ὥστε καὶ διασκευάσασθαι ῥάδιον ἔσται πρὸς ὀλίγους δικαστὰς καὶ συνδεκάσαι, πολὺ ἧττον <δὲ> δικαίως δικάζειν. (8) πρὸς δὲ τούτοις οἴεσθαι χρὴ καὶ ἑορτὰς ἄγειν χρῆναι Ἀθηναίους, ἐν αἷς οὐχ οἷόν τε δικάζειν· καὶ ἄγουσι μὲν ἑορτὰς διπλασίους ἢ οἱ ἄλλοι· ἀλλ' ἐγὼ μὲν τίθημι ἴσας τῇ ὀλιγίστας ἀγούσῃ πόλει.

τούτων τοίνυν τοιούτων ὄντων οὔ φημι οἷόν τ' εἶναι ἄλλως ἔχειν τὰ πράγματα Ἀθήνησιν ἢ ὥσπερ νῦν ἔχει, πλὴν εἰ κατὰ μικρόν τι οἷόν τε τὸ μὲν ἀφελεῖν τὸ δὲ προσθεῖναι. πολὺ δ' οὐχ οἷόν τε μετακινεῖν, ὥστε μὴ οὐχὶ τῆς δημοκρατίας ἀφαιρεῖν τι. (9) ὥστε μὲν γὰρ βέλτιον ἔχειν τὴν πολιτείαν, οἷόν τε πολλὰ ἐξευρεῖν· ὥστε μέντοι ὑπάρχειν μὲν δημοκρατίαν εἶναι, ἀρκούντως δὲ τοῦτο ἐξευρεῖν ὅπως δὴ βέλτιον πολιτεύσονται, οὐ ῥᾴδιον, πλὴν ὅτι ἄρτι εἶπον κατὰ μικρόν τι προσθέντα ἢ ἀφελόντα.

3.5 ἀστρατείας Brodaeus, Bowersock: στρατιᾶς AC; στρατιὰς M; στρατιὰ B; στρατηγικὰς Lipsius, perhaps στρατηγικὰς <δίκας> Brock & Heath

3.6 οἴεσθαι <χρὴ> Wachsmuth, Bowersock: or alternatively οἴεσθε with no insertion Marr

3.7 συνδεκάσαι Matthiae, Bowersock: συνδικάσαι ABCM
     <δὲ> Kalinka, Bowersock

3.8 ὀλιγίστας CM, Bowersock: ὀλιγούσας AB

3.9 ὅπως δὴ Bowersock: ὅπως δὲ ABM; ὅπως C; sentence perhaps corrupt Marr and appoint guards for prisoners. (5) All these things have to happen every year. Then, intermittently, they have to judge cases of avoidance of military service and any other sudden crime which may occur, i.e. if any people commit an unusual act of arrogance or of impiety. And there are many more items which I completely pass over. I have mentioned the most important, apart from the assessments of tribute. This usually takes place every four years.

(6) Well then, ought one to think that they ought not to deal with all these cases? Let someone say which ought not to be dealt with there. But if we have to agree that they ought to judge them all, the process is one which needs to go on throughout the year, since not even now when they do judge throughout the year are they in a position to stop all the wrongdoers, because of the large size of the population. (7) All right, but someone will say that they do have to judge cases, but that fewer people ought to do the judging. In that case there will need to be only a few judges in each court, unless they make the number of courts small; and then, with only a few judges, it will be easy to make an arrangement and to bribe them, and they will be much less likely to judge justly. (8) Furthermore, one has to take into consideration the fact that the Athenians ought to hold festivals, during which they do not have the ability to judge lawsuits. And they actually hold twice as many festivals as the others do. But I am assuming that they only hold as many as the state which holds the fewest.

Since these things are so, I maintain that there is not the ability for public business at Athens to be different from the way it is now, except in so far as there is the ability to remove or add something just to a slight extent. There is no ability to make a substantial change, without removing some element of the democracy itself. (9) It is possible to devise many ways to make the constitution a better one; but to devise one effective enough to result in their definitely having a better constitution, while still remaining a democracy, is not easy, except, as I have just said, by adding or removing something just to a slight extent.

(10) δοκοῦσι δὲ Ἀθηναῖοι καὶ τοῦτο οὐκ ὀρθῶς βουλεύεσθαι, ὅτι τοὺς χείρους αἱροῦνται ἐν ταῖς πόλεσι ταῖς στασιαζούσαις. οἱ δὲ τοῦτο γνώμῃ ποιοῦσιν· εἰ μὲν γὰρ ᾑροῦντο τοὺς βελτίους, ᾑροῦντ' ἂν οὐχὶ τοὺς ταὐτὰ γιγνώσκοντας σφίσιν αὐτοῖς. ἐν οὐδεμίᾳ γὰρ πόλει τὸ βέλτιστον εὔνουν ἐστὶ τῷ δήμῳ, ἀλλὰ τὸ κάκιστον ἐν ἑκάστῃ ἐστὶ πόλει εὔνουν τῷ δήμῳ· οἱ γὰρ ὅμοιοι τοῖς ὁμοίοις εὔνοοί εἰσι. διὰ ταῦτα οὖν Ἀθηναῖοι τὰ σφίσιν αὐτοῖς προσήκοντα αἱροῦνται. (11) ὁποσάκις δὲ ἐπεχείρησαν αἱρεῖσθαι τοὺς βελτίστους, οὐ συνήνεγκεν αὐτοῖς· ἀλλ' ἐντὸς ὀλίγου χρόνου ὁ δῆμος ἐδούλευσεν ὁ ἐν Βοιωτοῖς· τοῦτο δέ, ὅτε Μιλησίων εἵλοντο τοὺς βελτίστους, ἐντὸς ὀλίγου χρόνου ἀποστάντες τὸν δῆμον κατέκοψαν· τοῦτο δέ, ὅτε εἵλοντο Λακεδαιμονίους ἀντὶ Μεσσηνίων, ἐντὸς ὀλίγου χρόνου Λακεδαιμόνιοι καταστρεψάμενοι Μεσσηνίους ἐπολέμουν Ἀθηναίοις.

(12) ὑπολάβοι δέ τις ἂν ὡς "οὐδεὶς ἄρα ἀδίκως ἠτίμωται Ἀθήνησιν;" ἐγὼ δέ φημί τινας εἶναι οἳ ἀδίκως ἠτίμωνται, ὀλίγοι μέντοι τινές· ἀλλ' οὐκ ὀλίγων δεῖ τῶν ἐπιθησομένων τῇ δημοκρατίᾳ τῇ Ἀθήνησιν. ἐπεί τοι καὶ οὕτως ἔχει, οὐ δεῖ ἐνθυμεῖσθαι ἀνθρώπους εἴ τινες δικαίως ἠτίμωνται ἀλλ' εἴ τινες ἀδίκως. (13) πῶς ἂν οὖν ἀδίκως οἴοιτό τις ἂν τοὺς πολλοὺς ἠτιμῶσθαι Ἀθήνησιν, ὅπου ὁ δῆμός ἐστιν ὁ ἄρχων τὰς ἀρχάς; ἐκ δὲ τοῦ μὴ δικαίως ἄρχειν μηδὲ λέγειν τὰ δίκαια <μηδὲ> πράττειν, ἐκ τοιούτων ἄτιμοί εἰσιν Ἀθήνησι. ταῦτα χρὴ λογιζόμενον μὴ νομίζειν εἶναί τι δεινὸν ἀπὸ τῶν ἀτίμων Ἀθήνησιν.

3.10–11 perhaps displaced from between 2. 17 and 18 Marr
3.10   τοῦτο οὐκ ὀρθῶς Morus: τοῦτό μοι οὐκ ὀρθῶς ABCM, Bowersock
          οἱ δὲ Marchant: οἳ δὲ Kalinka, Bowersock
3.12   οὐ δεῖ H. Fränkel, Bowersock: οὐδὲν ABCM; perhaps οὐδὲν <δεινὸν τῇ δημοκρατίᾳ
          τῇ Ἀθήνησιν·> οὐ <γὰρ> δεῖ Marr

(10) On the following point also the Athenians are thought to have a mistaken policy, in that they take the side of the inferior classes in states which are involved in a civil war. But they do this with good reason. If they took the side of the better classes, they would be supporting those who do not have the same views as themselves. For in no state is the best element well disposed to the *demos*; rather in every state it is the worst element which is well disposed to the *demos*. For like is well disposed to like. That is why the Athenians choose to support the side which is related to themselves. (11) Whenever they have attempted to take the side of the best men, it has not worked out well for them; thus, within a short time, the *demos* in Boeotia were enslaved. Again, when they chose to support the best men at Miletus, within a short time they had revolted and massacred the *demos* there. Again, when they chose to support the Spartans instead of the Messenians, within a short time the Spartans had subdued the Messenians, and were at war with the Athenians.

(12) Someone might object, 'Has no one then been unjustly disfranchised at Athens?' I reply that there are indeed some who have been unjustly disfranchised, but only a few. However, one needs more than a few to make an attack on the democracy at Athens. Since this is indeed the case, one must not count those people who have been justly disfranchised, but only those who have been so unjustly. (13) For how could anyone think that the majority of people have been unjustly disfranchised at Athens, a state where it is the *demos* who hold the political offices? It is from failing to hold office justly, or to say or do what is just, that men are disfranchised at Athens. Taking this into account, one has to conclude that there is nothing to fear from the disfranchised at Athens.

COMMENTARY

1.1. But with regard to the Athenians' constitution . . . : The author opens his work with a programmatic statement, in which, after making clear his personal distaste for democracy as a political constitution in general, and Athenian democracy in particular, he announces that he is going to demonstrate two things, (*a*) that the Athenians effectively preserve their constitution by doing the things for which they are criticised by 'the rest of the Greeks', and (*b*) that they also transact their public business effectively, despite these criticisms.

This division corresponds to a division of the subject matter in the work between chapters 1 and 2 and most of chapter 3. In chapters 1 and 2 he deals with a string of imagined criticisms of particular practices and policies to be found in the system, all of which he claims are deliberately arranged to be as they are, in order to preserve the constitution and benefit the *demos.* In chapter 3 he turns to details of the administration and the processing of public business, which he claims the Athenians deal with slowly, but as effectively as it is possible for them, given the size of the population and the mass of business they have to deal with. The language in 1.1 is deliberately picked up in 3.1 (περὶ τῆς Ἀθηναίων πολιτείας / τὸν . . . τρόπον / οὐκ ἐπαινῶ / ἐπειδήπερ ἔδοξεν / εὖ . . . διασῴζεσθαι / ἐπέδειξα), where, in an obviously summarising section, the author claims to have completed the first of the two objectives announced in 1.1 (see on 3.1). Similarly διαπράττονται (meaning 'transact public business') in 1.1, which is used with reference to his second objective, is picked up and repeated four times in 3.2–4, where he has turned to dealing with this second topic, administration.

The overall sense of the final sentence of 1.1 is reasonably clear, but the author's expression in detail is rather awkward. ἁμαρτάνειν here must mean 'do / act badly or mistakenly' (this is shown by, *e.g.,* 1.16, 2.1). In effect it is the opposite of εὖ διασῴζονται a few words earlier. The adverb εὖ (= 'effectively', 'successfully') is to be taken with both verbs διασῴζονται and διαπράττονται, although it is formally attached only to διασῴζονται. τἆλλα, however, is problematic. This is usually translated as 'the other things', and taken grammatically as the direct object of διαπράττονται. But that does not give very clear sense: in the expression 'transact their other public business', what business is 'their other public business' being distinguished from? It may be better to take τἆλλα as essentially adverbial here, in the sense 'for the rest', 'secondly', 'also' (*cf.* LSJ *s.v.* ἄλλος, II. 6 and 8). The relative clause starting with ἃ will then be an internal accusative, formally with διαπράττονται (= 'conduct their public business in the respects in which'), but like εὖ belonging in sense with both verbs. The whole sentence can then be translated as 'Given that they have decided that things should be as they are, I shall demonstrate how effectively they preserve their constitution and also (how effectively they) transact their public business, in (all) those respects in which the rest of the Greeks think they act mistakenly'.

Why did X insert the confusing τᾶλλα at all? The sentence would be easier without it. It is there, probably, partly because he wished to indicate that there will be two parts to his treatise (*i.e.* in the present division chapters 1–2 and most of 3), something which is otherwise not clearly signalled in 1.1, and partly for stylistic reasons – it enables him to complete an apparent chiasmus, διασώζονται (A^1) τὴν πολιτείαν (B^1), τᾶλλα (B^2) διαπράττονται (A^2). Compare 1.11, where the word ἐνίους performs a similar function, completing a contrived chiasmus.

1.1. But: This word (δὲ) looks odd coming in the opening sentence of the work, but it should not be removed from the text: there are parallels for the usage (*cf.*, *e.g.*, Xen. *Apology* 1, which begins Σωκράτους δὲ . . .). In addition, we know that in antiquity the *Constitution of the Athenians* and the *Constitution of the Lacedaemonians* were regarded as a single book. Diogenes Laertius (II. 57) refers to this, and puts the Athenian part first (*cf.* Introduction, p. 6). But all the surviving manuscripts have them in the reverse order, with the Spartan *Constitution* preceding the Athenian, and it may be that the δὲ here was inserted by an early commentator to provide a connecting link between this book and the (preceding) *Constitution of the Lacedaemonians*, at the time when they were considered to be a single book.

1.1. the Athenians' constitution: The title given in the manuscripts to the work derives from these opening words, and was probably assigned to it by a later scholar, rather than by the author himself (see Introduction, p. 2). X himself makes it quite clear in this opening section that he is writing a subjective argumentative treatise, not a constitutional history or institutional survey of Athens. One should note in particular the heavy verbal repetition, and the immediate triple use of the first person of the verb. Incidentally, one could hardly have a clearer statement than we are given in 1. 1 of X's political position with regard to the democratic constitution: he does not approve of it.

1.1. the worthless men . . . the valuable: πονηροί and χρηστοί are X's favourite class-label terms (see Introduction, section 8). *Poneros/oi* occurs seven times in the treatise, and the abstract *poneria* twice; *chrestos/oi* fourteen times. Again the author's political position is made clear. This is the traditional terminology of the upper class anti-democrat, for whom the *demos* are inherently *poneroi* (see Introduction, section 8).

1.1. they . . . they . . . they . . . they . . . they: Throughout the treatise the Athenians are consistently referred to in the third person. This has the effect of, to some extent, 'distancing' X from his main subject. But this need not be a spatial distance, and the usage cannot be cited to support the view of Frisch, 91–8, and others, that X wrote his treatise outside Attica (see Introduction, pp. 14–15, and pp. 138–9, below). The 'distancing' third person, and the frequent use of the word αὐτόθι to refer to Athens (see 1.2 and p. 63, below), would be perfectly appropriate in a lecture or an academic discussion paper (see Introduction, pp. 14–15).

1.1. I shall demonstrate: The verb ἀποδείκνυμι in the sense 'demonstrate by argument', 'prove', is a favourite word of (but is not peculiar to) philosophers and orators: this again is appropriate to an academic discussion (see Introduction, p. 15). *Cf.* ἐπιδείκνυμι in 3.1.

1.1. the rest of the Greeks: X contrasts Athens with the whole of the rest of the Greek world. For similar exaggerated contrasts *cf.* 2.8, 11, 3.8. The implication that Athenian democracy was a unique phenomenon in the Greek world is false. There were a number of other democracies, and in these states the Athenian model, with its associated tolerance and culture, was no doubt much admired (as Pericles claims, at Thuc. II. 41.1). What X actually means is 'their *critics* in the rest of the Greek world'. The phrase (with τοῖς ἄλλοις) here surely indicates that the 'opponents' whose arguments he is going to take issue with repeatedly throughout the treatise (first mentioned explicitly at 1.4), are, or are to be thought of as, non-Athenians, probably primarily Spartans (see Introduction, section 5). The treatise therefore cannot be a work like Andocides' *To his Comrades* (cited by Kalinka 40), *i.e.* a political pamphlet addressed to and delivered before the fellow-members of his Athenian club or *hetaireia*. It is equally unlikely to have been composed for delivery at a symposium. It is possible that, on occasions, some non-Athenians were present at the symposia of the Athenian well-to-do (though the evidence suggests that the guests were usually fellow-citizens), but the contributions made at symposia seem, when original, to have been tailored to a witty, light-hearted atmosphere, in which polemical political debate would have been badly out of place (*cf.* Ar. *Wasps* 1170–1264, Pl. *Symposium*). The likeliest setting for X's treatise is provided by the circle of the sophists and their pupils, in which the merits and demerits of different forms of constitution may have been debated from different points of view (*cf.* Introduction, section 5; also Kalinka 52–4, Forrest [1975], 43–5).

1.2–9. This passage coheres together. It is concerned with the political power exercised by the *demos* at Athens, through (*a*) holding offices, (*b*) serving on the council (*boule*) and (*c*) attending and proposing motions in the assembly. Three criticisms of existing practice are cited, and attributed to unnamed opponents (at 1.4, 6 and 7). In each case X proceeds to answer them. His replies do not take the form of denials or rebuttals. He accepts that the criticised practices do occur, and he shares his interlocutors' disapproval of them in themselves. But he argues that these are an inevitable consequence of the fact that Athens is a democracy. He assumes throughout the treatise that the citizen body is divided into two classes, the *demos* and his own class, the rich few or *oligoi*, and that these two classes are always and everywhere bitterly opposed to each other. Hence, if the *demos* wish the democratic constitution to continue, they have to dominate the state politically, however uneducated they may be, and however poor the decisions they make. If the *demos* were to allow the *oligoi* into positions of power, they would be damaging their own interests, since such men are inherently hostile to the *demos*, and would inevitably use their power to reduce the *demos* to total subservience.

The subject of office-holding is introduced at 1.2 and is dealt with in §§2–5. However, X's argument in 1.2 is not what we might expect, and comes as something of a surprise. He asserts that the *demos* are actually justified (*cf.* δίκαιοι) in dominating the political offices at Athens, because it is they who provide the manpower and expertise for the Athenian navy, and it is because of the navy that Athens is a powerful state.

He then (1.3) deals with an exception. The *demos* do not completely monopolise office-holding at Athens. There are some offices they do not hold, and do not wish to hold. These are the top military posts, such as the generalship, *strategia*, and the cavalry command, *hipparchia,* military offices on which the very safety of the state depends.

The evidence suggests that X is right in claiming that these posts were still, in the later fifth century, filled by members of the Athenian upper classes (see the entries for many of them in Davies, *APF*; of course such men did not necessarily share his political prejudices). The main reasons why this was so were, no doubt, (*a*) that they required a special expertise, which, up to now, only such people had the time and resources to acquire, and this fact was sensibly recognised by the *demos*, and (*b*) appointment to these offices was made not by allotment (as for most civilian offices) but by election (and often re-election) of those who were perceived to be the best candidates. X, however, offers two much less creditable reasons why the *demos* do not wish to hold these offices: (*c*) they do not wish to accept such a big responsibility, and (*d*) these offices are unpaid, so the *demos* would not benefit financially from holding them.

At this point (end of 1.3) X has taken up what is to become the *leitmotif* of the treatise – the Athenian *demos* looks only to its own advantage, its economic and political self-interest, and everything in the democratic system of government at Athens is deliberately arranged to be as it is, in order best to preserve the system and maintain the maximum flow of advantages to the *demos*. This argument is then developed in §§4–9, a passage in which X deals with three imagined criticisms of the system (at 4, 6 and 7), and, indeed, it pervades the whole of the rest of the treatise.

Thus the argument in 1.2, that the *demos* apparently deserve to hold the political offices, seems somewhat out of kilter and inconsistent with what we find in the rest of the work, where the issue of justification is not mentioned again. Why then does X introduce it at all? It is possible that he is responding here to an argument which was put forward by some anti-democratic theorists to justify a constitution where political rights were either wholly or in part restricted to the hoplite class, *i.e.* those wealthy enough to be able to provide themselves with the heavy arms and armour of an infantryman. This actually happened at Athens in 411 (Thuc. VIII. 65.3, 97.1). Such a constitution could be, and was, justified on the grounds that this was the class on which the power and the security of the state depended (*cf. e.g.* Arist. *Politics* III. 1279b 2–5).

It may be that at 1.2 X is deliberately turning this argument against its usual proponents. In other words, the assumed interlocutors who feature throughout the treatise from 1.4 onwards are implicitly in the background at 1.2 as well. X points out that, on the basis of the traditional objector's argument that the class which gives the state its military power and security should be the one which holds the political power, at Athens the Athenian *demos*, who provide most of the naval manpower, are justified in holding political power and dominating the political offices.

If we interpret 1.2 as a reply, like so much else in the treatise, to an assumed interlocutor's criticism of the system (in this case not actually cited by X), that would also explain 'next' in ἔπειτα δὲ ὃ ἔνιοι θαυμάζουσιν at the beginning of 1.4, a phrase which implies that he has *already* responded to a previous criticism, and that the one cited at 1.4 is not the first to be dealt with. We should note also the first person verb ἐρῶ at the beginning of 1.2. That is often an indication of a *reply* by X to an opponent's point (see Introduction, sections 5 and 9, and Appendixes 1 and 5).

X is undoubtedly factually correct in his claim at 1.2 that it was the Athenian navy which gave Athens its power. This became absolutely clear in the early years of the Peloponnesian War, *i.e.* the 420s, but it was becoming evident well before that. This passage therefore cannot in itself be used to support a date for the treatise in the 420s.

X is also correct in his claim that the citizens who crewed and operated the Athenian navy were what he calls the *demos, i.e.* the *thetes*, the poorest of the four Solonian census classes (*cf.* Ar. *Acharnians* 162–3, [Arist.] *Ath Pol.* 27. 1) – though we do not know to what extent non-Athenians (*e.g.* Thuc. I. 121.3, 143.1, VII. 13.2, 63.3–4) were employed to row Athenian ships (*cf.* pp. 80, 97, below). At the beginning of the Peloponnesian War the Athenians had no less than 300 triremes, oared fighting ships (Thuc. II. 13.8).

*1.2. the poor and the **demos** . . . the well-born and the rich:* These are not two different groups. For X, who is fond of these 'label lists' (*cf.* 1.4, 6, 7, 14, 2.10, 14, 18), often in contrast, the poor *are* the *demos* and *vice-versa*, and similarly the rich *are* the well-born (though we see in such men as Cleon and Nicias that by the late fifth century that was in fact not always true: p. 65, below): he regards the terms as interchangeable (see Introduction, section 8).

1.2. there: The word αὐτόθι occurs seven times in the treatise (at 1.2, 10 [twice], 11, 13, 3.1, 6), and always refers to Athens. For the precise sense of this word, and its implications for the place of composition of the treatise, see Introduction, section 5. Its use does not imply that X is writing his treatise somewhere other than Athens.

1.2. having more: The Greek expression πλέον ἔχειν is vague, as the English translation indicates. But the context shows that X is thinking here of political power rather than economic advantages. πλέον ἔχειν here is picked up by πλέον νέμουσι in 1. 4.

1.2. than the hoplites and the well–born and the valuable: The contrast shows that sometimes, for X, the *demos* does not include the hoplites, the heavily armed infantry, made up of citizens who could afford the requisite hoplite armour and weapons (see Introduction, section 7). On the other hand, when he writes at the end of this section of the *demos'* holding paid offices, the hoplites are tacitly included, since it was probably only with Athens' reduced citizen numbers after the Peloponnesian War that the ban on the *thetes'* holding office ceased to be enforced (*cf.* [Arist.] *Ath. Pol.* 7.4). He draws the line at different levels to suit his argument in different places (*cf.* Introduction, pp. 21–2; pp. 99–100, 122, below). Note that for the extreme oligarchs of 411 the five thousand privileged (hoplite) citizens were 'outright *demos*' (Thuc. VIII. 92.11).

1.2. both the allotted and the elective offices: The use of the lot and election were the two regular methods used at Athens for choosing public officials (*cf.* the survey in [Arist.] *Ath. Pol.* 43–62). By the later fifth century almost all civilian officials, including the archons, were chosen by lot (in the case of the archons, a two-stage allotment). The generals, *strategoi* (see on 1.3, below) and other military officials, and a few civilian officials thought to require expertise, were elected by the assembly.

1.2. any citizen who wishes should be allowed to have his say: The expression ὁ βουλόμενος was common in Athenian, and more generally in Greek, political and legal contexts. However, the phrase ὁ βουλόμενος is more applicable to speaking in the assembly (where the herald formally asked, τίς ἀγορεύειν βούλεται; 'Who wishes to speak?' *e.g.* Ar. *Acharnians* 45), or to prosecuting in those cases which were not limited to the family of the injured party (*e.g.* [Arist.] *Ath. Pol.* 9.1) than to the holding of office, the ostensible subject of §§2–5, and it is probably just tacked on here to signal a point to be introduced later (in §6).

1.3. safety to the whole **demos** *. . .* ***danger:*** X's point is that, because the danger caused by a poorly performed (military) office will affect large numbers of their fellows, individual members of the *demos* do not want to take the responsibility of holding such offices. There is a deliberate contrast between these offices and those which will bring the holder 'domestic benefit', *i.e.* personal financial gain.

1.3. well conducted . . . not well conducted: X has just used the word *chrestos* in its political-class-label sense (1.1). It is one of his favourite such terms (see Introduction, section 8, and Appendix 4). Here, however, with χρησταὶ . . . μὴ χρησταὶ he immediately switches to a non-political use of the word, *i.e.* 'well managed', 'not well managed'. This is clearly the sense required by the context.

1.3. have an allotted share in the generalships or the cavalry commands: X does not of course mean to imply that these offices were chosen by use of the lot. They were elective (*cf.* above). The reason why X inserts his parenthesis here is that the use of the lot was thought to be a quintessentially democratic procedure, much more so than election (*e.g.* Arist. *Politics* IV. 1294b 7–10 – though as a means of apportioning offices between men considered equally eligible allotment was not in fact used only in democracies). If an office was one which was acquired by use of the lot, that in itself would signify that it was available to the *demos*. X is really making two points here: (*a*) the *demos* do not put themselves forward as candidates for election to these important military offices, and (*b*) they do not wish them to become offices which are allocated by use of the lot.

1.3 the demos *do not want to have any share in these:* How valid is this claim? The assembly's election of Cleon (*cf.* p. 130, below) to a special command at Pylos and Sphacteria in the summer of 425, and his successful campaign there (Thuc. IV. 26–39), do not invalidate X's thesis here. Although it is likely (though not certain) that Cleon was actually appointed *strategos* (*e.g.* Rhodes on Thuc. IV. 29.1), the decision was an extraordinary one. Though he was what Thucydides calls a 'champion of the *demos*', προστάτης τοῦ δήμου, Cleon was not at all lower-class. He was the son of a rich but non-aristocratic father (Davies, *APF*, 318; W. R. Connor, *The New Politicians of Fifth-Century Athens* [Princeton UP, 1971], 151–68, noting that Nicias, despite his more traditional persona, was similar to Cleon in background). Though there may well have been men from a similar background in X's own circle (see Rhodes in R. Brock and S. Hodkinson [eds], *Alternatives to Athens* [OUP, 2000], 119–36 at 131–2), a man such as Cleon, combining a non-aristocratic background with populist politics, could from a traditionalist viewpoint be despised and depicted as a lower-class upstart (*cf.*, *e.g.*, Ar. *Knights* 178–94). So a man like X might have regarded Cleon's generalships as an example of this office's being held by the *demos*; on that score, it could be argued that it is less likely that this passage could have been written after Cleon's subsequent success in the regular elections for the generalship of 424/3, 423/2 (possibly) and 422/1. However, men from the traditional upper class remained prominent among the generals to the end of the Peloponnesian War, and the military role of a man like Cleon was exceptional and would not necessarily have inhibited X from making this essentially valid generalisation.

1.3. For the demos *know:* The verb γιγνώσκειν (with its cognate noun, γνώμη) is a key word in X's treatise. It is coupled with *demos* some twelve times (see Appendix 5). In X's view, the Athenian *demos,* for all its ignorance and lack of education, nevertheless instinctively knows what it is doing politically.

1.3. leaving them for the most able to hold: Elsewhere, at 2.18, X uses δυνάμενος, participle of δύνασθαι, as a class label, = 'man of influence' (see Introduction, section 8, and Appendix 4), and the cognate adjective δύνατος can also be used in this way (*e.g.* Thuc. II. 65.2). Here, however, X uses the superlative δυνατωτάτους in its natural, non-political, sense of most 'able', 'capable', though, of course, the most able in this area were also, in his view, the men of influence, his own class as opposed to the *demos*.

1.3. those offices which involve receipt of pay and domestic benefit: This comment is a significant indication of X's prejudices. For him the *demos*' motivation in holding office is simply self-enrichment (and the protection of their political domination, *cf.* 1.4–5), not personal honour (*time*), let alone a sense of civic responsibility. Political principle is something which his jaundiced world-view does not recognise.

X's implication here that the *strategia* was an unpaid office is only partly true. Presumably the generals, along with the men they commanded, did by the time of the Peloponnesian War receive payment, intended primarily as a maintenance grant, when on campaign (*cf.* [Arist.] *Ath. Pol.* 24.1, 27.2), though there is no text which explicitly mentions the payment of generals.

1.4–5 cohere together. X asserts that there is an inherent and universal opposition between the two classes into which he divides Athenian (and every other) society. See Introduction, section 7. At the beginning of §4 we have the first explicit example of what is to become a pervasive motif throughout the work – the view of an imagined opponent or opponents is cited or alluded to, and X proceeds to respond. These views are invariably criticisms of some aspect or practice of the democratic system of government. X's replies do not rebut the criticism, still less do they support the principles of democracy. Rather, in each case, he points out that the criticised practice is not accidental, or an aberration. It is deliberately designed to be as it is, because that way the democratic system itself is best preserved, and the *demos* effectively ensure that they gain the maximum advantages for themselves (*cf.* Introduction, section 6).

1.4. Next, a thing which some people are surprised at: ἔπειτα here picks up πρῶτον in 1.2. Although this is the first explicit reference to opponents and their views, it is possible that we are to understand that an opponent's criticism underlies what is said at 1.2 as well (see p. 63, above). The imagined opponents are invariably unnamed and unidentified, *e.g.*, in 1.4–7, 'some people', 'someone', 'someone'. Here they 'are surprised at' (θαυμάζουσιν), *i.e.* they object to, a practice, with the implication that it is not what they are used to (*cf.* 1.11).

1.4. they assign more: πλέον νέμουσι picks up πλέον ἔχειν in 1. 2. It refers to political power here, primarily office-holding, which has been the subject of 1.2–3. Having dealt with the implicit objection that office-holding should be restricted to the class through whose military efforts the safety and power of the state is secured (in Athens this is actually the *demos, i.e.* the *thetes,* who man the navy), X now proceeds to argue that the Athenian *demos,* by holding a major share ('assign more') of the political offices of the state, at the expense of the upper classes, ensure the preservation of the democratic system as a whole. His argument here is based on one of his most fundamental political assumptions, that the citizen body is divided into two classes, and that these are inherently bitterly hostile to each other. Hence, if office-holding were restricted to the so-called *chrestoi* (*cf.* p. 60, above: the word is used twice in §4), they would inevitably use their position of power to damage the democratic constitution. The *demos* know this, they realise that, if they allowed only the *chrestoi* to be office-holders, they would create a 'strong opposition to themselves'. Thus, in X's view, a constitution in which members of the *demos* were excluded from office-holding simply could not work, since there cannot ever be any cooperation between the *demos* and the *chrestoi.* This for X is a universal law of human nature and society (πάσῃ γῇ, §5).

1.4. and the common people: The expression οἱ δημοτικοί, 'the men of the *demos*', occurs three times in this section (and also at 1.6, 15, 2.18, 19). Other writers sometimes use δημοτικός of a democratically-inclined politician (*e.g.* Dem. XVIII. *Crown* 122), but for X the term is simply an occasional alternative to ὁ δῆμος, 'the *demos*'.

1.4. it will become clear that it is precisely through this practice that: X's reply starts here, at ἐν αὐτῷ τούτῳ φανοῦνται.

1.4. the poor . . . the poor . . . the rich: In this section, developing the contrast first made in §2, X puts a great deal of emphasis on the poverty of the *demos*. Their opponents are the opposite, rich. The point is taken up again at 1.5, where X offers a sociological explanation (based on their poverty) for the supposed moral and intellectual failings of the *demos*.

1.4. the inferior classes: οἱ χείρους is another characterising class label in X's treatise (see Introduction, section 8, and Appendix 4, for a detailed analysis of such words). χείρους has morally evaluative connotations, and is picked up by its opposite, τὸ βέλτιστον / οἱ βέλτιστοι = 'the best element', 'the best men', in 1.5 (see below).

1.4. by doing well . . . do well: εὖ πράττειν. The political rather than the economic aspect of doing well seems to be primary here (*cf.* p. 66, above), though there is no doubt an implication of the latter sense as well (see next note).

1.4. by increasing the numbers of themselves and their like: πολλοὶ (without the article) is used descriptively here, not as a class label (contrast 1.20 with p. 98, below). X's point seems to be that (*a*) the political and economic prosperity of the Athenian *demos* serves to increase their birth rate, and (*b*) because the *demos* are increasingly more numerous than the upper class, they can always outvote them in the assembly in support of their 'own' candidates for political office.

1.5. In this section X first provides a explanation of why there is such a fundamental political division and hostility between the two classes (something which he assumes to be the case throughout the treatise; see Introduction, section 7). In his view they possess totally different and opposite moral and intellectual qualities. These are by nature 'within' them. All the good qualities belong to the 'best men', *beltistoi*, and all the bad ones to the *demos* (see above on 'the inferior classes'). Interestingly, in the list of good qualities ascribed to the 'best men' he twice uses double negatives, 'the least . . . licentiousness and injustice', and only once a simple positive, 'the most scrupulousness over what is valuable'. By contrast, the *demos* have 'the greatest ignorance, indiscipline and worthlessness'. A very similar characterisation of the *demos* can be seen in the views attributed to Megabyxus in the constitutional debate attributed by Herodotus to the Persian conspirators of 522 (III. 80–3), a passage probably written shortly before X's treatise (for a more detailed consideration see Introduction, section 7).

Secondly, at the end of §5, X offers a more sociological explanation for this (alleged) phenomenon. The moral and intellectual failings of the *demos* are to some extent due to their poverty and lack of money. This is an interesting passage, which hints at a more sophisticated analysis than X provides elsewhere. But X is careful to qualify this explanation (note μᾶλλον, 'rather', hence our translation 'tends to'; and ἐνίοις, 'some people'). Poverty is only a partial and occasional reason for these failings. X believes these moral and intellectual differences between classes are mainly inherent (cf., e.g., 1.7, 2.19); they are in themselves part of the way the two classes are to be defined (see Introduction, section 8).

1.6. Someone might say: The next imagined objection is very clearly signalled. Here the optative εἴποι is used (cf. 1.7), as against the present indicative θαυμάζουσιν employed at 1. 4. But there is nothing significant in this variation (see Appendix 1).

We now move on from the topic of political office-holding (§§2–5) to that of collective decision-making (§§6–9). The criticism at 1. 6 is directed against the principle of universality involved in Athenian democracy, *i.e.* every citizen (πάντας) has a right to speak (*i.e.* in the assembly), and is eligible to be chosen and serve as a member of the council of five hundred, the *boule* (the verb βουλεύειν in the first sentence has its technical sense, = 'be a member of the *boule*'). These functions should, according to the imagined critic, be limited to 'the cleverest and the best men' (ἄριστοι is a synonym for βέλτιστοι). For X οἱ δεξιώτατοι ('the cleverest') is another class label: this particular expression has probably been prompted by what he has just said about the ignorance (ἀμαθία) of the *demos* in the last sentence of §5). A common line of argument used by opponents of democracy was that those with greater intelligence should play a greater part in government (an objection to which the Syracusan democrat Athenagoras replies in Thuc. VI. 39.1 – conceding that the intelligent, οἱ ξυνετοί, are best at deliberating, but adding that the many are best at listening and judging); and this foreshadows the view to be developed by Socrates and Plato that ruling is a skill (τέχνη) which is best performed by experts.

In reply, X 'defends' the existing practice – but not on grounds of principle (there is an interesting contrast in Pericles' statement of principle on these issues at Thuc. II. 37.1). His argument is based entirely on his already-enunciated thesis of inherent class conflict, that 'throughout the world the best element is opposed to democracy'. Hence, if only the 'best' and cleverest men discussed and formulated policy in the council and assembly, they would produce policies which would be to the advantage of their own class, but not to the advantage of the *demos*. Correspondingly the 'worthless' man, the *poneros* (the word occurs three times in §6), will propose what is in the interests of himself and his class.

The author's crude and simplistic class analysis does not accommodate the possibility that the 'best men' might concern themselves with the well-being of the citizen body as a whole. That was an argument sometimes put forward by the proponents of oligarchy, as a justification for their preferred system of government (*cf.*, *e.g.*, the words of Megabyxus at Hdt. III. 81.3, ἀρίστων δὲ ἀνδρῶν οἰκὸς ἄριστα βουλεύματα γίνεσθαι = 'it is reasonable to suppose that the best men will propose the best policies'); and Plato and Aristotle were to refine the threefold categorisation of constitutions with a good (*i.e.* beneficial to the whole community) and a bad version of each (*cf.* Introduction, section 6). Neither does X envisage the possibility that the self-interest of an individual member of the *demos* might be at variance with that of the *demos* as a whole (a phenomenon presented, *e.g.*, throughout Aristophanes' *Knights* through the figure of Paphlagon / Cleon). X here assumes automatic class loyalty on the part of all members of each class (*cf.* p. 15, above).

1.6. allow everyone in turn the right: There is no need to change the manuscripts' ἑξῆς to ἐξ ἴσης ('everyone an equal right'), which was proposed by Bergk and followed by Frisch and Bowersock: see O'Sullivan, 193. Universality rather than equality is the issue here, though 'in turn' is more applicable to the council than to the assembly: membership of the council changed annually. Pericles in his funeral oration (wrongly, as far as most civilian appointments were concerned) claims for Athens that 'in public life men gain preferment because of their deserts, when anybody has a good reputation for anything: what matters is not rotation (μέρος) but merit' (Thuc. II. 37.1). But he is perhaps thinking of the generals, who were elected (*cf.* p. 64, above).

1.6. their policy . . . is in their best interests: The middle verb βουλεύονται is here used in the more general, non-technical, sense (contrast the active βουλεύειν above). ἄριστα refers to what is best for the *demos*.

1.6. if only the valuable were to speak: I.e. to make speeches and propose motions in the assembly. The context requires us to understand 'only' here, as we also have to do before τοὺς δεξιωτάτους in the first sentence. The assembly and the council included *chrestoi*, but they did not have a privileged position there.

1.6. and be members of the council: It seems clear from the coupling with ἔλεγον that in the third sentence X reverts to the use of βουλεύειν primarily in its technical sense = 'be a member of the *boule*' (as in the first sentence of this section). But that sense is usually found only with the active form, and Morus therefore emended ἐβουλεύοντο here to ἐβούλευον. X does not seem to differentiate strictly between the active and middle forms of this verb (*cf.* the use of the active at 1.9 with the meaning expressed by the middle here), but in the absence of a good parallel for the middle in this technical sense, and with the middle used just above and the word following here beginning το–, it is better to suppose a copyist's error (dittography) and change to the active form.

1.6. good . . . not good . . . what is good: ἀγαθά . . . ἀγαθά . . . τὸ ἀγαθὸν here indicates that which is to the *demos*' advantage, in their class interest (*cf.* ἄριστα in the second sentence of this section).

1.6. any . . . person who wishes: For the expression ὁ βουλόμενος *cf.* p. 64, above. The words used by the herald in the assembly formally to open discussion of a topic, τίς ἀγορεύειν βούλεται; ('Who wishes to speak?'), deliberately called attention to the fact that it was open to any citizen present to speak and make proposals. We use 'person' here to translate ἄνθρωπος, which is used derogatively: of course, in

Athens, as elsewhere in Greece, only men were active citizens with the right to speak in the assembly.

1.7. Someone might say: At this point X deals with a subsidiary objection (again very clearly indicated). He has just asserted (in §6) that the reason why any Athenian citizen (not just the educated, well-to-do) is allowed to participate in decision-making (through serving on the council and speaking in the assembly) is that members of the *demos* will produce policies which are to the advantage of the *demos* as a class, whereas the *chrestoi* will not. But, it could be objected, given that such men are not clever or educated, how can they possibly *know* which policy will be the one to produce benefits for themselves and the *demos* as a class?

In his reply, X agrees that such men are indeed ignorant, in the sense of lacking in learning (ἀμαθία in §7 recalls the double use of ἀμαθία in 1.5, where on the second occasion it is coupled with ἀπαιδευσία, 'lack of education'), but they still know what they are doing politically. This is a key point for X (*cf.* 1.3), and he uses the words γιγνώσκειν / γνώμη some twelve times in the treatise with reference to the *demos* (p. 65, above, and Appendix 5). Thus in this section γιγνώσκουσιν deliberately picks up γνοίη. X argues that a man of the *demos,* despite his characteristic ignorance and worthlessness (πονηρία), has an instinctive loyalty or good will (εὔνοια) to his own class, and that in itself is enough to ensure that he proposes policies which are to their advantage, much more so than the instinctive ill will (κακόνοια is the opposite of εὔνοια) of the *chrestos,* for all his characteristic excellence (ἀρετή) and wisdom (σοφία). It is interesting to note that on this point X is very much at variance with the picture presented by Aristophanes throughout the *Knights* of 424 (with the exception of lines 1121–50), where the Athenian *demos* (through the character Demos) are portrayed as being politically naïve and ignorant, and so constantly deceived and robbed by their politicians (see pp. 133, 136, below).

Editors have pointed out certain similarities between X's argument at 1.7 and the anti-intellectual comments of Cleon in the Mytilene debate in 427, where a clever speech is used to attack the misguided cleverness which he attributes to his opponents (Thuc. III. 37.3). It is true that Cleon accepts the relative ignorance (ἀμαθία) of the common people (οἱ . . . φαυλότεροι τῶν ἀνθρώπων), in comparison with the cleverness (δεξιότης) of the intelligentsia (οἱ ξυνετώτεροι) – but (and here Cleon is at odds with X) he claims that the common people have 'prudence', 'common sense' (σωφροσύνη), and that that is what makes the uneducated generally better at managing public affairs than intellectuals, whose cleverness breeds licentiousness (ἀκολασία). Cleon would no doubt have seen X's treatise as exemplifying just the kind of cleverness to which he was objecting.

1.8–9. X now takes the implicit point of the argument of 1.6 a stage further. He asserts explicitly that not only would the best and cleverest men, if they had decision-making authority, not produce policies which bring good things (ἀγαθά) to the *demos*; they would positively discriminate against the *demos.* They would 'pass laws' (*i.e.* draw up a constitution) to suit themselves, and would then totally exclude the *demos* from political life – a state of affairs which X thoroughly approves of (*cf.* τούτων τῶν ἀγαθῶν, §9). The *demos* realise all this, and that is why they are not prepared to accept a constitution in which only the best and cleverest men propose and decide policy.

However, X slightly complicates his basic argument in 1.8–9 by introducing into it (*a*) a contrast between 'freedom' (and 'rule') on the one hand, and 'slavery' on the other, and (*b*) the concept of *eunomia* (and its opposite, *kakonomia*). See notes below.

1.8. a state would not be the best: In his use of the word βελτίστη here X does not imply that the *chrestoi* would, if policy-making were in their hands, rule in the best interests of the community *as a whole* (though that was sometimes a claim made on behalf of oligarchy: see pp. 68–9, above). That is not his view, as we can see very clearly in 1.9. So for him here 'the best *polis*' is simply one in which 'the best men'have political control and rule in the interests of their class.

1.8–9. the demos do not wish ... while they themselves are slaves ... reduced to slavery: X refers to 'slavery' twice in this passage, but he is not using the term in its literal sense here. δουλεύειν and δουλεία are used figuratively, in the sense 'loss of political rights', as at 1.11 (τοῖς ἀνδραπόδοις δουλεύειν) and 1.18 (δοῦλοι του δήμου). For this sense one may compare Thuc. I. 98.4 (where ἐδουλώθη is used of Naxos' loss of political independence in contrast to ἠνδραπόδισαν in §§1–2 of the literal enslavement of Eïon and Scyros). Similarly, its opposite, ἐλεύθερος (= 'free'), a word which is also used twice in 1.8, here means not `free-born' but 'free to do what it wants politically'; hence the linking additions that go with it (ἄρχειν, 'rule', and ἰσχύει, 'is strong'). In Thuc. VIII. 48.5 Phrynichus says that the allied states do not want to be slaves (δουλεύειν) either with oligarchy or with democracy, so much as to be free (ἐλεύθεροι) with whichever kind of constitution they may have, and in VIII. 64 Thucydides himself agrees with that.

1.8–9. governed well ... good government ... good government: There is a triple repetition by X here of what is surely intended to be a significant word (the opposite condition, κακονομία, 'bad government', is mentioned also). The noun *eunomia* and the cognate verb *eunomeisthai* in Greek combine the sense of 'obedience to the laws / constitution' with that of 'having good laws / a good constitution'. More significantly, although the word is used in a general sense by Solon (fr. 4. 32 West), it was, from an early period, applied specifically to the constitution of Sparta: *eunomia* is cited as the title of a poem by the Spartan Tyrtaeus (frs. 1–4 West) by Aristotle, *Politics* V. 1306b 39–1307a 1, and by the fifth century the word could be used virtually as a synonym for the Spartan constitution (Hdt. I. 66.1, Thuc. I. 18.1, both using the cognate verb, *cf.* Plut. *Lycurgus* 5.4). That X has this more particularised sense of the word in mind in his threefold use of the word at 1.8–9 is confirmed by the closely following direct reference to 'Lacedaemon', *i.e.* Sparta, at 1.11 (a rare example of specific detail in the treatise), where the context is similar, *i.e.* the citing of different, and allegedly better, practice elsewhere. These two closely connected passages strongly suggest that X's assumed interlocutors are to be thought of primarily as Spartans (see Introduction, section 5).

1.8–9. you consider . . . you are looking for . . . you will find: Here there is a sudden introduction of the second person singular σύ to refer to the assumed interlocutor / opponent, who previously has been referred to only in the third person (singular at 1.6 and 7, plural at 1.4). The third person reference returns at the beginning of 1.11 (εἰ δέ τις . . . θαυμάζει), but the lively second person singular recurs in slightly different usages in 1.10–12, first within an imagined objection (σοι at 1.10, where ἐγώ seems to refer to X), then as part of the exchange between X and his imagined interlocutor at 1.11 ('my slave . . . you . . . your slave . . . me . . . my slave . . . you'). We should also note the use of the first person plural (twice) at 1.12. These variations on the normal pattern, of third person imagined opponent(s), and first person singular author's reply, add an element of immediacy and liveliness to the treatise, and lend support to the hypothesis that the work was originally intended to be delivered orally as a contribution to an academic debate (see Introduction, section 5).

1.9. draw up the laws for them: τοὺς νόμους here refers particularly to constitutional laws. Bowersock prints the manuscripts' αὐτοῖς, but translates Müller-Strübing's αὑτοῖς, 'in their own interest'. However, given the reference to εὐνομία, good government, above, X's claim here is more probably simply that the most able men, given the chance, will draw up a (new) constitution for the state than that they will enact laws conducive to their own, rather than the *demos*', advantage. Of course, such a constitution will naturally discriminate against the *demos*. It is interesting to note that the oligarchic revolutionaries of 411 did just that, producing two draft constitutions, perhaps at the time of the formal inauguration of the régime of the Four Hundred ([Arist.] *Ath. Pol.* 30–1, with Rhodes *ad loc.*); and in 404 the Thirty were expected, and perhaps themselves at first intended, to draw up a constitution, though they did not in fact do so (Xen. *Hellenica* II. 3.2, 11, *cf.* [Arist.] *Ath. Pol.* 35.1–2).

1.9. the valuable men will punish the worthless ones: In what way? At first sight it may seem that X is using the verb κολάζειν here to denote legal punishment, *i.e.* the *poneroi* will be punished in the courts for breaking the laws drawn up by the cleverest men. This is possible, but it is more likely that X is not being so specific, and that 'punish' is more political than legal here (κολάσουσιν probably picks up ἀκολασία in 1.5). So formal law-breaking need not be involved. The *poneroi* will be 'punished' simply for being what they are, the natural opponents of the ruling *chrestoi*. That is precisely what happened to opponents of the Thirty in 404–403, with Critias cynically justifying the ruthless action taken (Xen. *Hellenica* II. 3. 15–16).

1.9. decide policy . . . be members of the council: See 1.6 for a similar mixed use of the verb βουλεύειν. Here one might expect the middle form rather than the active on the first occasion, but both active and middle are used with the meaning 'deliberate', 'make policy'.

1.9. for the state: As with πόλις . . . βελτίστη at 1. 8, περὶ τῆς πόλεως here does not imply that X thinks that an oligarchy of the best men will rule in the interests of the community as a whole. The sense is simply 'make policy for the state', *i.e.* 'rule'. The words thus distinguish this more general use of βουλεύειν from the technical sense in which the word is used in the next line.

1.9. wild persons: For the derogatory ἀνθρώπους here *cf.* p. 70, above. Editors compare Thucydides' notorious description of Cleon's promise in the Pylos debate in 425, 'wild though it was (καίπερ μανιώδης οὖσα), Cleon's promise was fulfilled' (Thuc. IV. 39.3). The strong word μαινομένους comes as a surprise here, and it is not used by X again. Although the verb μαίνεσθαι is not necessarily as strong as the English 'be mad', its use is still very striking in a political treatise like this. As usual, X is generalising, but he may well in his use of the word here have in mind Cleon's notorious promise, and the reaction to it. (This does not, of course imply that he must have read Thucydides' account of the debate: Thucydides employs a descriptive word which was probably used publicly by Cleon's enemies at the time.) X could have got it from any of them subsequently, and it seems quite likely that he was related to or closely associated with some of the 'sensible men' whose condescending sneers against Cleon at the time of the Pylos debate are also recorded by Thucydides (IV. 28.5).

1.9. to attend meetings of the assembly: This seems to be an extra point, added after 'to be members of the council or to speak' (βουλεύειν οὐδὲ λέγειν), a phrase which echoes λέγειν . . . μηδὲ βουλεύειν at the beginning of 1.6. This presumably denotes a further restriction, *i.e.* in a state with *eunomia* such persons, in addition to being prevented from being members of the council and speaking at meetings of the assembly, will also be prevented from meeting (and voting) in the assembly at all. Indeed (X concludes) they will quickly lose all their political rights, and a good thing too!

1.10–12. At the beginning of §10 X moves on to a completely new topic, which occupies §§10–12, and is introduced by a new imagined criticism. The passage is concerned with slaves and metics, and the first imagined objection is to the soft treatment of, and comfortable life supposedly enjoyed by, slaves and metics at Athens. The criticism is not signalled by a clear introductory tag (as at 1.4, 6, 7), but it is indicated by δ' αὖ, 'but again', and comes in the form of an unattributed direct quotation of the critical view. This occupies the whole of the first sentence of §10, which should, therefore, for the sake of clarity be placed within inverted commas. X's reply starts in the second sentence, and is emphatically indicated by ἐγὼ φράσω (note the personal pronoun). As usual, he does not deny the allegation. He accepts that the practice is as described, but explains the thinking behind it (οὖ δ' ἕνεκέν ἐστι τοῦτο), which makes it inevitable that it should be so. There are two further imagined criticisms of the treatment of slaves and metics, both of which X 'answers', in §11. In §12 he reiterates his main point, and emphasises that it applies just as much to metics as to slaves.

But why does he take up this particular topic here? The link with what precedes is by no means clear. There is virtually no thematic connexion. Rather, the topic has been suggested by the use of the words δουλεύειν and δουλεία in 1.8–9. In other words, the figurative use of the term 'slavery' in a political argument (see p. 71, above) has suggested the topic of actual slavery (1.10–12). Cf. Osborne, 2–3, who remarks on this tendency of X to let a word or topic mentioned in passing suggest his next topic, as a 'conversational' feature. This is a good example of X's technical weakness in transitions between topics.

1.10. and the metics: Metics were resident foreigners, non-Athenians, but they were free men. In this passage X seems virtually to equate slaves with metics (and with freed slaves, who, being non-Athenians, ranked as metics). Of course, as commentators point out, the two groups had very different legal statuses, but X joins them together here because he is concentrating on certain aspects of the way in which non-citizens were treated at Athens which were applicable to both slaves and metics, and where the treatment is regarded as unacceptably lenient by his assumed interlocutors. These are (*a*) their legal protection against being physically assaulted by citizens, hence their undesirable degree of indiscipline, (*b*) the wealthy lifestyle enjoyed by some of them, derived from getting paid employment from the state (*cf.* pp. 77–8, below), and (*c*) the lack of a general climate of fear at Athens.

Frisch, 204, argues that 'metics' in the opening sentence is just a 'headline' word, which does not actually apply to the first point, about protection from physical assault, but only to the subsequent points about the state's economic dependence on these inferior status groups. But such a restrictive interpretation seems very doubtful, given that the author's reply in the second part of 1.10 explicitly mentions metics (twice). It seems much more likely that metics are in X's mind in everything he says in this section (§§10–12), and that even where he refers only to slaves he intends metics to be included as well. This is surely indicated by the final reiterating paragraph at 1.12.

1.10. the slaves and the metics at Athens enjoy extreme licence, and it is not possible to strike them: To what extent does this allegation correspond to the facts? There is evidence that slaves at Athens did have some legal protection against assault, under the terms of the law about *hybris*, outrage (*cf.* Dem. XXI. *Meidias* 47–50, Aeschin. I. *Timarchus* 15–17), though this applied only in the cases of citizens other than their owner. He himself could ill treat them, though not kill them, with impunity (*cf.* Lycurgus *Leocrates* 65). *A fortiori*, protection under this heading (*i.e.* the law of *hybris*) must have applied to metics too.

The real motivation behind this limited protection was no doubt primarily social, to prevent the public demonstration of that degree of anti-social behaviour on the part of a citizen which was felt to be an affront to his fellows, and a threat to the communal values necessary for the survival of the *polis* (see D. M. MacDowell, *The Law in Classical Athens* [London: Thames and Hudson / Cornell UP, 1978], 129–32, N. R. E. Fisher, *Hybris* [Warminster: Aris and Phillips, 1992], 36, 40, 58–60). It was perhaps partly humanitarian as well.

However, the explanation offered at 1.10 by X for the legal protection afforded to slaves (and others) at Athens is odd, even by his standards. In the two following points (in §11) his explanation centres entirely on the economic dependence which, in his view, the Athenian state has on slaves and metics. We therefore expect some use of the economic argument here too. But we do not get it. Instead, X claims that, since one cannot tell a slave from a citizen simply by looking at him, the Athenians have been forced to extend legal protection against physical assault to slaves, since, if it were not there, citizens would be at risk of being beaten up in public in the mistaken belief that they were really (only) slaves. This is so cynical and absurd that one suspects it may be a joke!

1.10. nor will a slave step aside for you: This is presumably because he knows he is not in danger of being violently pushed or kicked out of the way. This seems a rather trivial complaint to make, but such lack of deference in public by the lower orders was an aspect of Athenian public life which clearly rankled with some anti-democrats (*cf.* Pl. *Republic* VIII. 562 c).

1.10. their local practice: This word (ἐπιχώριον) is not padding; it has a point here. It implies a contrast with practice somewhere else, and that somewhere else is, specifically, Sparta and Laconia (note the direct reference to "Lacedaemon" in §11, a rare example of a specific detail in the treatise). In fact a contrast with Sparta is implicit throughout §§10–12.

A famous, or infamous, passage from Myron of Priene (*FGrH* 106 F 2, cited by Ath. XIV. 657c–d, and translated in P. Cartledge, *Sparta and Lakonia: A Regional History* [London: Routledge, ²2002], 305), is horrifyingly explicit about the Spartan treatment of helots, who suffered routine annual beatings, 'so that they would never forget they were slaves', who had to wear a distinctive servile dress, a dogskin cap and skins, and whose masters were punished if they allowed their helots to grow fat. In other words, there was a very visible difference, apparent at first sight, between Spartan citizens and helots in Laconia. You knew at once that the person you were beating up was a helot; there was no problem about that.

That is the reason why X replies as he does in 1.10. At Athens, by contrast with Sparta and Laconia, there was no such instantly visible differentiation. Slaves did not have to wear a distinctively servile dress. X does not bother to explain why not, but no doubt the main reason was that in Athens, unlike Laconia, where the helots were in some sense communally owned (*cf.* Arist. *Politics* II. 1263a 35, Xen. *Constitution of the Lacedaemonians* 6.3), most slaves were privately owned, thus making it difficult to enforce such a requirement.

1.10. the* demos *there are no better dressed than the slaves and the metics:

According to Thucydides (I. 6.3–4), writing at the end of the fifth century, the older men among the Athenian upper classes had only recently given up wearing elaborate clothes and ornaments (unsuitable for, and therefore a mark of those not needing to engage in, manual work: he thinks the Ionians had copied this from Athens, but more probably the fashion had travelled in the other direction), and the preference for a simpler style which had begun in Sparta had become general in Greece. In the mid fourth century the wealthy speaker of [Dem.] XLVII. *Evergus and Mnesibulus* 61 complains that his opponents tried to take his son from his house thinking that he was a slave.

X does not mean to imply that the Athenian *demos* in his time dressed particularly shabbily by the standards of other Greek states (there is no evidence for that), though he may be thinking in part of the change mentioned by Thucydides. His main point must be that the Athenians' slaves were not dressed in a distinctively humiliating way: not only were Sparta's helots required to wear a distinctive costume, but it was perhaps normal elsewhere that slaves were worse dressed than free men (*cf., e.g.*, Hom. *Od.* XIV. 341–3, XXIV. 249–57). But there is perhaps also a suggestion here that too many ordinary Athenians could be seen out and about in their everyday working clothes (for which see Kalinka, 126–9, Frisch, 207–8). As M. M. Austin and P. Vidal-Naquet shrewdly point out (*Economic and Social History of Ancient Greece: An Introduction* [London: Batsford / U. of California P., 1977], 283 on no. 74), 'what the author here finds most striking is ultimately less the insolence of slaves and metics at Athens than the massive public presence of the common people'.

1.10. nor are they any better in their appearance: This is an afterthought, but it *is* a further point, and thus τὰ εἴδη must refer to something different from dress. But what? Surely not to size, *i.e.* height or bulk: slaves in general are not likely to have been inferior in physique to citizens; and (despite Xen. *Constitution of the Lacedaemonians* 1.10) there do not seem to have been any noticeable differences in this respect between Athenians and Spartans.

It may perhaps refer to hairstyle. It was common practice in Greece for slaves to have close-cropped hair (*cf.* Eur. *Electra* 107–9, Ar. *Birds* 911), and they are sometimes depicted in this way in Athenian vase paintings: see K. Joss, 'Reconstructing the Slave: An Examination of Slave Representation in the Greek Polis' (St. Andrews Ph.D. thesis, 2006), 97–112, esp. 101–2. But at Athens long hair for citizens, together with elaborate clothing, had gone out of fashion by the later fifth century. Indeed, long hair had come to be seen by then as a peculiarly Spartan feature (Hdt. VII. 20, Xen. *Constitution of the Lacedaemonians* 11.3, Plut. *Lycurgus* 22.1: it was inconvenient for those who had to engage in physical labour, as the Spartan citizens did not), and those few Athenians who wore their hair long (an affectation on the part of some rich young men) were regarded with suspicion during the Archidamian War as Spartan sympathisers (Ar. *Knights* 580, 1121–2, *Clouds* 14, *Wasps* 466). Thus X's point here may be that in Athens, again in contrast to Sparta, one cannot immediately distinguish between citizens and slaves on the basis of hairstyle either. Both slaves and the Athenian *demos* wear their hair short, and, in this respect too, they look the same.

1.11. If anyone is also surprised at the fact: This time the imagined criticism is clearly signalled, and the καὶ (= 'also') before τοῦτο shows that the first sentence of the preceding §10 has also to be understood as an imagined objection (see pp. 73–4, above). What we have now is a *second* criticism. X's reply starts at καὶ τοῦτο γνώμῃ φανεῖεν ἂν ποιοῦντες . . . and continues down to ἐλευθέρους ἀφιέναι.

1.11. that they allow the slaves to live luxuriously there and, some of them, in a grand style: The objection here is to the allegedly wealthy and luxurious life-style enjoyed by some slaves at Athens (not all: the addition of ἐνίους limits the extent of the 'abuse'). X agrees that this happens, but explains that it is an inevitable consequence of the fact that Athens is a naval power (which itself, as he has explained at 1.2, is an essential feature of the democracy). Naval power entails, according to X, that the citizens should 'be slaves to the slaves' (τοῖς ἀνδραπόδοις δουλεύειν). This is a striking expression, in which τοῖς ἀνδραπόδοις is, as normal, used literally, but δουλεύειν is obviously used figuratively (*cf.* 1.8, 9), in the sense 'be totally dependent (economically) upon'. Indeed, economic necessity is the central argument of 1.11–12. But how exactly is this dependence shown? X's answer comes in the last part of the second sentence. Although the text is corrupt, the sense seems to be that the *demos* exploit the wealth of their slaves to benefit themselves economically, by 'milking' them of their earnings (λαμβάνωμεν . . . τὰς ἀποφοράς), and then further by charging them a fee to manumit them (ἐλευθέρους ἀφιέναι). This is a source of income on which, he claims, the Athenian citizens have become dependent.

What are the facts? Was it really possible for slaves to become wealthy at Athens, and, if so, what was the connection with Athenian naval power? It seems clear that X is here thinking primarily of the payment of public money, and we have detailed inscriptional evidence for payments made by the state to slaves (and metics) for building work done on the Erechtheum temple construction in the last decade of the fifth century (*e.g. IG* i^3 476: extracts translated Austin and Vidal-Naquet [*cf.* p. 76], 276–82 no. 73). Some of these workers were carpenters, *i.e.* woodworkers, rather than masons, and it seems very likely that, although we have no direct evidence, slaves were also employed as skilled workmen in the construction and maintenance of the Athenian fleet, and were paid by the state in the same way as those who worked on the Erechtheum. That would provide the connection with naval power which is central to X's argument here. This is that Athens' power depends on having a large navy; ships have constantly to be constructed or repaired; that requires a large skilled workforce (see p. 80, below); hence slaves have to be so employed. Their owners, are of course, quite happy about that, since much of the earnings of these 'wealthy' slaves will be creamed off by them as their masters. Indeed, they have, in his view, become completely dependent on this source of income.

X says nothing about metics in this section, but later (1.12) he asserts explicitly that they too were needed as skilled workmen in the construction of the fleet (διὰ τὸ ναυτικόν). The main weakness in his argument in 1.11 is gross exaggeration (even with his limiting 'some'). It seems unlikely that the numbers of skilled slave workmen so employed were very large, or that they could ever become 'wealthy' on their earnings (one drachma a day was paid to those working on the Erechtheum), or that their masters' dependence on these earnings was as total as he alleges.

1.11. in order that we may take their earnings: The manuscript reading λαμβάνων μὲν πράττῃ τὰς ἀποφοράς is obviously corrupt. The emendation λαμβάνωμεν ἃς πράττει ἀποφοράς is simple and restores sense (cf. p. 79, below, for the first person plural). Cf. G. Bechtle, 'A Note on Pseudo-Xenophon, *The Constitution of the Athenians* 1.11', *CQ* n.s. 46 (1996), 564–6, who agrees with us about the meaning of this section but does not champion any particular emendation.

1.11. to manumit them: Literally 'to let them go free'. The point is that slaves who earned money were in a position to buy their freedom from their master for an agreed fee. In such cases masters could make money by charging more than the sum they had paid to buy the slave originally. Of course, a master did not have to make such an agreement, however 'wealthy' a slave might become. It is a gross exaggeration to suggest, as X does here, that such arrangements were 'necessary'. For a study of manumission in Greece see R. Zelnick-Abramovitz, *Not Wholly Free* (*Mnemosyne* Supp. 266, 2005).

1.11. But in Lacedaemon: This is a very significant detail – the only place-reference (apart from those to Athens) in the treatise, before 3.11. It comes abruptly and without amplification, but the clear implication is that the imagined interlocutor here is a Spartan. There are some other passages which may suggest that X envisages himself to be arguing primarily with a Spartan opponent or opponents (1.8–9, 13, 2.13), but none is as explicit as this (see Introduction, section 5).

1.11. And in a state where there are rich slaves . . . my slave should fear you: In the manuscripts this sentence follows . . . ἐλευθέρους ἀφιέναι, but, to make sense of X's argument from there to the end of §11, it must be transposed to the end of the section, after ἐν δὲ τῇ Λακεδαίμονι . . . κινδυνεύειν περὶ ἑαυτοῦ (see Marr [1996] for the detailed argument).

We thus have, first, a further criticism about the treatment of slaves at Athens, one which comes specifically from a Spartan, who is envisaged as saying, 'In Sparta my slave fears [or 'would fear'] you'. The directly quoted objection, without an introductory tag, is similar to that at the beginning of 1.10. The interlocutor asserts that the slaves, *i.e.* the helots, at Sparta live in a climate of general fear. There, 'my slave fears you' (*i.e.* any Spartan citizen, not just me, his master). The helots, though allocated to work for individual masters, were owned by the Spartan state, the community, and could be used (and abused) by others wherever and whenever needed (cf. p. 75, above). According to Plutarch, there was actually a cult of Fear at Sparta (*Cleomenes* 9. 1): fear was so endemic it was deified.

The implication of the imagined criticism is that, by contrast, there is, regrettably, no such climate of fear for slaves at Athens. X's reply to this begins at ἐὰν δὲ δεδίῃ ... His argument is again based on the notion of economic necessity. Thus, in a state where slaves must fear all citizens alike, where 'your slave fears me', there is a risk that they may have to give protection money to anyone who threatens to abuse them physically. That cannot happen at Sparta, because the helots have no money, but it certainly can in a state like Athens, where slaves supposedly can become 'rich' (as explained above), and there it will be highly disadvantageous to their owners, who will lose out economically if their slaves are giving away protection money to other citizens. That is the reason, according to X, why the Athenians have given some legal protection to slaves, ensuring that they do not have to live in a climate of fear, constantly afraid of assault by citizens other than their owner.

It can be seen that the transposition of one sentence to the end of §11 restores coherence to what is otherwise an incomprehensible passage. X's argument in the second part of §11 is, in fact, a rather more serious reply than that given in §10 to what was essentially the same criticism, levelled against the (in fact very limited) legal protection enjoyed by slaves at Athens.

1.12. we have established: The double use of the first person plural in §12, with reference to Athens, is a decisive indication of the author's nationality: X is an Athenian (*cf.* 2.11–12). The first person plural here makes it easier to accept the emendation λαμβάνωμεν in the second sentence of 1.11 (*cf.* above).

1.12. equality of free speech: In Greek ἰσηγορία can be used in a constitutional sense, virtually as a synonym for *demokratia* (*cf.* Hdt. V. 78). But X is here using the word in its more specific and literal sense of 'equality of free speech'. He surely has in mind Athens' distinctive *parrhesia*, 'outspokenness', which is often cited as a characteristic feature of Athenian democracy (the word first appears in Euripides, *e.g. Hippolytus* 422, and Aristophanes, *e.g. Thesmophoriazusae* 541). His claim is that, out of economic necessity, the Athenians have extended it to non-citizen groups, metics and slaves. There may be something in his claims. One thinks of the cheeky slave Xanthias in Ar. *Frogs*, and Demosthenes actually boasts about the extension of *parrhesia* to non-citizen groups at Athens (IX. *Philippic 3.* 3). But X's formulation of his point as usual involves some exaggeration. Outspokenness on the part of non-citizens may have been an (atypical) social phenomenon at Athens, but neither slaves nor metics had any 'equality of free speech' when it came to meetings of the assembly and political debate there. That was restricted to (male) citizens.

It is interesting that Plato makes Socrates put forward a similar allegation to that of X here, in an absurdly exaggerated passage (*Republic* VIII. 563a–b) which should be required reading for anyone who takes Plato's criticisms of democracy seriously.

1.12. as between metics and citizens: Metics are referred to three times in §12. X thus makes it quite clear in this summarising section that his argument throughout

§§10–12 applies to metics as well as to slaves, even if they are not specifically mentioned in §11. ἀστός like πολίτης denotes 'citizen': in so far as they differ, ἀστός emphasises a man's citizen birth while πολίτης emphasises his current possession of citizen rights (*e.g.* Hansen in M. H. Hansen and T. H. Nielsen [eds], *An Inventory of Archaic and Classical Poleis* [OUP, 2004], 47).

1.12. since the city needs metics because of the great number of their skills and the requirements of the fleet: διὰ τὸ ναυτικόν here deliberately picks up ναυτικὴ δυναμίς in 1.11, and τῶν τεχνῶν makes it clearer than in §11 that what X has in mind is the state's need to employ metics and slaves as a skilled work force in the construction and repair of its triremes, warships. The inscription already referred to (p. 77, above) attests metics employed (and paid) by the Athenian state as woodcarvers, carpenters, sawyers, joiners, painters, gilders and labourers, – thus nicely illustrating X's point here. One suspects that what he says in 1.11–12 actually applied much more to metics than to slaves. Of course, a metic's earnings could not be 'creamed off', as a slave's could be by his owner. The metics were free men, entitled to keep their earnings. But X's point in §12 is that the Athenians had to encourage metics to come to live in Attica, they had to entice and pamper them, because they needed a skilled metic workforce to keep up the required trireme production.

It is true that metics were sometimes enlisted (as well as citizens) as oarsmen to crew the triremes, *e.g.* in 428 (Thuc. III. 16), as indeed were slaves (*cf.* p. 97, below). But non-citizen oarsmen were usually paid volunteers who were not otherwise resident in Athens as metics, and almost certainly metic oarsmen are not what X has in mind here, since throughout §§11–12 the emphasis is on the economic infrastructure of trades and skills which the building and maintenance of a large fleet inevitably generates.

There were large numbers of metics in Athens and Attica, and they were important for the Athenian economy (see in general D. Whitehead, *The Ideology of the Athenian Metic* [*PCPS* Supp. 4, 1977]; the fact that, unless granted a special dispensation, metics could not own land or a house in Attica meant that Athens' metics were active in areas other than agriculture), and that in itself would be reason enough for X to introduce them into his argument here. But, given that X's interlocutor is specifically envisaged as a Spartan in this passage, there may be a particular reason for the antipathy to the idea of resident foreigners which seems to underlie the discussion in 1.10–12. Sparta was notoriously xenophobic, and had periodic expulsions of foreign visitors (*xenelasiai, cf. e.g.* Thuc. I. 144.2). Other Greeks had no rights of sojourn, even as an inferior group, in Sparta and Laconia. Metic status did not exist there, and that was how Spartans wanted it to be.

1.13. A new topic is introduced and dealt with in this section: the typically aristocratic leisure pursuits of physical exercise (athletics) and musical performances. The imagined criticism is that at Athens these activities have gone out of fashion. In reply, X argues that in fact they are still there, but they have been 'nationalised', so that, although individual members of the *demos* do not organise and practise such activities in their personal or family life, they are carried on at the state level, where they are financed by the rich and enjoyed by the *demos*, who also receive payment for participating in them.

The connection with the previous passage (1.10–12 on slavery) is not obvious, but it may perhaps be through the reference to Sparta in 1.11. Compulsory physical training for every individual citizen was one of the most distinctive characteristics of Spartan society (*cf. e.g.* Pericles' comment at Thuc. II. 39.1). Having specifically mentioned Sparta to make a contrast with Athens with regard to the treatment of slaves, X now turns to another feature of Athenian society where, supposedly, there is a contrast with Sparta in particular. Hence the opening words, τοὺς δὲ γυμναζομένους αὐτόθι.

The envisaged criticism at the beginning of §13 is not given an explicit attribution to an imagined third party ('some people', 'someone' or 'you'). It is simply cited, as at 1.10 (pp. 73–4, above). Here, however, X begins his reply within the first sentence, starting at the participle γνούς, which is emphatic, and carries a strongly causal sense = 'it is (not) because they think . . . but because'. We may compare 1.14 for a similar opening sentence, where the criticism is cited and X begins his reply to it, starting with a causal participle, all in the one sentence. γνούς here is picked up for emphasis by γιγνώσκουσιν. For the *demos*' knowing what they are doing see p. 70, above.

1.13. have made it unfashionable: καταλέλυκεν, from καταλύειν, cannot here mean 'has put a stop to', in the sense of 'ban' or 'abolish'. There is no evidence that such a thing ever happened. On the contrary, it seems quite clear that private athletic and musical activities continued to be practised by members of the Athenian upper classes in the later fifth century (*cf.* Ar. *Knights* 579–80, *Clouds* 72–8, *Wasps* 1219–64). The verb is being used here (as part of a typical exaggeration) in the sense 'make unfashionable', 'bring into disrepute' (*cf.* [Andoc.] IV. *Alcibiades* 39: τὰ γυμνάσια καταλύων), and the point of the criticism (which X naturally accepts as an accurate statement of the facts) is similar to that made by the Right Argument in Ar. *Clouds* 961–83 (note Wrong Argument's castigation of traditional educational practices as 'archaic' at line 984).

1.13. not because they think . . . but because they know: <οὐ> νομίζων . . . γνοὺς <δὲ> is an emendation by Orelli of the manuscript text, which as it stands is nonsensical. The passage is marked as 'clearly corrupt' by Bowersock, but this simple emendation restores perfect sense.

1.13. they cannot afford to: δυνατός, agreeing with δῆμος, is a correction found in C. The reading of the other manuscripts, δυνατά, which gives the same sense, is more awkward but possible. Here 'ability' refers to financial ability.

In his reply X, as usual, simply accepts the cited criticism as an accurate statement of the facts, and proceeds to explain the true motive behind what has happened. In this case, he argues, it is not that the *demos* regard athletics and musical activities as unfitting in themselves (on the contrary, they regard them as a fine thing, καλὸν). Rather it is that they cannot afford to pursue such traditional activities privately. Therefore they have 'nationalised' these activities: they are now financed by wealthy individuals, chosen by the state.

X is referring to the system (best known from Athens but attested in other Greek states too) of imposing 'liturgies' on wealthy individuals, *i.e.* a requirement to accept personal responsibility for and to finance various public institutions and services. On liturgies in general see, *e.g.*, M. H. Hansen, *The Athenian Democracy in the Age of Demosthenes* (London: Duckworth [Bristol Classical Paperbacks] / University of Oklahoma Press, [2]1999), 110–2; also Davies, *APF*, xx–xxiv. Here X refers in particular to the *choregia* and *gymnasiarchia*, *i.e.* the financing of performers in choral and athletic competitions at public festivals. These were extensive in Athens in the late fifth century. Both athletic and musical contests were held as part of the Panathenaea ([Arist.] *Ath. Pol.* 60.1, 3, Plut. *Pericles* 13.11), and dramatic and dithyrambic choruses were an important part of the Lenaea and Dionysia festivals ([Arist.] *Ath. Pol.* 56.3, with Rhodes *ad loc.*). On the number of festival liturgies see J. K. Davies, 'Demosthenes on Liturgies: A Note', *JHS* 87 (1967), 33–41, and on the *choregia* in general see P. Wilson, *The Athenian Institution of the Khoregia* (CUP, 2000).

1.13. trireme provisions: X here introduces a further point, the obligation of the Athenian rich to perform trierarchies, *i.e.* to finance the triremes which constituted the Athenian fleet. This is something which is not relevant to the argument about athletic and musical activities, with which he has been concerned in §13 so far, and is not really appropriate here. But X has included it because the trierarchy was another liturgy (as well as the *choregia* and *gymnasiarchia*) which the rich had to perform. Indeed, it was not just another liturgy, but a vitally important one. The Athenian fleet, the basis of Athenian power, and the key factor in securing the rule of the *demos* (*cf.* 1.2) is in X's mind throughout the treatise, and it has just been referred to twice in the previous passage (1.11 and 12). Hence the apparently irrelevant mention of the trierarchy here. On the trierarchy see especially V. Gabrielsen, *Financing the Athenian Fleet* (Johns Hopkins UP, 1994).

1.13. provide the choruses . . . take part in them: The point throughout this refrain, with the active being followed by the passive form of the verb, is the contrast between those who provide the public service (the rich, who must pay for it) and those who benefit by being paid to participate in it, as members of choruses and other teams of performers or as crews of ships (the *demos*). The men who rowed the ships were indeed largely the poorer men (though a proportion of them were non-citizens: *cf.* pp. 63, 80, above, 97, below). It is not clear how many of the performers were members of the lower classes: wealth and residence in or near the city would be the two factors making it easier for some men than for others to be available for training, and D. Pritchard argues that most of the performers will in fact have been from the élite ('Kleisthenes, Participation and the Dithyrambic Contests of Late

Archaic and Classical Athens', *Phoen.* 58 [2004], 208–28; *cf.* Wilson, *The Athenian Institution of the Khoregia*, 75–7).

1.13. Thus: The reading οὖν (in M) gives a slightly better sense in this context than γοῦν (in ABC), which would mean 'at any rate'.

1.13. a right to receive money: X here spells out more clearly that the *demos* benefit not merely as spectators of shows which the rich liturgists pay for but as performers and oarsmen on whom the rich spend their money. However, he conflates and confuses two separate activities and procedures. The rowers in the fleet were paid a salary, but not normally by the trierarch as part of his trierarchy (though when money due from the state was not provided, or when they wanted to recruit good crews, trierarchs sometimes had to or chose to make payments themselves, instead of or in addition to the payment made by the state: *e.g.* Thuc. VI. 31.3): their salaries came directly from the state treasury, and were the responsibility of the serving *strategoi* (*e.g.* [Dem.] L. *Polycles* 10–15). In the case of the *demos'* alleged ability to 'receive money' through public athletic and musical competitions, it is possible, but unlikely, that X is thinking of the prizes given to the winners. These could sometimes be cash prizes (*cf.* [Arist.] *Ath. Pol.* 60.3), but, obviously, only a small proportion of the contestants would benefit in this way. Furthermore, unlike rowers in the fleet, the contestants in these activities were not paid a salary for participating. However, the expenses involved in providing training, equipment, and costumes for the participants were defrayed by the gymnasiarch or choregus, and that must be what X has in mind in his rather misleadingly formulated assertion here. The dramatic choruses were quite small, but the dithyrambic ones seem to have involved much larger numbers of citizens, ten men's and ten boys' choruses of fifty each year at the Dionysia and five men's and five boys' at the Thargelia ([Arist.] *Ath. Pol.* 56.3; for choruses of fifty, schol. Aeschin. I. *Timarchus* 10 [29 Dilts], *cf.* Antiphon VI. *Chorister* 22), and they are probably what X is primarily thinking of in 'singing . . . and dancing'. See p. 150, below.

1.13. for singing and running and dancing and sailing: The order of the participles is odd. We should expect 'singing' and 'dancing', often performed by the same people on the same occasions, to be placed next to each other. But X seems unconcerned by such compositional niceties.

1.13. so as to get wealth for themselves and to make the rich poorer: There is no doubt that liturgies could be expensive (*cf.* Davies, *APF*, xxi–xxii). There were safeguards against exploitation in the rules which limited what could be required of a man (to perform a festival liturgy one year in two, Dem. XX. *Leptines* 8; a trierarchy one year in three, Isaeus VII. *Apollodorus* 38), but the competiveness encouraged by the system, and the desire to build up a store of *charis* ('gratitude') on which to draw if they came under political attack, led some men to perform more liturgies and to spend more money on them than was strictly necessary (notice the claims made by the speaker of Lysias XXI. *Defence on a Charge of Taking Bribes* 1–5; and for building up a store of *charis* see Lysias XVI. *Mantitheus* 17). The system of liturgies was a means of getting the rich to spend their money in ways useful to the city, but X's claim that the sole motivation behind the system was to enrich the *demos* and impoverish the rich is perverse and absurd (*cf.* pp. 65–6, above).

1.13. And in the lawcourts . . . their own advantage: The last sentence of 1.13 surely does not belong here. It is an abrupt and isolated comment, which is totally unconnected with anything which has preceded or with the first part of the section on the allies which is to follow. It reads more like a view of his imagined interlocutors than of X himself, and, as such, may belong after the opening sentence of 1.16, which is certainly a more appropriate context, *i.e.* part of the imagined complaint about the treatment of allies in Athenian courts which introduces that section (see Marr [1983], 48–9).

Conversely, the passage 2.9–10 (on public festivals, exercise grounds and baths) fits better here, after the substance of 1.13, than where it is placed in the manuscripts (see pp. 112–3, below). It is possible that 2.9–10 was omitted from its original position after 1.13, and then wrongly inserted where it now is. This may have left a gap in the text at the end of 1.13, which was filled by the insertion of these words, by some copyist who thought they provided some sort of connection with 1.14–18, a new topic – the harassment of rich allies – which starts, rather abruptly, at 1.14.

In any case, it is clear that this final sentence of 1.13 should be bracketed, as an indication that, wherever the words come from, they do not belong here.

1.14. But with regard to their allies . . . because they know that the ruler is necessarily hated by the ruled: A major new topic is introduced here, and five sections (§§14–18) are devoted to it. The passage is concerned with Athens' relations with her Aegean allies in the Delian League, as is evident from the word ἐκπλέοντες (= 'sailing out') in the first sentence (*cf.* Thucydides' usage of ξύμμαχοι, *e.g.* at II. 13.3): these were now in various degrees subordinate to Athens and (with the exception of Chios and Methymna on Lesbos) tribute-paying (*cf.* 2.1).

The first imagined criticism which X deals with (in §14) is that the Athenian *demos* discriminate against, and persecute, the upper classes, the *chrestoi*, in these allied states, and instead support the *demos*, the *poneroi*, there. In reply, X argues that the Athenian *demos* have no choice but to do this, if they wish to keep control of their empire, *arche*. If the upper classes are allowed to flourish in these allied states (it is implied), they will successfully revolt against Athenian rule, and so 'the empire of the Athenian *demos* will only last for a very short time'. X will return to this topic in 3.10–11.

This argument, that self-preservation necessitates the action criticised, is similar to that of 1.4–9. It assumes a universal and innate opposition between the two social classes into which X divides not just Athens, but all Greek states. However debatable the original assumption, once it is accepted the subsequent argument is logical enough. There is, however, some awkwardness in his combining the claim that 'the ruler is necessarily (ἀνάγκη is one of X's favourite words: see Introduction, section 9, and Appendix 5) hated by the ruled' (for this generalisation *cf.* Pericles' last speech. Thuc. II. 63.1, 64.5) with the suggestion that if the cities were ruled by the upper classes they would soon shake off their subservience to Athens. The first claim, by itself, should entail that any government in an allied state, whether oligarchic or democratic, would resent being part of the Athenian empire and would seek to revolt against it; but the second implies the view expressed by Diodotus in the debate on Mytilene in 427, that 'the *demos* in all the cities are well disposed to you' (Thuc. III. 47.2, rejecting what Cleon had said about Mytilene in 39.6). X seems to take it for granted, somewhat debatably, that the 'natural' form of government in any of these states, if Athens did not support the democrats, would invariably be oligarchy, just as the Athenian *arche* is for him essentially the *arche* of the *demos*. It looks as though X has taken the impressive-sounding generalisation about the ruler's necessarily being hated by the ruled from some contemporary work of sophistic political theory, and has inserted it into his argument here without realising that, logically, it does not fit very well (*cf.* 2.20 for a similar procedure, and see Appendix 7.4).

The first sentence of 1.14 is structurally similar to the first sentence of 1.13, in that the criticism is cited, and then the author begins his reply to it, all in the same sentence. In each case the reply starts with a strongly emphatic causal participle (here γιγνώσκοντες, for which *cf.* p. 70, above). In 1.14 a clear indication of the imagined criticism is provided by ὡς δοκοῦσι, which literally = 'as they are thought to' (*i.e.* by my interlocutors), since X often uses the tag δοκεῖ or δοκοῦσι in an opening sentence to signal an opponent's criticism (*e.g.* at 1.16, 2.1, 3.10). Hence here we are to understand that the pejorative συκοφαντοῦσιν (*cf.* p. 86, below) and the forceful μισοῦσι are words used not by him, but by his interlocutors (see Marr [1983], 49, 53), though he does not demur at their use.

Naturally, X accepts that the criticism, that the Athenians oppress the upper classes in the allied states, is an accurate statement of the facts. By way of 'reply' he argues that they have no choice but to do so, if they want their *arche* to continue. But how valid is the criticism in fact? The evidence suggests that it is, at the least, a gross exaggeration. Although Athens was widely seen as a champion of democracy and Sparta of oligarchy (*e.g.* Thuc. III. 82.1), the Athenian state did not routinely intervene to suppress oligarchic governments in allied states. The oligarchic government in Chios, for instance, remained undisturbed for many years until the revolt in 412. Usually it was only after revolts that the Athenians intervened and imposed democracies: τοὺς μὲν χρηστοὺς ἀτιμοῦσι . . . τοὺς δὲ πονηροὺς αὔξουσιν here could refer both to that and to the favouring in the Athenian courts of democratic, pro-Athenian over oligarchic, anti-Athenian leaders from the cities (*cf.* notes below). An inscribed record of a settlement imposed by Athens after a revolt survives in the case of Chalcis, recovered in 446 (ML 52 = *IG* i³ 40, trans. Fornara 103). Interestingly, this decree actually mentions all four types of punishment which

X specifies in §14 (lines 4–9 of the decree mention loss of citizen rights, exile, death, and confiscation of property). But the decree also contains an undertaking by the Athenians not to do any of these things without a trial (line 9), a crucial safeguard which X ignores in §14, where his vagueness gives the impression that the Athenian *demos* simply enforce their political will as they wish, as an imperial power ruling over weaker, dependent states.

X is right here only in so far as, when allied revolts occurred, the revolts were often led by the oligarchically-inclined upper classes, and the *demos* sometimes remained lukewarm at best. The extent to which Athenian rule was hated only by the upper classes in the cities and was popular with the *demos* has been much disputed since G. E. M. de Ste. Croix argued that that was the case in 'The Character of the Athenian Empire', *Historia* 3 (1954/5), 1–41. In the revolt of Mytilene in 428–427 (almost certainly alluded to in 1.15: see notes) the oligarchs who led it were not supported by the *demos* (Thuc. III. 27 – though he suggests that the *demos* were not so much pro-Athenian as reduced to desperation by hunger); in the debate on what to do with Mytilene after the revolt was suppressed, Cleon argued that all the Mytilenaeans had opposed Athens but Diodotus contradicted him and won the debate (*cf.* above). For a summary of discussion on the issue see Rhodes, *The Athenian Empire* (*G&R New Surveys* 17 [1985; [2]1993]), 36–8 with 43–4. Probably Thucydides' view that all the subjects hated Athenian rule and de Ste. Croix' view that only the upper-class subjects did are both over-simplified; one group of men who did have strong reason to be pro-Athenian comprised the local democratic leaders who were in a strong position in their cities with Athenian backing, but might lose that strong position if Athenian backing were removed.

1.14. bring malicious charges: Although X does not mention lawcourts in §14, it must be the case that the punishments he here refers to, *i.e.* loss of citizen rights, confiscation of property, exile and death, are those which were imposed by courts (especially Athenian courts) after a trial. This is most clearly implied by the word συκοφαντοῦσιν in the opening sentence. This verb (and its cognate nouns, συκοφάντης and συκοφαντία) always has abusive connotations. It carries associations of false allegations and sophistic quibbling, and sometimes of monetary motivation, in legal prosecutions. There is a detailed examination of Athenian 'sycophancy' and the 'sycophant' in P. Cartledge *et al.* (eds), *Nomos: Essays in Athenian Law, Politics and Society* (CUP, 1990), in two articles with differing conclusions, by R. Osborne (83–102) and D. Harvey (103–121).

It seems likely (Marr [1983] 53) that the word was a coinage of comedy which passed into everyday use, invented in the period immediately after the Athenian decree of which the Megarians complained in 432 (its earliest extant appearance is in Ar. *Acharnians*, of 425). It was first applied to individuals who brought prosecutions (through the procedure known as *phasis*, whereby a successful prosecutor was entitled to one half of the fine, if the defendant was convicted) against those who allegedly imported contraband goods into Attica. Subsequently the term acquired a wider application (*e.g.* Ar. *Knights* 437), and an increased pejorative sense, and was used to characterise any prosecution which was allegedly brought from malicious and / or mercenary motives. The earliest extant use of the word with regard to the treatment specifically of allies (other than here) is at Ar. *Birds* 1410–69, *i.e.* in 414. The Thirty in 404–403 are said to have repealed clauses in Solon's laws which required the exercise of discretion by jurors and so provided an opportunity for 'sycophants', and to have begun their régime well by eliminating undesirable categories of men including 'sycophants' ([Arist.] *Ath. Pol.* 35.2–3); and by the later fourth century *sykophantia* was a prosecutable offence ([Arist.] *Ath. Pol.* 43.5, 59.3). But that law was almost certainly enacted much later than the date of X's treatise.

There is evidence that Athenian individuals did sometimes bring prosecutions against well-to-do members of allied states, perhaps not always with honest motives (*cf.* Ar. *Knights* 328, 1408, *Peace* 639–40), and that such prosecutors and their 'summoners' were often resented abroad (*cf. e.g.* Ar. *Birds* 1410–69). This point will be further examined in the notes on 1.16.

1.14. if the rich and strong come into power: ἰσχυροὶ is the second adjective in all the manuscripts here. It provides an awkward and apparently tautological expression in combination with the verb ἰσχύσουσιν, but it should not be emended to χρηστοὶ (so Heinrich: accepted, *e.g.*, by Bowersock), since Stobaeus (*Flor.* XLIII. 50) has ἰσχυροὶ in his quotation of the passage, and it is obviously being used here together with πλούσιοι as a class label, a variant on χρηστοί (see Introduction, section 8, and Appendix 4).

1.14. they take away the political rights of the valuable: The reference here is to *atimia*, which was a formal judicial punishment, in which the type and range of rights removed could vary. See 3.12–13 with p. 165, below.

1.14. promote the interests of the worthless: Presumably through their support for and establishment of democratic constitutions, under which such men have political power, and also the through sympathetic treatment given to democratic leaders by Athenian courts (*cf.* 1.16 with p. 91, below).

1.14. but the valuable men at Athens try to protect the valuable men within the allied states: This must refer to legal, not political, support. There is no evidence that the Athenian upper classes ever wanted to give up the empire, or that they sympathised with oligarchic rebellion, *e.g.* with the perpetrators of the Mytilene revolt. Diodotus, who spoke against the wholesale punishment of the Mytileneans, made it clear that he was trying to save the innocent *demos,* not the guilty oligarchs (Thuc. III. 47). In 411, however, Athenian oligarchs, while not wanting to give up the empire, wanted to change from democracy to oligarchy in the allied states as well as in Athens, though Phrynichus said (and Thucydides himself agreed) that what the allies wanted was neither democracy dependent on Athens nor oligarchy dependent on Athens but freedom (Thuc. VIII. 48.5, 64).

Rather, X here has in mind individuals like the orator Antiphon, who wrote defence speeches for allied defendants up in court at Athens (*e.g.* Antiphon V. *On the Murder of Herodes*) and allied states contesting tribute increases (*e.g.* fr. A. 2 Maidment, *On the Tribute of Samothrace*), or Archeptolemus, who in some way opposed the prosecution of rich allies by the 'demagogue' Cleon (Ar. *Knights* 326–7). These two men were certainly Athenian *chrestoi*, and they both took a leading part in the oligarchic revolution of 411 (Thuc. VIII. 68.1, 90.1, [Plut.] *Lives of the Ten Orators* 834a–b). On Antiphon, and the possibility that he was X's tutor, see p. 140, below.

1.14. since they realise that it is good for themselves always to protect the best men in the allied states: In what way was it good for them? Perhaps politically (*cf.* the promises of the Athenian oligarchs in 411, above), but the context here seems judicial rather than political. X may have in mind a mutual support system whereby wealthy Greek aristocrats would look after their fellows if they were exiled from their own states. But more probably he simply accepts the common view that democrats found democrats elsewhere more congenial and oligarchs found oligarchs elsewhere more congenial (*cf.* 3.10 and, *e.g.*, Thuc. V. 29.1, 31.6).

1.15. Someone might say that . . . payments of money: A further criticism, within the context of the treatment of the allies, is clearly indicated here. The objection is that the Athenians ought to treat their allies in such a way as to allow them to prosper economically (*i.e.* with a lighter touch) This would mean that Athens in turn would benefit, by being able to receive the allies' tribute regularly and perhaps at a higher rate (χρήματα εἰσφέρειν here clearly refers to the payment of tribute): that would be enough to keep Athens strong. It is worth noting that neither here nor elsewhere in 1.14–18 does X envisage his interlocutors as attacking the *arche* as such. The Athenian upper classes gained much from the empire (see conveniently Hornblower in S. Hornblower and M. C. Greenstock, *The Athenian Empire* [LACTOR 1³, 1984], 146–8 Note E), as X was doubtless well aware.

In reply X accepts the implication that the allies are not treated with a light enough touch. Indeed, he suggests there has recently been a deliberate move by the Athenian *demos* to a situation of tighter constraint and greater economic exploitation of the allies than had previously been involved in the regular process of tribute assessment and collection. On the face of it his language, especially ἕνα ἕκαστον Ἀθηναίων ἔχειν, ἐκείνους δὲ ὅσον ζῆν, seems to be a reference to the expropriation of, and settlement by Athenians on, allied territory, through the imposition of a cleruchy. But this was not a form of control practised systematically by Athens over its allies. It usually happened only after serious revolts. When it did, the local inhabitants were sometimes expelled (*e.g.* at Hestiaea in 446: Thuc. I. 114.3); but often the original owners were retained as tenants or hired labourers on land whose ownership had been transferred to Athenians (R. Zelnick-Abramovitz, 'Settlers and Dispossessed in the Athenian Empire', *Mnem.*⁴ 57 [2004], 325–45). The most obvious example of the imposition of a cleruchy in circumstances which fit X's description here exactly was the settlement imposed on Mytilene in 427, after its failed revolt, when the land was confiscated and distributed to 2,700 Athenian cleruchs, but the Mytilenaeans themselves were not expelled (Thuc. III. 50.2). Instead, they agreed to pay these cleruchs a rent of two minas per year each (note here τὰ τῶν συμμάχων χρήματα), while themselves continuing to cultivate the land (ἐργάζεσθαι here corresponds closely to εἰργάζοντο in Thucydides).

1.15. only what is enough to survive on: In other words they are economically constrained much more tightly than if they merely paid the normal tribute. Again, this description suggests the Mytilene situation, where an annual payment of 54 talents to the cleruchs (who received almost 4 obols per day each) was considerably more than the pre-425 tribute assessment of any other allied state, and fell directly on the former owners of the land (the highest levels of tribute were, before the Peloponnesian War, 30 talents from Aegina and from Thasos; but in what can be restored of the optimistic assessment list of 425, perhaps 75 talents from Abdera and 60 talents from Thasos: see R. Meiggs, *The Athenian Empire* [OUP, 1972], 538–61 Appendix 14).

If Thucydides' language at III. 50.2 mirrors that of the formal decision taken in 427, the marked similarity of X's words here makes it a strong possibility (*pace* Frisch, 223) that Kalinka (155) and other scholars were right in their conclusion that, beneath the characteristic generalisation and exaggeration, he is thinking here specifically of the assembly's treatment of Mytilene in 427. In that case the treatise must have been written after that date, though probably not long after, as the event is still in his mind.

How long did this situation at Mytilene last? It appears that the cleruchy was subsequently withdrawn, since an inscription (*IG* i³ 66, translated S. Hornblower and M. C. Greenstock, *The Athenian Empire* [LACTOR 1³, 1984], p. 140 no. 169 / R. Osborne, *The Athenian Empire* [LACTOR 1⁴, 2000], p. 63 no. 134) and a speech (Antiphon V. *Murder of Herodes* 77) refer to the Mytilenaeans' having the right to occupy their own property. How long before Antiphon's speech (*c.* 415) this happened is unknown.

1.15. without being able to plot revolt: It was certainly the case that one of the purposes of an Athenian cleruchy was to serve as a potential garrison (and it has been pointed out that the rent paid to the cleruchs was more or less equivalent to the stipend paid to hoplites: see Hornblower's commentary on Thuc. III. 50.2), able to act immediately against any local uprising. But X skates over the fact that cleruchies were usually imposed only when there had been a *prior* revolt, to deter a repetition, and, it is misleading of him to suggest, as he does here, that Athens now routinely rules its Aegean allies by means of imposed cleruchies. Indeed, he contradicts himself on this point at 2.1, where he characterises the allies generally as 'tribute-paying' (οἳ φέρουσι τὸν φόρον).

1.16. On this point too, it is thought that the Athenian* demos *act ill-advisedly: A further criticism is now envisaged, still within the context of the Athenian *demos*' treatment of their allies. The criticism is directed against the (alleged) compulsory transfer of jurisdiction (ἀναγκάζουσι πλεῖν ἐπὶ δίκας) from the courts of these allied states to the Athenian lawcourts, the *dikasteria*. This topic takes up three sections (§§16–18).

The author's reply begins at οἱ δὲ ἀντιλογίζονται, an interesting variation in which X cheekily puts his explanation into the mouths of the Athenians. Thus they themselves (implausibly) admit their entirely selfish and self-interested motivation (a constant theme for X) behind the practice under discussion. Most, though not all, of these self-confessed advantages are financial. They deliberately make money out of forcing allied litigants to travel to, and stay in, Athens for their judicial proceedings. The first advantage briefly enumerated is clearly financial (they receive pay for jury service), but then X turns to a *political* advantage, the ability to protect Athenian sympathisers, members (and particularly leaders) of the *demos*, in allied states, who, if trials were held locally, would be judicially ruined by their powerful opponents. This point is similar to that made in 1.14 (τοὺς . . . πονηροὺς αὔξουσιν), though it is further developed here, and, interestingly, X now admits that there are some active political supporters of Athens and the Athenian *demos* within the allied states.

After the intervention of this essentially political argument in the second part of §16, X reverts to arguments centring on the economic advantages which Athens derives from the transfer of allied jurisdiction to the Athenian lawcourts. This aspect occupies all of §17 and is perhaps in the background also in §18.

1.16. they compel the allies to sail to Athens for lawsuits: What are the facts about the transfer of jurisdiction from allied to Athenian courts? As usual, it seems that X is exaggerating and over-simplifying. About the middle of the century Athens interfered in the judicial freedom of some individual states. For instance, the decree for Chalcis of (almost certainly) 446/5 (ML 52 = *IG* i³ 40, trans. Fornara 103), in an amendment proposed by Archestratus (lines 70–6), specifies that 'Chalcidians shall be punished in Chalcis, just as Athenians are punished in Athens, except where the sentence is of exile, death, or loss of citizen rights (*atimia*). In these instances there shall be a right of appeal (*ephesis*) to the *heliaea* [court] of the *thesmothetai* at Athens.' Here it seems that in the case of certain serious offences there was a right of appeal, *ephesis* (which could be exercised apparently by either defendant or prosecutor: in some circumstances *ephesis* denotes compulsory transfer, but 'appeal' seems to be the right translation here), from the allied to the Athenian courts. But in the case of Erythrae, probably in the late 450s, Athens seems to have insisted that exiles should not be reinstated and men in Erythrae should not be exiled without the authority of Athens (ML 40 = *IG* i³ 14, trans. Fornara 71, lines 26–9): this is not just a right of appeal but compulsory reference for confirmation by the Athenians.

X's work is not the only literary text which suggests that later the Athenians imposed a general limitation. According to Antiphon V. *Murder of Herodes* 47 (*c.* 415), 'It is not permitted even to a<n allied> city to sentence anyone to death without <the authority of> the Athenians'; less, specifically, Chamaeleon fr. 44 Wehrli, quoted by Ath. IX. 407b, mentions something which occurred 'when the Athenians were transferring the island lawsuits to the city'. It does appear likely that eventually Athens reserved to itself the right to impose the severest penalties even in cases between citizens of the same allied city. However, the picture presented by X in 1.16–18, which implies a total termination by the Athenians of *all* allied local jurisdiction, is seriously misleading.

This interference with the allies' judicial autonomy was, no doubt, motivated primarily by defensive political considerations, since the Athenians wished to protect their friends in the allied states by preventing their powerful opponents from exploiting deferential local courts to ruin them for essentially political reasons (as X here cheerfully admits they would, if they could!).

1.16. But they list on the other side of the balance sheet: In this metaphor from accounting we have an unusual variation on the reply formula, where the responses are elsewhere always expressed as X's own. With οἱ δὲ (Marchant) X might in theory either be attributing the response to 'others', replying to an unexpressed οἱ μὲν ('some') who voiced the objection, or attributing it to the Athenian *demos* itself; but an attribution to the *demos* is more pointed, and is surely what X intends here. The relative οἳ δὲ (some editors including Bowersock) is not used in this way in classical prose. In fact the arguments which X presents are obviously his own, as elsewhere. Hence there is no attempt to correct the exaggeration, or to defend the justice of the procedure, only an unashamed enumeration of all the advantages (mostly economic) which Athens gained by having allied citizens come there for their judicial business. As we might expect, in reality the Athenians, when pressed on this point (*e.g.* those at Sparta in 432), strongly asserted that their lawcourts did function justly and impartially in cases involving allied citizens (Thuc. I. 76.3–77. 2).

1.16. that from the legal deposits they receive their jury pay throughout the year: This is an absurd exaggeration. The deposits which litigants had to pay to the state in advance in *dikai* (private lawsuits) were only a small fraction of the total value of the lawsuit (*e.g.* 30 drachmae for a suit involving anything between 1,000 and 10,000 drachmae). They cannot possibly in themselves have been enough to finance jury pay (*misthos*) for a year. In the 420s jurymen were paid 3 obols per day. If we assume (as Hate-Cleon does at Ar. *Wasps* 661–3) that all the 6,000 empanelled jurymen (see p. 94, below) were employed on jury service on every available day of the year (about 240 days), that would produce a total annual expenditure of 120 talents. This is certainly a big overestimate of the cost of judicial *misthos*: the actual number of court days will have been *c.* 175–225, and not all of the 6,000 jurors will have been needed every day (see M. H. Hansen, 'How Often Did the Athenian *Dicasteria* Meet?' *GRBS* 20 [1979], 243–6, *cf. The Athenian Democracy in the Age of Demosthenes* [London: Duckworth (Bristol Classical Paperbacks) / University of Oklahoma Press, ²1999], 186–7); but, even if the actual figure was only a third of that amount, say 40 talents, it cannot have been made up just from litigants' deposits. One suspects that X has in mind *fines* (*cf.* Ar. *Knights* 1359–60) as well as deposits here. But as the text stands he does not say so, and the exaggeration is so gross that it may be that we should restore καὶ τῶν ζημιῶν ('and from the fines') to the text here, after ἀπὸ τῶν πρυτανείων.

1.16. that ... they receive: λαμβάνειν is infinitive of indirect statement, dependent on ἀντιλογίζονται (hence 'that' in the translation). But in the next sentence X switches to the indicative with διοικοῦσι, etc.

1.16. resentment against the Athenians: X sometimes omits the article with Ἀθηναῖοι: *cf.* 3.1, 10.

1.17. the Athenian demos profit in the following ways: In this section X reverts from political to economic gain, and lists four different ways in which the Athenian *demos* profit financially (κερδαίνει) from having allied citizens travel to Athens for judicial proceedings. They are: (*a*) the one per cent tax in the Piraeus, (*b*) having rooms for rent, (*c*) hiring out a pair of animals or a slave to carry belongings, (*d*) the auctioneer's fee. In his list X does seem not to distinguish between the profits made by individuals (*b*, *c* and *d*), and those accruing to the state as a whole (*a*). For X these are all equally advantages derived by the *demos.*

The vividly envisaged details here, in which one sees the foreigner land at the Piraeus, pass through the customs, rent a room for the night, then next day hire a carriage or a slave to carry his belongings up to the town, and make use of an auctioneer, are another indication that X himself is an Athenian, to whom it was all familiar, and would be significant even if we did not have the first person plurals of 1.12 (Frisch, 227, is acute on this point).

1.17. the one per cent tax in the Piraeus brings in more for the state: This must refer to a customs tax of some sort. It may be an early version of the tax that was levied on all imports and exports passing through the port of Piraeus at a rate of 2% after the Peloponnesian War (Andoc. I. *Mysteries* 133–4), although the foreigners coming to Athens for trials transferred from their own states were not importing goods. A passage in Ar. *Wasps*, which is surely relevant given the play's date of 422, refers to 'the many one per cent taxes', and also to 'deposits', 'harbour taxes' (*i.e.* harbour charges of some kind) and 'rents', as all being part of the total revenues of the state (656–60).

1.17. he does better: The manuscripts have the infinitive πράττειν here. But we have just had a nominative subject (ἡ ἑκατοστὴ) with indicative ἐστι understood, and another indicative πράττουσι follows two sentences later, so it is better to follow Schneider in restoring the indicative, and to suppose that the corruption occurred under the influence of μισθοφοροῦν in the next sentence. We have also to understand ἄμεινον πράττει as the apodosis to εἴ τῳ συνοικία ἐστίν.

1.17. anyone who has a carriage or a slave for hire: μισθοφοροῦν is an explanatory infinitive after ζεῦγός and ἀνδράποδον. These are slaves who could be hired out as porters – an economically profitable use of slaves (particularly for those Athenians who lived in the Piraeus) which X has not mentioned at 1.11–12. No doubt slaves were often used in this role (*cf.* Xanthias in Aristophanes' *Frogs*).

1.17. the auctioneers do better: The basic meaning of κῆρυξ is 'herald'. Frisch and Bowersock take the reference to be to the official herald of the assembly, who formally started proceedings and who introduced official foreign visitors (Ar. *Acharnians* 43–64). But he did not have any independent authority, being responsible to the presiding officers (*prytaneis*); and, in any case, X is surely not referring to the assembly here.

In the later fourth century each lawcourt had a herald who called the selected jurors to their assigned courts ([Arist.] *Ath. Pol.* 64.3, 66.1), and, later, summoned them to vote at the end of the proceedings, and then announced the result ([Arist.] *Ath. Pol.* 68.4, 69.1). It seems reasonable to assume that such heralds, for these latter purposes at least, went back to the later fifth century, and Kalinka thought that it is to these judicial heralds that X is referring here. In what way could they benefit financially from the visits of these allied litigants? X does not explain, but we should have to assume that he is alluding to the sort of minor palm-greasing of officials which he mentions more explicitly at 3.3. Possibly it was necessary for such a litigant to register his arrival in Athens, and his availability for proceedings, with a dicastic herald. Until his presence was officially accepted, he would be wasting his money and time. Hence the need to tip the herald generously.

However, a more specialised meaning of κῆρυξ is 'auctioneer' (*e.g.* Theophr. fr. 97 Wimmer), and when *kerykes* are mentioned after the hiring-out of lodging-houses, carriages and slaves that is surely the most likely meaning here. Auctioneers may have been involved both in hiring-out and (in the case of carriages and slaves) in selling.

1.18. In addition to this . . . they would honour: πρὸς δὲ τούτοις shows that X is making a further point in this section, *i.e.* members of the *demos* also derive considerable *psychological* advantages from being personally flattered and fawned on by allied litigants, who need to secure their good will before and during their trials. If the system were not as it is, the only Athenians whom allied citizens would need to court would be those who went out from Athens in an official capacity, and whom they encountered at home, *i.e.* 'the generals and the trierarchs and ambassadors', and the various officials sent from Athens to allied cities (see pp. 95–6, below). X does not say so here, but his implication is that at any rate the generals, trierarchs and ambassadors are not themselves members of the *demos* (*cf.* 1.3, 13, where it is explicit).

It is not necessary to assume that in this section X is implying bribery, the giving of gifts by allied litigants to Athenian jurymen. It is true that a passage in Ar. *Wasps*, 675–9, refers to a variety of gifts made by visiting allied citizens. But these are gifts allegedly made to politicians, not jurors, and another passage of *Wasps*, 550–75, strongly attests the great psychological boost to their self-esteem which the system afforded the ordinary Athenians, when they were serving as jurymen. That seems clearly to be X's point in 1.18, and there is no reason to doubt that it did happen.

1.18. each and every one of the allies has been compelled to flatter the Athenian demos: X's point here is that, before the case, outside the courthouse, the allied litigant has to flatter any member of the *demos* he meets, since, as far as he is concerned, anyone might be a member of the jury allocated to his case. This was something which X assumes was not known by the litigants in advance. In the later fourth century there was a complicated procedure for allotting jurors to courts on a daily basis, to make sure they were not known in advance (*cf.* [Arist.] *Ath. Pol.* 63–6). This did not exist in the fifth century, when panels seem to have been assigned to particular courts throughout the year (*cf., e.g.,* D. M. MacDowell, *The Law in Classical Athens* [London: Thames and Hudson / Cornell UP, 1978], 36, citing Ar. *Wasps* 242–4, 303–5). But even so, litigants, especially from abroad, would often not have known who their jurors were going to be. The emphatic nominative εἷς ἕκαστος here is logically misplaced: what X ought to have said that litigants from the allied states have to flatter every single member of the Athenian *demos*. The contrast is between a limited number of Athenian officials who descend on the allied states (εἰ μὲν . . . τοὺς ἐκπλέοντας . . . μόνους) and the entire body of the *demos* (νῦν δ᾽ . . . τὸν δῆμον), every one of whom the allied litigants must pay court to under present arrangements.

1.18 has been compelled . . . is compelled: This repetition for emphasis repeats and reinforces ἀναγκάζουσι in 1.16. The motif of Athenian compulsion is dominant in 1.16–18.

1.18. to appear as a defendant or as a prosecutor: Literally 'to pay and to exact the penalty'.

1.18. this indeed is the law at Athens: The insertion of this explanatory gloss, with its emphasising δὴ, again implies that X's assumed interlocutors (unlike him) are non-Athenian, and also suggests that they have a different judicial system. It is worth noting that Sparta entirely lacked a citizen judiciary. The administration of justice there was in the hands of the council of thirty elders (*gerousia*) and / or the five ephors (*cf.* D. M. MacDowell, *Spartan Law* [Edinburgh: Scottish Academic Press, 1986], 126–35).

At Athens, by contrast, 6,000 citizens were empanelled as registered jurors in any one year ([Arist.] *Ath. Pol.* 24.3), juries selected for individual cases were several hundred or sometimes several thousand strong, and the *demos*' control of the lawcourts was regarded as a fundamental feature of the democratic constitution ([Arist.] *Ath. Pol.* 9.1, 41.2, Arist. *Politics* II. 1273b 41–1274a 11).

1. 18. And inside the courts he is compelled to beseech, and to grasp the hand of, anyone who enters: In §18 X seems to envisage two stages at which the visiting allied litigant must pay court to members of the *demos*. First outside the court, before the case, when he has to flatter everybody he meets; secondly, when he is inside the court, at which point he has to pay fawning attentions to the jurymen as they come in. A similar two-stage process of supplication is envisaged at Ar. *Wasps* 552–73. However, in the *Wasps* the physical touching is said to occur outside the court, at the earlier stage (553–4), and in fact that is a more likely time for it to have taken place. It was perhaps not possible for a litigant, once inside the courthouse, to grasp the hands of the members of the jury. X seems to be writing a little loosely here (*cf.* 2.16).

1.18. anyone who enters: The idea seems to be that, even at this stage, the allied litigant does not know who the actual jurymen are going to be. For him it could be anyone who comes into the court.

***1.18. the allies have become, rather, the slaves of the Athenian* demos:** δοῦλοι ('slaves') is used figuratively here, to indicate political subservience, as it is at 1. 8, 9, 11 (see notes). The point of μᾶλλον is that they are now dependent instead of (free) allies. There is an implicit contrast between their present and their former status (for this use of μᾶλλον to indicate a contrast *cf.* 2.8, 14, 19).

1.19–20. This is the final topic of chapter 1. X argues that, because of their official visits to, and possessions in, the territory of allied states overseas, the Athenians have all become experienced seamen. Hence they know how to operate triremes, the fighting ships of the Athenian navy, as soon as they get into them. The transition from the immediately preceding passage (16–18), on the advantages they gain by requiring their allies to come to Athens for judicial proceedings, seems abrupt. X does not introduce any new imagined criticism at the beginning of §19. So it seems that he regards this section as somehow still connected with what precedes. He is probably thinking back to §15. There (before devoting §§16–18 to advantages enjoyed by the *demos* in Athens at the expense of visiting allies) X has referred to the Athenian practice of establishing cleruchies, settlements of Athenian colonists, on the territory of their allies: this is the point reverted to in 19–20, where X argues that a further advantage of cleruchies, other than the obvious economic and military ones, is that, through the necessity of having to travel backwards and forwards to visit these overseas possessions, the *demos* (not specified here but clearly implied in the argument) have become experienced seamen, who can operate ships of war effectively, as soon as it becomes necessary.

The reason why X introduces this particular point here is that he wishes to prepare his readers / audience for the move to his next major topic, Athenian naval domination, and the strategic advantages enjoyed by a state which rules the sea. This starts at 2.1, and takes up much of chapter 2.

1.19. because of the land they have acquired in overseas territories, and the offices which take them abroad: κτῆσις or κτήματα ἐν τοῖς ὑπερορίοις can be used to denote possessions abroad which are privately owned by wealthy individuals (*IG* i³ 421–30; extracts ML 79, trans. Fornara 147. D; also Xen. *Mem.* II. 8.1), but here it is much more likely that X has in mind cleruchy land, which was confiscated from

Athens' Aegean allies and allocated to members of the *demos* for settlement in large numbers (see pp. 88–9, above). No doubt this necessitated a good deal of maritime travel to and fro in passenger and cargo boats.

In his reference to *archai* ('offices') here, X is presumably not thinking of generals and ambassadors, who for him are not members of the *demos* (*cf.* 1.3, 18). Rather, he has in mind such overseas administrative officials as *archontes* (governors), and *episkopoi* (inspectors), who are frequently attested in decrees of the later fifth century as operating in allied states. Indeed, according to the papyrus text of [Arist.] *Ath. Pol.* 24. 3 there were some 700 such officials serving abroad in any one year (though this 700, coming after 700 internal officials, may well be a scribal error). If there was a significant number of such officials, they will have been drawn from a wider social background than the generals and ambassadors, through probably still not from what X regards as the *demos*. However, what he is really concerned with in this section is not officials but cleruchs.

1.19. they have learned to row without noticing it: This seems an odd comment. There is no doubt that many thousands of Athenians were skilled seamen. Even the Athenian cavalry, *hippeis*, could row, and did so for instance on the expedition against Corinth in 425 (Ar. *Knights* 601). Their massive superiority in the techniques of seamanship, and their opponents' lack of experience and problems in acquiring these skills, were crucial facts, strongly stressed *e.g.* by Pericles in a speech in 432 (Thuc. I. 142–3). In that speech Pericles lays repeated emphasis on the Athenians' μελετᾶν, practising (Thuc. I. 142.7–9), just as X does in 1.20, where the repetition perhaps deliberately echoes Pericles' comments (see p. 121, below, on 2.14–16).

On the other hand, X's claim in 1.19–20, that this great technical superiority comes simply from the practice the Athenians get in peace-time maritime activities, through having to serve as officials abroad and visit their overseas possessions, with the implication that they do not train specifically for naval warfare, is surprising. Plutarch, *Pericles* 11.4 refers to a pre-war Periclean policy of regular patrols by squadrons of triremes, through which large numbers of citizens learned naval skills. We do not know what source Plutarch had for this statement: some naval patrolling is surely what we would expect, given that the Athenians needed to keep the Aegean secure, and to enforce tribute payment in peace-time as well as in war. But we do not know how large these patrols were, or how often they were deployed, and they would not necessarily have provided large numbers of citizens with experience in rowing. Indeed, X denies that they needed to mount naval patrols at all (1.16).

Probably the point underlying X's comment here ('without noticing it') is his, and his interlocutors', awareness that the Athenians, despite their concentration on naval power, had no comprehensive and compulsory programme of naval training for their citizens which in any way corresponded to the *agoge*, the compulsory military education for all Spartan citizens, which formed the basis of Sparta's hoplite supremacy. Compare the comment in Pericles' funeral speech: 'They [the enemy, and particularly the Spartans] start right from their youth to pursue manliness by arduous training, while we live a relaxed life but none the less go to confront the dangers to which we are equal' (Thuc. II. 39.1). An implied contrast with Sparta here would fit the hypothesis that the imagined interlocutors are regarded primarily as Spartan (cf. Introduction, section 5, and p. 78, above).

1.19. both they themselves and their slaves: Pace Bowersock, who translates 'associates', this must be the sense of ἀκόλουθοι here (cf. the parallel οἰκέτην in the next sentence). X uses several terms for 'slave', most often δοῦλος (unlike the others, often figurative), but also these two and ἀνδράποδον. It is interesting that he takes it for granted that any citizen, *i.e.* any member of the *demos*, will have a slave.

On the face of it, X seems to be suggesting, through his phrase 'both themselves and their slaves', that slaves as well as citizens were sometimes used as rowers in the Athenian navy. The usual view of scholars is that they were not, or at least were not until the battle of Arginusae in 406, when the use of slaves was, it is argued, an exceptional occurrence, at a time of great national crisis (cf. Ar. *Frogs* 190–1); and this was one of J. D. Smart's reasons for dating the work after that battle ('The Athenian Empire', *Phoen.* 31 [1977], 245–57 at 250 n. 12). But the evidence is not absolutely conclusive on this point. B. Jordan, *The Athenian Navy in the Classical Period* (*U. Calif. Pub. Class. Stud.* 13 [1975]), 240–68, after an article published in *CSCA* 2 (1969), 183–207, argues on the basis of the word *hyperesia* that the Athenians regularly used slave rowers. That is certainly wrong, but a stronger argument has been presented by A. J. Graham, 'Thucydides VII 13.2 and the Crews of Athenian Triremes', *TAPA* 122 (1992), 257–70, and 'Thucydides VII 13.2 and the Crews of Athenian Triremes: An Addendum', 128 (1998), 83–114. The Athenians may have used slave rowers on occasions even during the Archidamian War, and, if so, that would explain X's two specific references to slaves in §19, which would otherwise be pointless.

1.19. learn the naval terminology: Seamen traditionally have had a language of their own, which has the effect of reinforcing their group identity, and making outsiders feel inadequate. X shows good insight in mentioning this point. He has an interest in esoteric vocabulary (cf. 2.8), and is here probably thinking not so much of nautical metaphors taken into everyday language as of specialised naval terms, such as ὑποζώματα (the 'undergirdles' running between prow and stern to strengthen a ship: *e.g. IG* ii² 1629 = RO 100, 133–4, on which see J. S. Morrison, J. F. Coates and N. B. Rankov, *The Athenian Trireme* [CUP, ²2000], 169–71); and ἐντερόνεια ('ship-intestines', used in Ar. *Knights* 1185), may be another instance of this (A. H. Sommerstein *ad loc.* [Aris and Phillips, 1981] suggests that it is either a technical term or slang).

1.20. They become good steersmen also: This is a reference to a different nautical activity from rowing, which X has dealt with in §19. He now turns to the art of steering, controlling the direction of a ship by using its rudder (cf. Ar. *Knights* 541–2). He argues that the Athenians learn this skill partly through their general experience of sea-voyaging (see next note), and partly through actual practice in using the rudder. The practice is done either on a passenger boat or on a cargo ship. After this practice in steering non-military boats, they have graduated to steering triremes, warships. In the final sentence of §20 X seems to sum up the whole of 1.19–20: the Athenians have already learned, as an essential part of their civilian lives, all the important naval-warfare skills, both rowing and steering, before they embark on their warships.

1.20. through experience gained in their voyaging: He has in mind here their knowledge of such matters as position, currents, and winds, which they have gained simply from their frequent maritime travelling.

1.20. boat . . . cargo ship: For this contrast between a πλοῖον ('boat' in general) and a ὁλκάς (large cargo ship) cf. Thuc. VII. 7.3 with the note in K. J. Dover's small edition (OUP, 1965). Both were vessels used for non-military purposes, in contrast to triremes, warships.

1.20. and from there some have passed on to triremes: This is awkwardly expressed. What X means is that the Athenians have learned the art of steering, through practising in various ships of peace-time, and, as a result of that, they are all able to steer ships of war as soon as they get into them. X would have made his meaning clearer if he had simply written ἐντεῦθεν δ' instead of οἱ δ' ἐντεῦθεν here. The contrast between 'some' and 'others' has already been completed, and we do not need another subdivision of the grammatical subject.

1.20. the many are able: The expression οἱ . . . πολλοὶ probably has its class-label sense here (see Introduction, section 8): it is the equivalent of τὸ πλῆθος (2.18). It is true that X uses this expression in its neutral sense of 'the majority' at 3.13 (see p. 167, below), but that sense here would provide his argument with an unnecessarily weak conclusion. The whole point of 1.19–20 is that *all* of the lower classes at Athens (even the slaves), not just a majority, have learned in advance the naval skills necessary to operate triremes in war. The expression οἱ πολλοί is frequently used by contemporary authors in this social sense (*cf. e.g.* Thuc. I. 6.4, Eur. *Electra* 382), and in this passage which obviously refers to the *demos* (without, however, explicitly using the word) we might expect X's summarising sentence to contain a typical class-label expression to make up for that absence, and to underline his point.

1.20. to operate their ships: ἐλαύνειν (= 'drive', *cf.* 1.2) must here include both 'rowing' (the subject of §19) and 'steering' (the subject of §20). The final sentence seems to sum up the whole argument of 1.19–20, that the Athenians have learned all the necessary nautical skills, both rowing and steering, before they get into their warships. In §19, where X is concerned specifically with rowing, the words τῇ κώπῃ are attached to the infinitive ἐλαύνειν to indicate that it has a more specific sense there.

   X does not mention sailing skills anywhere in 1.19–20. In fact, commercial ships were normally powered by sails rather than by oars, and even triremes had sails. But what X is really concerned about in this passage is the effortless ability of the Athenians to operate triremes in naval warfare, and in the actual battles at sea a trireme's sails were not used (*cf.* J. S. Morrison, J. F. Coates and N. B. Rankov, *The Athenian Trireme* [CUP, ²2000], 175–8). What mattered was speed (generated by the rowers) and direction (controlled by the steersmen).

2.1. At this point X moves on to a major new topic, Athens' concentration of its resources on naval power, and the immense military and strategic advantages which Athens enjoys by virtue of being 'the ruler of the sea'. This topic is developed at some length, in §§2–13 of chapter 2.

The connexion with the preceding sections comes partly by way of a deliberate contrast, *i.e.* at Athens everyone knows how to row and steer ships, and therefore can serve in the navy (1.19–20), but 'as for their hoplite force . . . ' (first words of 2.1), partly from a continuation of the theme of relations with the allies, which occupied 1.14–18. Thus in 2.1–3 X makes the further point that the geographical situation of Athens' allies is such as to make them particularly vulnerable to a dominant naval power.

At first sight there might appear to be a difference between the type of argument which X deploys in 2.2–13, which is concerned with the advantages gained by Athens as a state, through its sea-power, and that of chapter 1, which is concerned with the class advantages the *demos* derives from having a democratic constitution. But the difference is more apparent than real, as we can see from 1.2, where X makes it clear that the *demos*' continued political power at home (and hence its class advantage) is a direct consequence of the fact that it mans the navy, and it is the navy which gives the city its power.

2.1. *their hoplite force and the view that this is not at all an Athenian strong point:* The presence of the word δοκεῖ (= 'is thought') shows that what we have here is another imagined interlocutor's criticism (see Introduction, section 5, Appendix 1; and *cf.* 1.14, 16, 3.10). X's reply begins immediately, within the same sentence, at οὕτω καθέστηκεν (= 'they have set it up to be as it is'), *i.e.* they deliberately, as a matter of policy, keep their hoplite force comparatively weak, and, correspondingly, concentrate the resources which they have heavily on their navy. As far as their hoplite infantry is concerned, their only requirement is that it should be stronger than that of their Aegean allies. They regard it as acceptable for it to be weaker and smaller than that of their enemies (Wilamowitz's correction of the manuscript reading μείζους, 'greater', to ὀλείζους, 'fewer', is necessary to the sense and has been generally accepted).

An implication of X's argument here may be that some Athenian citizens who qualified as hoplites (which was probably equivalent to qualifying for membership of the third of the four Solonian property classes, the *zeugitai*) were in fact used in the navy, in addition to the *thetes*, to add to the body of oarsmen. We have evidence that this did sometimes happen, *e.g.* in 428 in an attack on the Isthmus of Corinth

(Thuc. III. 16.1), and hoplites sent to strengthen the siege of Mytilene acted as their own oarsmen to cross the Aegean (Thuc. III. 18.3–4). Even the elite cavalry, the *hippeis*, could on occasions be pressed into service as oarsmen (*cf.* Ar. *Knights* 600–3). This must have been disconcerting to X's imagined interlocutors, especially if they are considered as Spartans (the hoplite community *par excellence*), who presumably thought, as he did (1.2, 2.14), that the hoplites were not part of the *demos*. In his reply to their criticism here X again demonstrates that the traditional conservative view is naïve and simple-minded.

According to Thucydides (II. 13.6), there were in all some 13,000 Athenian hoplites in 431 (plus 16,000 in the lowest and highest age groups, and metics, all engaged in garrison duty). This was not an inconsiderable force, as the Spartan king, Archidamus, recognised (Thuc. I. 80.3), but all social classes in Athens were depleted by the plague in the early 420s, and when caught unprepared Athens' hoplites were not strong enough to defeat the Thebans at Delium in 424 (*cf.* below). They were not used to defend Plataea in 429, and they were never risked in a pitched battle against the invasions of Attica by the Spartans and their allies in 431, 430, 428, 427 or 425. This was indeed, as X asserts, a deliberate policy, established on the advice of Pericles (Thuc. I. 143.5, II. 13.2).

The implication of everything X says in 2.1–6 is that the Athenians, the 'rulers of the sea', will not use their hoplite army in any kind of direct confrontation with a powerful land force. But in the autumn of 424 a plan to make the Boeotians divide their forces failed and the Athenians were soundly defeated by a substantial Boeotian force in the battle of Delium: nearly 1,000 hoplites and a general, Hippocrates, were killed (Thuc. IV. 76–7, 89–101). It seems highly unlikely that X could argue as he does here if he were writing after that battle, or at least within a couple of years after it. This is a strong indication of a date for the treatise earlier than the end of 424 (*cf.* Introduction, p. 5, and pp. 120–1, below).

2.1. than their enemies: τῶν μὲν πολεμίων is contrasted with τῶν δὲ συμμάχων, their allies. The use of the word 'enemies' here does not necessarily on its own imply that there is an enemy, whom the Athenians are fighting against, at the time when X is writing; it could be purely theoretical. But in view of what follows, particularly 2.14–16, it is much more likely that it does refer to a definite enemy, which is now taking definite action against the Athenians.

2.1. stronger even on land: It is hard to make sense of the phrase κράτιστοί εἰσι here, though the reading is found in all the manuscripts. We surely need a comparative rather than a superlative form, and εἰσι seems otiose. We suggest (*cf.* Marr [1983], 41–2) that we should read κρείττους instead of κράτιστοί εἰσι. This restores sense to the passage, viz. 'They hold that they are weaker and fewer (in hoplites) than their enemies, but stronger even on land (let alone on the sea) than their tribute-paying allies, and they think that their hoplite force is quite sufficient for them as long as they remain stronger (in hoplites) than these allies'. καὶ before κατὰ γῆν is adverbial, = 'even by land'.

2.1. than their tribute-paying allies: The relative clause οἳ φέρουσι τὸν φόρον is added here to differentiate Athens' allies in the Delian League from those states like Plataea, Corcyra, and Acarnania, which were politically independent, and had voluntarily entered into individual alliances with the Athenians. This is the first of the passages which imply that the allies currently pay tribute (*cf.* 3.2, 5): nearly all scholars regard it as an indication that this work was written before the replacement of tribute with a harbour tax in 413 (Thuc. VII. 28.4); but M. J. Fontana, *L'Athenaion Politeia dal V secolo a. C.* (Palermo: Cappugi, 1968), 32–3, arguing for a later date, noted that it is generally thought that the tribute was reintroduced not later than 410.

By 431 only Chios and the cities on Lesbos of the members of the Delian League did not pay tribute (*phoros*) to Athens, and in 427, Mytilene, the main city of Lesbos, lost its independence after its failed revolt. The members of the Delian League were still technically 'allies' of Athens, and were often so referred to by the Athenians (*cf.* Thuc. III. 37.2, Ar. *Knights* 839), but they were all (including Chios and Lesbos) subject to Athens' authority in their foreign policy, and they had no choice but to have the same 'enemies' as Athens had. Hence they they could also be referred to as Athens' *arche*, 'empire' (*e.g.* Pericles in his funeral speech, Thuc. II. 36.2), and as 'the cities which Athens rules' (*e.g. IG* i^3 156.14–15).

Naturally the Athenians were concerned to guard against the possibility that these allies might revolt against Athenian rule, as happened in the case of Potidaea in 432 and Mytilene in 428. Therefore, as X argues here, the Athenians needed to have a hoplite force which was strong enough to defeat their allies' infantry, since that would enable them successfully to establish themselves on an allied state's territory and prosecute a siege, in the event that it did revolt (*cf.* Thuc. I. 62–4, III. 18).

2.2–3. X now moves to an elaboration of the strategic advantages enjoyed by a dominant naval power like Athens, which make it easier for the Athenians to control their allies than for a land power to control its allies. He envisages the possibility of small subject states combining together into a larger force, and then rebelling against the ruling power. His argument proceeds by way of contrast. That may pose a problem for a land power controlling mainland allies, but, he claims, it is not a problem for a dominant sea power. He then goes on to explain why not.

He first deals with subject states which are islands (§2). Here he asserts that such island states will not be able to combine by 'synoecism' into a single entity, because their location on separate islands keeps them physically apart, and, if they were to attempt to combine politically and militarily, the ruling power, in as much as it dominates the sea, would be able physically to prevent them from doing so. Furthermore, even if such island states did somehow manage to escape the notice of the rulers of the sea in transporting themselves and their resources into one place, the large population so created would not be able to sustain itself long on the produce possible on a single island. So they would die of starvation, X suggests at the end of this section.

Secondly, in 2.3, he turns to those subject allies of Athens which are situated 'on the mainland' (*i.e.* the Thracian and Asiatic coasts of the Aegean, and the Hellespont). He maintains that they too (even though not kept physically apart by the sea) are at the mercy of the rulers of the sea, because, to survive, they need to import and export goods. This they cannot do unless they are 'compliant to' (ὑπήκοος) the rulers of the sea. X's argument here would be much clearer if he had stated what presumably was for him too obvious to state, that all, or virtually all, of the mainland states in the League were coastal, maritime, cities, and thus easily blockaded by the rulers of the sea.

2.2. *natural advantage:* κατὰ τύχην here does not mean 'by chance', 'by accident'. Frisch, 240, rightly argues that it means 'in the nature of things'. *Tyche* denotes conditions determined by nature, geography, as against anything that might be obtained by human endeavour (*cf.* the cognate verb τυγχάνειν, used in exactly the same way at 2.16). The meaning is that 'they also enjoy the following natural advantage', *i.e.* for keeping control over their subject allies.

2.2. *to unite their small cities and fight all together:* In 432, under the influence of Perdiccas of Macedon, the coastal towns of the Chalcidice, acting in concert with Potidaea, revolted against Athens, and 'synoecised', *i.e.* they combined militarily and politically, and indeed physically, by moving to a single centre at Olynthus (Thuc. I. 58.2). The Athenians were able eventually to recapture coastal Potidaea, in early 429 (Thuc. II. 70), but not to capture Olynthus, which was some distance inland (and which was to be one of the states offered a special status in the Peace of Nicias in 421: Thuc. V. 18.5–6). The language used by Thucydides, 'migrate (ἀνοικίσασθαι) to Olynthus and make this a single strong city' (*cf.* ἀνεῳκίζοντό a few lines later), is similar to that found here in X (συνοικισθέντας); and συνοικίζειν (used in the active of the directing individual or city, in the middle and passive of the communities combining: *e.g.* Thuc. II. 15.2) is a technical term for this kind of union.

Proponents of an early date for X's work have argued that these events falsified X's claims here, and that consequently he must have written his treatise before the synoecism of Olynthus in 432 (*e.g.* H. U. Instinsky, *Die Abfassungszeit der Schrift vom Staate der Athener* [Freiburg im Breisgau dissertation, 1933], 20–1), or that X is not using the verb in its technical sense (*e.g.* Frisch, Bowersock). But these events support rather than falsify X's claim, since Potidaea, which occupied a coastal site and had not taken part in the synoecism, eventually capitulated, but the synoecised Olynthus did not. It is probable that X is using the verb in its technical sense here; and, if his work is correctly dated 425–424 (*cf.* Introduction, section 3), very likely that he has the synoecism of Olynthus in mind.

2.2. *rulers of the sea:* This expression becomes a refrain for X throughout 2.2–16. The single compound word, θαλασσοκράτορες ('thalassocrats'), used here and at 2.14, is consistently spelled with double sigma in the manuscripts. This is an Ionic form (fifth-century Attic inscriptions and comedy use double tau instead of double sigma, though Thucydides and Xenophon, the orator Antiphon and tragedy use double sigma). It has been suggested that the preservation of the Ionic form of this compound by a writer who otherwise always uses the Attic dialect (*e.g.* θάλαττα here) indicates that the word, and hence the concept of 'thalassocracy', originated in Ionia (*cf.* Hdt. V. 83.2, and the verb at III. 122.2).

The whole section on the 'rulers of the sea' recalls Pericles' dictum in 432 that, in a conflict with the Peloponnesians, 'control of the sea is vital' μέγα γὰρ τὸ τῆς θαλάσσης κράτος (Thuc. I. 143.5). Pericles' strategy for Athens in the Peloponnesian War relied on maintaining Athens' supremacy at sea while not risking a defeat on land (*cf.* Thuc. II. 13.2, 65.7): we need have no doubt that Pericles did in his public speeches stress the importance of controlling the sea, and X here is merely enlarging on a view and a strategy which will have been widely known in Athens at the time and subsequently.

2.2. they will die of starvation: Does X have the revolt and siege of Mytilene in 428–427 in mind here? According to Thucydides Mytilene was effectively starved into surrender by the besieging Athenians, when the upper-class leaders armed the members of the *demos* but they refused to continue the struggle (Thuc. III. 27–8). We have suggested that X does have the revolt of Mytilene in mind at 1.15 (see pp. 88–9, above), but it is doubtful whether there is any allusion to Mytilene here. The cities which were combined with Mytilene were all situated on the island of Lesbos in the first place. This is not the possibility which X envisages at 2.2–3, and by 'they will die of starvation' he means simply that not enough food could be produced by the one island to which people would migrate as the result of a synoecism to support such a greatly increased population.

2.3. As for those states subject to Athens' rule which are situated on the mainland: In 2.2–3 X simply divides the members of the Delian League into those at sea, *i.e.* islanders, and those on land / on the mainland, reflecting the differences with regard to Athens' ability to control them. In fact, the official division which is attested was more detailed, and differently based. Some of the early tribute quota lists (the lists from 453 onwards of the $^1/_{60}$ of each state's tribute which was given as an offering to Athena) show a tendency to group states in regions, from 442 (list 12: *IG* i^3 269) there is a formal arrangement in five regions (Caria, Ionia, the Hellespont, the Thraceward region, and the Islands), in or soon after 437 (list 17: *IG* i^3 274) the Carian district is absorbed in the Ionian; and this organisation is found also in assessment lists (425/4: *IG* i^3 71; extracts ML 69, trans. Fornara 136) and is reflected in decrees (*e.g. IG* i^3 71. 4–6) and in Thuc. II. 9. 4.

2.3. the big ones are kept in subjection through fear, the small ones very much so through need: Continuing his categorisation from the point of view of Athenian control, X makes a distinction between large (coastal) allies and small ones, in terms of what factors keep them subject to Athens. But what exactly is his point? The following sentence suggests that the 'need' he refers to here is economic need.

The smaller states, with little agricultural territory, need to import vital foodstuffs, like grain (in return for manufactured goods or other local specialities, which they export). But to engage in such traffic they depend on the good will and support of the dominant sea-power. The large states can survive economically on their own produce, but they cannot take an independent political line against the power of Athens' fleet, which they fear. No doubt the smaller allies also feared Athens, but, in their case, their need of Athens' support, to ensure their economic survival, is greater than their fear. This seems to be the thinking underlying the rather forced contrast here.

However, X's fondness for exaggeration leads him to undermine this distinction when, in the following sentence, he goes on to assert that all states need to import or export goods, and thus are dependent on the rulers of the sea. In other words all Athens' allies are kept in subjection through need, not just the small ones.

2.3. need to import or export something: The second decree, of 426/5, in Athens' *dossier* of decrees for Methone, on the Macedonian coast (ML 65 = *IG* i³ 61, trans. Fornara 128, lines 32–56 at 34–41), and decrees for Aphytis on Pallene, the western prong of Chalcidice (*IG* i³ 62, 63), show that Athens did sometimes intervene in the trade of allied states, in particular to regulate their importing of corn from the Black Sea, *via* Byzantium. There was a board of *Hellespontophylakes*, guardians of the Hellespont, with the duty of enforcing what Athens allowed and forbade. Methone and Aphytis exemplified exactly what X refers to here, *i.e.* small, economically dependent, mainland allies, and it is likely that in §3 he is thinking of the controls and the exemptions from them of which we find instances in these decrees.

2.3. will not be open to it, unless it is compliant: The implication is clear, that Athens will impose a naval blockade on any recalcitrant subject-ally (*cf.* 2.12).

2.4–5. X continues the contrast, begun at 2.2, between the leading naval power and the leading land power. Having shown in §§2–3 that Athens as the dominant naval power is more easily able to control its subject allies, he now goes on to argue that the 'rulers of the sea' also enjoy advantages over the rulers of the land in terms of the strategy they can pursue in a war against their enemies: they can more easily devastate the territory of the enemy (§4), and more easily undertake military expeditions far from home (§5).

In these two sections X refers in apparently general terms to the 'rulers of the sea', but his argument is not a purely theoretical one. By the 'rulers of the sea' he clearly means the Athenians, just as he has specified them to be such in §§2–3 (where αὐτοῖς identifies the Athenians in §2 and they are mentioned again by name in §3). Correspondingly, the 'rulers of the land' referred to in 2.4 must be the Spartans. Furthermore, the 'more powerful' mentioned in 2.4, whose land he claims can more easily be ravaged by the rulers of the sea, must be those more powerful *on land, i.e.* the Spartans and their allies. In other words, the context of the comparison between the dominant Greek sea power and the dominant land power has now become one in which a *conflict* is assumed between the two. It could be that this is just an imaginary scenario, but it is much more likely that it corresponds to something which had happened, or was happening, in the real world, and, if so, that conflict can hardly be anything other than the Peloponnesian War, which began in 431. Indeed, the strategy envisaged by X in 2.4–5 (and subsequently), namely, sea-borne raids on the enemy's agricultural land, and long distance expeditions abroad, was very much the strategy successfully pursued by the Athenians in the first part of that war, the so-called Archidamian War of 431–421.

Thus in the first two years of the war, 431 and 430, the Athenians' response to the Peloponnesian invasions of Attica was to send out large naval expeditions to the Peloponnese and beyond, which did indeed make landings but re-embark and move on when they encountered opposition (*e.g.* Thuc. II. 25). The Athenian attack on Corinthian territory, in an expedition sent across the Saronic Gulf in 425 (Thuc. IV. 42–5), was another action which well demonstrated the validity of X's strategic claims here. Very probably X has campaigns of this kind in mind here, as he could well do if (as we believe: see Introduction, section 3) he was writing in 425–424. Athens' successes at Pylos in 425 and at Cythera in 424 did not involve landing and then moving on, but, rather, establishing a settled Athenian base in the enemy's territory; and X probably alludes to them in §13 (*cf.* below), but not here.

2.4. have the ability to do only sometimes: There is a contrast here. X's point is that the sea power can do it whenever they choose, the land power only (not expressed in the Greek, but we must understand this word) sometimes. The point is then amplified in the rest of 2.4–5.

2.4. to sail along the coast and put in: With παραπλεῖν ('sail along') we have to supply 'and put in'. In 2.5, where the verb is repeated, the expression of a destination is added.

2.4. the one which responds with its infantry: παραβοηθεῖν is normally used to mean 'come to help', and here would refer to the local forces coming to the defence of the position which the sea-borne raiders have attacked (*cf.*Osborne's translation), so that this sentence would be enlarging on what was stated in the previous sentence: the sea power can disembark but, if it encounters opposition, re-embark and sail away, whereas the land power whose territory is raided can only react, and is helpless if the raiders do not stay to be defeated but depart. Some commentators have thought this rather illogical here. The main contrast in 2.4–5 is between the dominant sea power and the dominant land power, and X ought here to be focusing on the greater ease and safety (ἧττον ἀπορεῖ means 'has less of a problem') enjoyed by an attacking sea power, because of its superior mobility, as against a land power trying to do the same thing. It has therefore been suggested that X is using the word παραβοηθῶν here in the sense 'attack', 'invade', or else that the text should be emended (*e.g.* παραποήσων, 'to do the same thing', *i.e.* raiding enemy territory, Kalinka). But to diverge from his main point, to note that when the sea power does make raids it has the advantage over the land power whose territory it raids, is a shift of which X is perfectly capable. His comparison slides into an assumption of conflict between the sea power and the land power (*cf.* pp. 104–5, above).

2.5. to sail as far as you like away from their own country: The use of the second person singular, present tense (βούλει) is probably colloquial. What is at issue here is the ability of a dominant sea power to undertake a significant long-distance voyage, not merely to cruise around the Aegean. Does any specific action underlie X's generalisation here? He may well have in mind the Athenian expeditionary force which was sent to Sicily in 427, and which was able to remain there for three years (Thuc. III. 86, IV. 58–65).

2.5. whereas the rulers of the land do not have the ability to undertake a journey of many days away from their country: This very definite assertion was spectacularly disproved by the Spartan general Brasidas' remarkable march right through Thessaly to Chalcidice in the summer of 424 (Thuc. IV. 78–9). Brasidas did not have to 'fight to win his way through' Thessaly. The Thessalians had sent help to Athens in 431 (Thuc. II. 22.2–3), but had not been involved in the war since then except to attack the Spartan colony at Heraclea near Thermopylae (Thuc. III. 93.2); at the time of Brasidas' march 'the mass of the Thessalians had always been well disposed to the Athenians', but the Thessalians 'were ruled by oligarchic cliques', and, despite opposition, there were men willing to escort Brasidas, so that by a combination of speed and propaganda he was able to get through.

Hence this passage has been frequently cited as providing one of the strongest indications of a *terminus ante quem* for the treatise. It is argued that it must have been written before Brasidas' march in the summer of 424. Some caution is needed. It is not wholly impossible that X should have written a passage after an episode which directly undermines what he says; and in this case the essential validity of X's general strategic point here was borne out by the subsequent inability of the Spartans on two occasions, in 423 and 422, to reinforce Brasidas or repeat the stratagem (Thuc. IV. 132.2–3, V. 13). The Thessalians, now aware of the situation, barred any further passage through their territory, the Spartans did not attempt to force their way through, and Brasidas' death in battle at Amphipolis in 422 effectively ended the threat posed by his force to Athenian interests in the north Aegean (Thuc. V. 6–13).

Nevertheless, it does seem very unlikely that X's strategic claim here, and hence his treatise, could have been written in the immediate aftermath of Brasidas' march. Thucydides underlines what a striking achievement that was (IV. 78.2). It must have been in everybody's minds in the year following it. X's comment could perhaps have been written after 422, when subsequent events had shown Brasidas' march to have been a one-off. But other indications of date do not support a date for the treatise later than 422 (*e.g.* 2.13, 14, 16; see notes *ad locc.*), and we do believe that X was writing before Brasidas' journey (*cf.* Introduction, p. 5).

2.5. progress is slow: *I.e.* in comparison to travel by ship.

2.5. cannot carry provisions sufficient for a long period: During their invasions of Attica, the Spartans and their allies brought their provisions with them (Thuc. II. 10.1, III. 1.3). These were carried, not by the hoplites, but by their attendants, usually slaves (*cf.* Thuc. VII. 75.5). This is the method of supplying an army which X has in mind here; but a land force away from home for a long time would need to find provisions locally after consuming what it had been able to take with it. On the number of days' provisions taken by an army, in the case of Athens usually three, see W. K. Pritchett, *Ancient Greek Military Practices*, i (*U. Calif. Pub. Class. Stud.* 7 [1971]), reissued as *The Greek State at War*, i (U. of California P., 1974), 32–4.

2.5. it is possible for the seafarer to disembark wherever he is stronger: Greek triremes were not self-sufficient or self-contained: nearly all the space was taken up by the rowers, and it was not possible to cook or sleep on board. They were also vulnerable to bad weather. The 'rulers of the sea' therefore needed to put in to land regularly. They could not stay on board their ship for weeks on end (see A. W. Gomme, 'A Forgotten Factor in Greek Naval Strategy', *JHS* 53 [1933], 16–24, revised in his *Essays in Greek History and Literature* [Oxford; Blackwell, 1937], 190–203 ch. 10). This limitation is the reason why X adds the qualification in the last sentence of §5.

2.5. and, wherever he is not the stronger, not to disembark at this point of the land, but to sail along the coast: The words οὗ δ' ἂν μὴ ᾖ, μὴ ἀποβῆναι ('and, wherever ... not to disembark') are missing from the manuscripts at this point but are necessary to make sense of the passage. They are present only in C, not here but after ταύτης τῆς γῆς – probably as a conjecture rather than as an authentic survival of the original text. We have followed Kalinka and other editors in accepting them but placing them before ταύτῃ (Hermann's correction of ταύτης) τῆς γῆς, where they give the required meaning.

2.6. In this section X argues that a strong sea power is better able than a strong land power to withstand food shortages caused by crop diseases (νόσοι): it is able to import the necessary provisions from faraway areas, which are 'healthy', *i.e.*, not affected by the disease.

But what exactly is the connexion of thought (indicated by ἔπειτα, 'further') with the preceding sections? The reference to 'ravaging the territory' at the beginning of 2.4 seems to be the key point. The word τέμνειν there alludes to the cutting down of food crops, *i.e.* wheat and barley and (much harder to destroy) olives and vines. That was precisely what was done by both sides in their respective attacks on their opponents' territory during the early years of the Archidamian War (*cf.*, *e.g.*, Thuc. II. 19.2, 25, 31.2, 55.1, using τέμνειν in the first and last of those passages; Ar. *Acharnians* 512). Having explained in 2.4–5 the advantages which the dominant sea power has over the land power in the strategy of destroying the enemy's crops, X now turns to a *second* way in which crops can be damaged – not by human action, but by natural causes. He argues that, when that type of damage occurs, the sea power is better able to withstand the loss. There is some incoherence here, since X has previously only been concerned with the *offensive* superiority enjoyed by the sea power in causing crop damage. He now adds to that a claim about their (defensive) superiority in being better able to cope with crop failures.

2.6. crop diseases which are the result of bad weather: The root sense of the word καρπός is 'fruit', but it frequently denotes cereal crops (fruits of the soil), and that specifically is what X has in mind here.

What is the point of the relative clause, which literally means 'which are from Zeus'? It is surely not inserted by X in order to affirm his commitment to a religious belief that crop failures were heaven-sent, decreed and caused by the gods (*cf.*, *e.g.*, Hes. *Works and Days* 242). X refers to the many religious festivals at Athens, and accepts that they have to be held (2.2, 4, 8), but there is nothing anywhere else in the treatise to suggest that he feels any need to demonstrate conventional piety or traditional religious belief. *Cf.* the language sometimes used by the not conspicuously religious Thucydides, *e.g.* 'the god' in I. 126.4.

It is much more likely that the relative clause is inserted here in order to characterise and define the word νόσους, *i.e.* 'I mean those particular diseases which come from Zeus'. In other words, X is referring to crop failures which are the result of *bad weather*. Zeus was the sky-god, and, as such, was responsible for the weather. See at greatest length Ar. *Clouds* 367–407; and at Ar. *Birds* 1501 the phrase τί γὰρ ὁ Ζεὺς ποιεῖ; ('What is Zeus doing?') means 'What is the weather like?' Here what is envisaged is bad weather (*i.e.* rain-storms), and the word 'Zeus' in combination with the verb ὕειν (= 'to rain') is well attested in the sense 'it is rainy weather' (*e.g.* Alcaeus fr. 338.1 Lobel and Page, Theophr. *Characters* 14.12; *cf.* Hdt. II. 13.3, ὕειν ὁ θεός, with Zeus mentioned later). This seems to have been something of a colloquial usage. Thus νόσους here refers not to biological or insect-produced diseases, but to 'sicknesses', 'illnesses', in the sense of failure due to stormy, rainy weather, which damaged the growing crops in the fields. This was by far the most common way in which crops could be adversely affected in the ancient world (*cf.* Ar. *Clouds* 1119–20).

It may be worth noting that just such a period of abnormal, unseasonal, bad weather had occurred in the spring of 425, when the Spartans and their allies had been forced to withdraw from Attica after an invasion lasting only 15 days (Thuc. IV. 6). Thucydides considers it worth mentioning, and adds that it occurred 'when the corn was still green', *i.e.* when it was most vulnerable to bad weather.

Given that this is the sense of νόσους here (*cf.* also νοσεῖ in the second sentence), it is not in the least significant for dating his work that X says nothing in §6 about the terrible plague (*nosos*) which first struck Athens in 430 (Thuc. II. 47–54, III. 87.1–3). That phenomenon (a human disease) had nothing to do with the point he is making here. Some commentators at this point have laid too much stress on the idea of disease in the sense of plague (*cf.*, *e.g.*, Frisch, 57, Moore, 52). That sense is not present here. Hence it cannot be argued from this passage that the work must have been written before the onset of the plague in 430.

2.6. imports ... reach the rulers of the sea: The verb ἀφικνεῖται (= 'arrives') has no subject: we have to understand 'imports' (of essential foodstuffs, especially grain). This is harsh, and it may be that a word has been lost.

One should note that in §6 X simply takes it for granted that corn and other essentials can be imported from abroad at will by the 'rulers of the sea'. He does not think it necessary to go into details, still less does he anticipate any problems arising in this area. This corresponds closely to the untroubled situation Athens was in until 413. Athens was wealthy enough to pay for imported corn, and strong enough to protect its passage.

2.6. from an area which is flourishing: εὐθενούσης (the Attic form to which Dindorf corrected the manuscripts' εὐθηνούσης) here indicates the opposite condition to that denoted by νόσους and νοσεῖ. Athens imported grain particularly from the Black Sea region, hundreds of miles away from Attica (e.g. Dem. XX. *Leptines* 31, RO 64.8–20). The Athenian navy did not itself transport imported corn (the triremes were unsuitable for carrying cargo: cf. p. 107, above), but they were able to protect the grain-carrying merchant ships from pirates and enemy attack (for their vulnerability cf., e.g., Hdt. VII. 147.2–3).

2.7–8. X now turns to the subject of Athens' ability to import foreign luxury goods (§7), and other things (§8), from abroad. He thus passes from the theme of the strategic and military advantages enjoyed by the rulers of the sea to that of economic and cultural advantages. The mention of imported corn at the end of 2.6 has led to the transition. Note that the argument is no longer put in the form of a generalisation about the 'rulers of the sea'. Rather we are told specifically that the Athenians have been able to do these things by virtue of their naval power (subjectless plural indicatives are used to start with, but the Athenians are directly named at the end of §8: cf. the explicit reference to the Athenians in 2.3); for the idea cf. Pericles in Thuc. II. 38. The nature of the comparison also seems to change in 2.7–8. Up to now it has been between the dominant sea-power (Athens) and the dominant land-power (Sparta), but here it appears to be between Athens and all the rest of the Greek world (§8).

2.7. lesser matters: X is aware that his assumed audience may not regard Athens' ability to import luxury foods as quite so significant an advantage as the military ones which he has discussed in 2.2–6.

2.7. luxury foods. Whatever the delicacy: The choice of words is significant here. Both εὐωχιῶν and ἡδύ indicate that X is thinking primarily of *food* luxuries (cf. Ar. *Acharnians* 1009). In the list which follows, the places mentioned seem to be paired, and deliberately grouped on a geographical basis, i.e., Sicily and Italy (west), Cyprus and Egypt (south), Lydia and Pontus (east and north). Only the Peloponnese is not paired (other than with 'or anywhere else'). Its inclusion here is odd, since it is not 'abroad', or even outside the Greek mainland (hence not somewhere which could only be reached and influenced by the rulers of the sea), and it was hardly a great source of luxurious or exotic foodstuffs.

An apparently similar list appears in a preserved fragment of Hermippus' *Phormophoroi* – a play which can be dated *c.* 425 (fr. 63 Kock / Edmonds = Kassel and Austin, quoted by Athenaeus, I. 27e–28a). Hermippus' list includes Syracuse (in Sicily), possibly Italy, Egypt (though not Cyprus), Phrygia and Paphlagonia (though not Lydia), and the Hellespont. It also mentions Arcadia, which might explain X's rather surprising reference to the Peloponnese here, if he had Hermippus' list in his mind when he wrote §7. But one should be cautious about drawing this inference: the items in Hermippus' much longer list are not confined to food, and it was a commonplace by the early 420s that the Athenians were able to import and enjoy all kinds of foreign luxuries (*cf.* Pericles at Thuc. II. 38.2; D. Braund, 'The Luxuries of Athenian Democracy', *G&R* n.s. 41 [1994], 41–8). The use of such lists was probably common in the comedy of the 420s, and X is probably echoing comedy, though not necessarily this play in particular. (For the theme *cf.* Ar. *Wasps* 655–724, and for another possible overlap between X and comedy see p. 152, below; and note the discussion of comedy in 2.18.) It is perhaps best to explain the mention of the Peloponnese at the end of the list in §7 as a pointed addition, due to the fact that X's assumed interlocutors are thought of as primarily Spartans (*cf.* 1.8–9, 10–11, 13, 2.1). The point will then be 'from everywhere, even your own backyard', *i.e.* X underlines the power of the rulers of the sea to acquire foodstuffs from absolutely anywhere.

2.8. every sort of language: φωνὴν πᾶσαν here refers not to dialect forms (as supposed by the translations of Frisch, Moore and Bowersock) but to words. X is concerned throughout §§7–8 with *extra*, additional, things which the Athenians have been able to acquire through being the 'rulers of the sea', and thus having contacts with, and being open to the influence of, foreigners abroad. Having mentioned luxury foods, he now refers to foreign loan-words, taken from other Greek, and indeed non-Greek (καὶ βαρβάρων at the end of §8 is explicit) countries. X clearly regards this larger vocabulary as a positive advantage (like the imported luxury foods), which Athens gains from being a dominant sea-power. In his commentary (pp. 52–3; but contrast his translation, cited above) Moore rightly takes this phrase as referring to foreign loan-words, but, perhaps influenced by a moralising passage of Cicero (*De Republica* II. 7), cited by Frisch, 254, he finds the lack of condemnation by X here 'surprising'. On the contrary, it is not surprising at all, but perfectly in accordance with X's thesis throughout chapter 2 – the advantages (of all kinds) which Athens and the Athenian *demos* enjoy, as a result of their being the 'rulers of the sea'. There is no moral disapproval of this on X's part.

X is interested in words, especially non-standard ones, as we can see from 1.19. What sort of words does he have in mind here? The explicit reference to *barbaroi* suggests that he is primarily thinking of non-Greek words, especially those which come from the Persian empire in the east. A remarkable sight at Athens in the later fifth century was the aviary of peacocks kept by Pyrilampes, a friend of Pericles, and then by his son, Demos (Antiphon frs. xvii Sauppe = B. 12 Maidment; Plut. *Pericles* 13.15). These birds seem to have originally been a present given to Pyrilampes when he went on an embassy to the Persian king. Peacocks actually come from India, part of which was, at that time, within the Persian empire. Demos was involved in some litigation with regard to these peacocks, and the orator Antiphon composed a speech for him (see Cartledge, 'Fowl Play: A Curious Lawsuit in Classical Athens', in P. A. Cartledge *et al.* [eds], *Nomos : Essays in Athenian Law, Politics, and Society* [CUP, 1990], 41–61, for a reconstruction of the circumstances of the case). It is interesting that the word for peacock, ταῶς, with its unusual internal aspirate (attested by the grammarian Tryphon, cited by Athenaeus), hence a particularly obvious non-Greek loan-word, was adopted into the everyday language of the Athenians (*cf. e.g.* Ar. *Acharnians* 63, *Birds* 102), despite its oddness for a Greek. Athenaeus (IX. 397a– 398b) on peacocks ends with a philological discussion about the unusual form of this word and the difficulty of representing it in Attic or Ionic spelling, and notes that the consciously literary Antiphon avoided it in his speech. ταῶς was surely just the sort of imported word which X has in mind here.

2.8. The other Greeks stick rather to their individual language: Instead of οἱ ἄλλοι X writes οἱ μὲν … μᾶλλον here, followed by 'Αθηναῖοι δὲ: for this use of μᾶλλον to indicate a contrast *cf.* 1.18, 2.14, 19. ἰδίᾳ here is an adjective, agreeing with φωνῇ etc.: it makes a contrast with κεκραμένη.

2.8. language and diet and dress: In the final summarising sentence of the section X extends his point about Athens' overseas acquisitions to διαίτῃ καὶ σχήματι: in these areas also, he claims, they have acquired items from abroad, in addition to their native ones. But what does διαίτῃ mean here? One sense of this word is very general: 'way of life', 'lifestyle'. If X is using the word in that sense here, it is not clear what in particular he is referring to. Possibly such things as Persian peacocks (see previous note) and parasols (Ar. *Birds* 1509: see M. C. Miller, *Athens and Persia in the Fifth Century B.C.* [CUP, 1997], 193–209). But it is odd that X should be so vague in a passage which is otherwise, for him, unusually specific. Another, more specific, sense of δίαιτα is 'régime', 'diet'. It is found in this sense mostly in the medical writers, but it seems to be used of the food régime of an athlete in training by Plato (*Republic* III. 404a). If X is using the word in this sense here, then he is directly referring back to what he has said in §7 about imported luxury foods, and φωνῇ καὶ διαίτῃ provides a summarising conclusion (typically, in reverse order) to the subject-matter of §§7–8 (*cf.* 1.12, 20).

However, σχήματι, 'dress', coming at the very end, is a new detail. X adds a reference to imported items of dress which the Athenians are able to acquire because they are 'rulers of the sea'. What is he thinking of in particular? The names given to certain types of shoes suggest they were originally of foreign origin, or at least that the style came originally from abroad. We hear of 'Persians' (Περσικαί), soft shoes for women (Ar. *Clouds* 151, *Lysistrata* 229, *Ecclesiazusae* 319) and 'Laconians'

(Λακωνικαί), smart town shoes for men (Ar. *Wasps* 1158, *Thesmophoriazusae* 142, *Ecclesiazusae* 74, 269).

But σχήματι suggests clothing rather than footwear, and we do have good evidence for an influx of fashionable non-Greek clothing into Athens in the 420s. Thus in Ar. *Wasps* (422 B.C.), 1131–56, Hate-Cleon persuades his father Love-Cleon to put on, instead of his threadbare countryman's cloak (τρίβων), a luxurious coat, which, he says, 'is called by some a Περσίς (Persian), and by others a καυνάκης'. Hate-Cleon waxes enthusiastic about the coat's being available in Sardis, and having been made in Ecbatana. In fact it seems that the *kaunakes* was of Assyrian rather than Persian origin (Pollux VII. 60), but it was clearly an exotic and expensive import. Miller, *Athens and Persia*, 153–87, discusses other items of imported foreign dress from the Persian empire, which seem to have appeared in Athens in the later fifth century, *e.g.* the *kandys*, a sort of jacket, and the *ependytes*, a tunic-like garment, made of linen or wool.

There is thus plenty of evidence to support X's point about imported foreign dress here. But why does he refer to dress here apparently only by way of an afterthought? Probably because his main interest in §8 is in imported language, foreign loan-words. But many of those very words denoted items of foreign dress (like *kaunakes* and *kandys*). Hence the addition of σχήματι. The thought of the words has suggested the thought of what some of the words denoted.

One might contrast what X says here in §8, about how the Athenians have been able to acquire additional, and (the implication is) classy items of clothing from abroad, with his remarks in 1.10, where he has asserted that the Athenian *demos* are no better dressed than their slaves. Of course, it will not have been ordinary members of the *demos* who wore exotic foreign clothes, but it was the naval power based to a considerable extent on the ordinary members of the *demos* which made those clothes available in Athens.

2.9–10. In this passage X starts by focusing on the sacrifices to the gods, and the associated public feasts, which occur outside the many Athenian temples and religious buildings dedicated to those gods. He argues that it is a deliberate policy of the *demos* that these temples are built, and sacrifices held, at the state's expense, so that they themselves may enjoy the associated feasts. In §10 he turns to the subject of exercise grounds (*gymnasia*), and baths. He argues, similarly, that the *demos,* by ensuring that the state provides these facilities, has secured for its own use and enjoyment something which its members could not individually afford for themselves.

This is a very awkwardly placed passage. It is not concerned with the theme of 2.2–8, the advantages which the Athenians gain from Athens' control of the sea, but, rather, with the advantages the *demos* gain from democracy (the *leitmotif* of chapter 1). Furthermore, the theme of 2.2–8 is resumed at §11, and continues down to §16, as though there had been no break at §§9–10. This passage would fit better after 1.

13, the section on liturgies (omitting the last sentence of 1.13: see p. 84, above, and *cf.* Frisch's commentary on this passage, pp. 254–5), and there is a strong argument for transposing it to that position. The politically partisan language of 2.9–10 is also much more appropriate to chapter 1. In chapter 2 it is not until §17 (after the long passage about the 'rulers of the sea' is finished) that X reverts to the sort of language and arguments about the *demos* which characterise chapter 1.

It has been suggested that εὐωχεῖσθαι and εὐωχούμενος in §9 deliberately pick up εὐωχιῶν, 'luxury foods', in 2.7 (M. Kupferschmid, *Zur Erklärung der pseudoxenophontischen 'Aθηναίων πολιτεία* [Hamburg dissertation, 1932], 49, thus providing a sort of link with the preceding section, a slender thread of continuity. It is true that X does sometimes use purely verbal rather than thematic links to join passages together (*cf.* 1.10 with p. 74, above), but the transition here is so abrupt, and the reversion back to the main theme at 2.11 equally so abrupt, that it is hard to believe that §§9–10 was originally placed in this position. One might equally well argue that, once the passage had for some reason been omitted from its original position at the end of 1.13, it was inserted here by a copyist, precisely because he thought there was some connexion between εὐωχιῶν in §7 and εὐωχεῖσθαι in §9.

2.9. As for sacrifices and sanctuaries and feasts and precincts: The structure of the first sentence of §9 is very awkward. It opens with four connected nouns all in the accusative case, placed at the beginning for emphasis. This forms the 'subject of the thought'. These nouns are then left suspended grammatically by the insertion of a clause in indirect speech, introduced by a causal participle, γνοὺς ὁ δῆμος ὅτι . . . That clause largely restates the idea established by the original nouns (though with verbs instead of nouns, and with only three verbs to correspond to the four nouns). After the eventual appearance of the main verb, ἐξηῦρεν, we get an indirect question introduced by ὅτῳ τρόπῳ, in which the final word ταῦτα, 'these things', the subject of the indirect question, refers back to the four original nouns. This is a clumsy piece of sentence construction. Although there are four nouns, there are really only two components to the 'subjects of thought', since the first and third, θυσίαι and ἑορταί, are virtually the same thing (sacrificial feasts), as are the second and fourth, ἱερά and τεμένη (religious sites).

R. Brock and M. Heath, 'Two Passages in Pseudo-Xenophon', *CQ* n.s. 45 (1995), 564–6 at 564–5, suggest that ἱερὰ should here be taken to mean 'rites' (*cf.* LSJ *s.v.* ἱερός, III. 1c), so that the four nouns at the beginning of the sentence form an ascending sequence. ἵστασθαι (= 'set up') is a generally accepted correction of the manuscript reading κτᾶσθαι (= 'obtain'), an easy corruption in uncial script (see Introduction, p. 29, and Bowersock [1966], 42, [1968], 468), though the verb is not used elsewhere of buildings. Brock and Heath note parallels for ἵστασθαι of establishing rites, but suggest καθίστασθαι as an alternative. However, we are not convinced that ἱερὰ means anything very different from τεμένη here.

2.9. set up sanctuaries and create a beautiful and great city to live in: In this expression the qualifying adjectives καλὴν and μεγάλην, with πόλιν but placed after the verb, carry the emphasis. We have translated οἰκεῖν as 'live' here, but there may also be a suggestion of another sense, 'manage', 'run' (*cf.* pp. 138–9, below).

The reference here must be to the building of temples in Athens and Attica in the fifth century, and particularly to the famous, and expensive, programme on the acropolis begun in 447/6 (Plut. *Pericles* 12–14). This included the Parthenon, which was completed in 433/2 (when that programme was wound up as the Peloponnesian War approached: ML 58 = *IG* i³ 52, trans. Fornara 119, probably to be dated 434/3). X argues here that the state as a whole (ἡ πόλις stands in contrast to ὁ δῆμος) pays for these splendid temples and their associated lavish sacrificial feasts, but the material enjoyment of them is gained by the *demos,* whose members are too poor to provide such enjoyments for themselves out of their own resources. They therefore ensure that other people, *i.e.* the rich, pay for them.

There is a hint, in 'beautiful and great city', that X recognises that *aesthetic* pleasure on the part of the citizens, as well as material pleasure, was a consideration involved in the building programme. Plutarch confirms that this was an important aspect of it (*Pericles* 14); Pericles at Thuc. II. 40.1 describes the Athenians as 'lovers of beauty without extravagance' (*i.e.* lovers of beauty unlike the Spartans, without extravagance unlike the Persians? see L. Kallet, '*Demos Tyrannos*: Wealth, Power and Economic Patronage' in K. A. Morgan [ed.], *Popular Tyranny* [University of Texas Press, 2003], 117–53 at 131–4), while according to *Hell. Oxy.* 17. 5 McKechnie and Kern = 20.5 Chambers 'the land of Athens was at that time the most expensively furnished in Greece'. But X is reluctant to credit the *demos* with any aesthetic or cultural sensibility, so he concludes the section by concentrating solely on the basic sensory pleasures, *i.e.* eating at the sacrificial feasts.

X is vague about the financing of these buildings, and the subsequent associated feasts. He implies that it was the rich Athenians, *i.e.* the *chrestoi*, who paid for them, presumably through taxation (*cf.* 3.2) since they were not financed by liturgies (*cf.* 1.13, 3.4). But Plutarch claims that the building programme, if not the sacrificial feasts, was paid for by using money diverted from the tribute paid by the members of the Delian League, whose treasury was now kept in Athens (*Pericles* 12), and that seems to have been the general view, admitted by Pericles. Weaknesses in the whole scenario constructed by B. D. Meritt *et al., The Athenian Tribute Lists,* iii (Princeton: Am. Sch. Class. Stud. Ath., 1950), 326–8, have been stressed by L. Kallet-Marx, 'Did Tribute Fund the Parthenon?' *Class. Ant.* 8 = *CSCA* 20 (1989), 252–66; but it remains a serious possibility that there was some diversion of unspent League funds to pay for the buildings, and a certainty that the availability of League funds to pay (for instance) for the Athenian navy left the Athenians with more money to spend for other purposes than they would otherwise have had. Beyond that, it is an important fact about the buildings of this period that they were funded from public money (including Delian League money), and not as earlier by rich individuals from their own pockets.

X's real point here, and the one he wants to stress, is that the *demos* derives the material (and aesthetic) enjoyment from all this, but does not itself pay anything for it.

2.9. to whom the victims are allocated: The flesh of the sacrificed animals was cooked and distributed to the participants. It is likely that these were the only occasions when many citizens were able to eat meat, an expensive food item. X here implies that the *demos* was the exclusive beneficiary of these public feasts. In fact they were open to all participating citizens, including the *chrestoi*, and the distribution of meat was not egalitarian but holders of particular positions received larger shares (*e.g. IG* ii² 334 = RO 81. *B*, 8–27).

2.10. exercise areas, changing rooms and baths of their own: X's argument here, as in 2.9, is that, by getting the state to provide these facilities at public expense, the *demos* has obtained access to things which its members could not individually afford to possess themselves. Only the rich, or some of them, can do that (for the qualifying ἐνίοις at the end of a generalised assertion *cf.* 1.11).

It is slightly odd that X includes γυμνάσια among the private facilities and παλαίστρας among the public ones, since γυμνάσιον seems normally to have been the word with the broader meaning. A *palaistra* was usually restricted in size, and used particularly for wrestling (παλαίειν) and boxing, whereas *gymnasia* were or included larger areas, sports-grounds suitable for activities like running and throwing the discus and javelin. X ignores this distinction, and uses the two words as interchangeable terms in the sense 'exercise areas'. There certainly were some public *gymnasia* at Athens in the later fifth century (though X's 'many' is probably an exaggeration), *e.g.* in the Academy, Lyceum and Cynosarges. According to Plutarch (*Cimon* 13.7), it was Cimon who transformed the Academy into a public park for walking and exercise.

Rich Athenians had fine houses in the Attic countryside (Thuc. II. 65.2), which no doubt included walled exercise areas for their private use. It is interesting to compare X's admission here that some of the rich did still have their private exercise areas with his assertion at 1.13, that the *demos* have 'made . . . unfashionable' private athletics (see p. 81, above).

The rare word λουτρῶνας at the end of the sentence picks up, and means the same thing as, the earlier λουτρά. It has been suggested that X is here referring merely to washing places, which were attached, like the changing rooms, *apodyteria*, to the *gymnasia*. This is possible, but it is likely that the *apodyteria* themselves contained some basic washing facilities, and the separate mention and deliberate repetition of λουτρά / λουτρῶνας suggests that X has in mind something quite separate, *i.e.* public baths. If so, this seems to be the earliest clear-cut evidence for the existence of public baths at Athens. The present tense οἰκοδομεῖται perhaps suggests that there was some current construction in progress at the time of writing. The references to 'bath houses' (βαλανεῖα) in Aristophanes seem to be to private, fee-charging institutions

(*e.g. Clouds* 837, 991, 1045, *Frogs* 708), though *Knights* 1060–1 perhaps implies
the existence of some public baths.

2.10. built for themselves ... of their own: The second ἰδίᾳ (= 'of their own') is
awkward here, since we have already had αὐτὸς αὐτῷ, which gives the required
sense, and it rather spoils the intended contrast between the rich and the *demos*.
δημοσίᾳ (= 'at public expense'), would have been more logical, as in the penultimate
sentence of 2.9; certainly X's implication, here as in 2.9, is that the *polis* as a whole
pays but the *demos* enjoy benefits which they could not themselves afford. Possibly
the second ἰδίᾳ should be deleted as a copyist's mistaken repetition of the earlier
one, but X is so fond of verbal repetition that it would be rash to remove it from the
text (see Appendix 6).

2.10. from these the mob derive more enjoyment than ... the well-to-do: Of
course, the rich at Athens were not excluded from the public parks and baths; X's
point presumably is that, since some of them had their own private exercise grounds
and bath-houses, they did not need or bother to visit the public ones, even though it
was they, in effect, who paid for them through their taxes.

2.10. the mob ... the few and the well-to-do: For X ὄχλος is a thoroughly pejorative
term, with connotations of instability and turbulence (*cf.* Thuc. IV. 28.3, VI. 63.2).
Like ὄχλος, the terms ὀλίγοι and εὐδαίμονες are used here for the first time as class-
labels (see Introduction, section 8, and Appendix 4). No distinction between these
two is intended. The 'few' *are* the 'well-to-do' (*cf.* 1.2 with p. 63, above). εὐδαίμων
means 'enjoying a good *daimon*', and hence 'prosperous', 'well-to-do', or 'rich'
(πλούσιος), the word used in the preceding sentence. This partisan terminology is
much more common in chapter 1, to which 2.9–10 may perhaps belong (see pp. 84,
112–3, above).

2.11–12. There is now a return to the theme of 2.2–8, the unique advantages Athens
gains through being the 'ruler of the sea'. The underlying contrast, however, is no
longer (as it was in 2.2–6) between the 'ruler of the sea' and the 'ruler of the land',
but between Athens as ruler of the sea and all the rest of the world, both Greek and
non-Greek – a thematic development which began in 2.7–8, where Athens was first
contrasted with the rest of the Greek world.

In this passage X argues that it is not possible for any other state to challenge
the domination of Athens as the ruler of the sea by building up a strong naval force
of its own. He focuses on the various raw materials essential for the creation of a
navy – timber; iron, copper and flax; wax – and he claims, first, that any state which
produces any of these items must gain the permission of the Athenians to export it
abroad, since such exports must go by sea, and the Athenians are the rulers of the
sea. Then, in §12, he argues that the Athenians will also prevent their 'rivals' (for
the meaning of this see p. 118, below) from transporting such materials by sea;
and, finally, he asserts that nowhere can one find these vital raw materials natively
occurring all together in the same place.

2.11. naval wealth: τὸν δὲ πλοῦτον μόνοι is the reading of all the manuscripts, but 'wealth' on its own cannot be right. Even X, with all his fondness for exaggeration, could not make the absurd claim that Athens is the only country in the whole world that can be wealthy. As becomes apparent, his argument here is concerned specifically with the raw materials necessary for the building and maintenance of a fleet, and the fact that some states 'are rich in' (πλουτεῖ, used twice, deliberately picks up πλοῦτον) one such thing , *e.g.* timber, some in another, *e.g.* iron or copper or flax, but none are rich in all, nor can they acquire them all. It is clear that he is concerned not with any sort of wealth, but only with the wealth represented by these particular commodities. Note also how ἔχειν here is picked up by πάντα ταῦτα ἔχω in §12. We need to insert one or two words here which will qualify πλοῦτον. Frisch, 258–9, suggests τὸν δ' ἐ<κ πλοῦ> πλοῦτον ('wealth which comes from voyaging'). This is palaeographically neat, but does not quite give the required sense. We suggest <ναυτικὸν> πλοῦτον ('naval wealth'), which does. It is at least certain that something has fallen out here, immediately before or after πλοῦτον, to give the sense required.

2.11. Where will it dispose of it: διαθήσεται is (typically for X) used twice in close succession. The verb διατίθεσθαι means 'arrange', and particularly 'distribute', 'dispose of'.

The clear implication of X's argument here is that Athens can, and will, employ a naval blockade against any state which produces any of these raw materials, if it does not like what that state is doing with them. Such producer-states will only be able to export these raw materials in the quantities, and to the destinations, which the Athenians approve of. This will effectively prevent any other state from becoming a rival naval power, because any state has to import by sea some or all of these materials.

The strategic argument in §11 seems to be pure theory on X's part. We have no evidence that Athens in the later fifth century did attempt to blockade any state which produced and exported these essential materials. In his speech in 432 the Spartan king Archidamus admitted that to challenge Athenian naval supremacy would be difficult and would take time, but he did not suggest that the existing (very inferior) Peloponnesian fleet could never be effectively supplemented because it was impossible to acquire the necessary raw materials (Thuc. I. 81.4). It is true that the Athenians imposed economic sanctions on Megara in or before 432 (*e.g.* Thuc. I. 67.4) and blockaded Megara in 427 (Thuc. III. 51), but the sanctions were in response to earlier hostile action by Megara, and by 427 Megara was an enemy state and the intention was primarily to stop goods entering rather than leaving Megara. However, from the 390s–380s we have an alliance between Amyntas III of Macedon and the Chalcidians which regulates exports of the Chalcidians and stipulates that they may not export fir (the preferred timber for shipbuilding) without giving advance notice to Amyntas (*SIG*^{3} 135 = RO 12, 9–18).

2.11. the consent of the ruler of the sea: At this point there is a switch from plural to singular. All the manuscripts have the singular τὸν ἄρχοντα in the third sentence of §11; only M has it in the second sentence, but it should be read there as well (*cf.* O'Sullivan, 193; but Kirchhoff and Bowersock read the plural τοὺς ἄρχοντας throughout). It looks as if there has been a (not very thorough) attempt by a copyist to establish consistency with the plural which was used earlier, in 2.2–6. But the arguments about strategy have been interrupted by §§7–8 (and maybe 9–10), and in §11 the singular τὸν ἄρχοντα fits rather better with the sudden introduction of the first person singular pronouns μοί and ἐγὼ which follow in §§11–12 (*cf.* below).

2.11. it is from these very materials that I get my ships: Timber was used in the construction of the triremes' hulls, iron for the beaks (fortified for ramming) and the anchors, copper for the inner fittings (to prevent rust), flax for the sails and ropes, and wax (mentioned here but not earlier) like pitch for caulking.

2.11. my ships: The sudden introduction of the first person pronoun μοί (*cf.* ἐγὼ, and also the plural ἡμῖν, in 2.12) enlivens what is otherwise a particularly theoretical and unspecific passage. X gives no precise details about where these vital raw materials might come from, and does not even refer to 'the Athenians' in §§11–12. As well as confirming that X is an Athenian (*cf.* 1.12), the personal touches here add a distinct debating-room tone to the treatise (*cf.* 1.11, and Introduction, section 5).

2.12. Furthermore, they will prevent any of our rivals: This is a further point (πρὸς δὲ τούτοις). But what is it? The Athenians are the subject of ἐάσουσιν. The object is provided by the relative clause, introduced by οἵτινες, *i.e.* 'whoever are our ἀντίπαλοι' (Renehan's οἷ τινες, 'to where any of our ἀντίπαλοι are', accepted by Bowersock, and O'Sullivan's [193] οὗ τινες, 'where any ... ', produce not a better but a worse sense). ἀντίπαλοι means 'rivals' rather than 'enemies', and ἄγειν means something different from 'dispose of' (the sense of διατίθεσθαι, used in §11). The verb means 'carry', and X is referring here not to the producers of raw materials themselves, or to Sparta, but to merchants from other states which can carry these materials as cargo. These are viewed as 'our rivals' because Athens itself was also a state in which a large number of citizen and metic traders were based. The most obvious rival to Athens in this area was Corinth, a merchant state which was also a political and military ally of Sparta, and the Corinthians are probably the people whom X is particularly alluding to here.

What X envisages here is the possibility that a producer of strategic raw materials might use a foreign merchant ship as a third party to carry these materials as a cargo to somewhere else (ἄλλοσε), a destination which the Athenians do not approve of. In that case the Athenians would take action, by threatening to 'stop them from using the sea'. In other words, they would directly attack merchant ships based in or trading with such states, if any of them tried to transport the raw materials in question as cargoes in their ships.

X's argument here is somewhat less theoretical than the one in §11. In fact, there is no direct evidence that Athens ever did attack merchant shipping during the Archidamian War (though Thuc. II. 69.1, on the blockade of Corinth by the Athenian fleet at Naupactus in 430/29, may refer to merchant ships as well as warships); but their opponents certainly did, in 431 and 430, and not just those ships carrying strategic materials (Thuc. II. 67.4, 69.1). These actions may have provided X with the germ of his idea here. For the first person plural pronoun ἡμῖν, which reads rather oddly after the third person plural verb, see p. 118, above.

2.12. Thus, despite producing nothing from my land, I possess all these materials: καὶ here means 'and so', and οὐδὲν ποιῶν goes closely with it in a concessive sense (= 'though producing nothing from the land'). πάντα ταῦτα (= 'all these things') refers to all the raw materials necessary for building ships, specified in 2.11. X is somewhat exaggerating here. It is true that the Athenians had to import copper and iron (from Cyprus), since these metals were not found locally; they also imported some timber (from Macedon: on Macedon and Thrace as the best sources of timber for shipbuilding see R. Meiggs, *Trees and Timber in the Ancient Mediterranean World* [OUP, 1982], 118–32, and *cf. SIG*³ 135 = RO 12, cited above). But both timber and wax (and possibly flax) were natively produced in Attica. The exaggeration is due to X's desire to make a forced rhetorical contrast between οὐδὲν and πάντα ταῦτα.

2.12. I possess ... because of the sea: For the first person pronoun ἐγὼ see p. 118, above. X's point is that Athens imports all these materials. Precisely because she is the ruler of the sea, she is the only state able to do so.

2.12. no other city has two of these things ... two or three of the materials: Another exaggeration. The cities of Cyprus certainly produced and exported both copper and iron. There is also a certain lack of logic in the addition of 'or three' (of the materials), since the point has already been made by 'any other combination of two', and the addition of 'or three' only weakens it. No doubt 'or three' was added by X as a concluding rhetorical flourish (so Frisch, 264), in despite of the logic.

The last three sentences of §12 constitute a further argument on X's part. So far, in §§11–12, he has demonstrated the impossibility of another state's building up a navy to challenge Athens' domination as the 'ruler of the sea'. For that to happen certain raw materials are necessary, and X has argued that the Athenians will not allow another state to acquire them. They will blockade any state which produces any of them, if it attempts to export the materials anywhere that Athens disapproves of, and they will attack and drive off the sea any merchant ships which try to transport them as cargo. So far so good, but it may be objected that X has assumed that such raw materials always have to be imported. What about states which produce them in their own territory? X's answer to this, at the end of §12, is that no state produces them all, indeed no state produces more than one. Thus it is not possible for any other state to build up a navy from its own native resources.

2.12. the land is flat: λεία means 'smooth', *i.e.* here 'flat'. X is right to say that (fir) trees grow in hilly terrain and flax on flat ground, so they are not found growing together, but he ignores the obvious possibility that a single state's territory may contain (as, *e.g.*, Attica did) both hilly and low-lying areas.

2.13. This is a brief, self-contained section, in which X argues that the rulers of the sea are able to devastate the territory of their enemies, by making use of topographical features which they have access to and can control, viz. a projecting headland, an offshore island, or a narrow strait. At first sight this is a rather similar strategic argument to that made at 2.4, but X clearly signals that he regards this as a further point (πρὸς τούτοις). The difference is that at 2.4 X was primarily concerned with the *superior mobility* enjoyed by the rulers of the sea, and what he seems to envisage there is a series of hit-and-run raids by sea-borne forces which withdraw quickly from each position attacked, the kind of operation which the Athenians carried out in 431–430. At 2.13, by contrast, he is concerned with the ability of a sea power to utilise a *fixed position* as a base for sustained ravaging of enemy territory.

2.13. *every mainland coast:* X has been criticised for gross exaggeration in this generalisation (*e.g.* by Frisch, 264). However, X does not say 'a headland and an island and a strait', but only 'a headland or an island or a strait'. The (characteristic) generalisation is still an exaggeration, but not such a serious one.

2.13. *projecting headland ... offshore island ... narrow strait:* This is a perfect description of the topography of the bay of Pylos in the south-west Peloponnese, with its headland at the northern end, the long offshore island of Sphacteria closing the bay, and the straits between the island and the shoreline. It is hard to imagine that X does not have the Pylos campaign of summer 425 in mind here (though Osborne, 4, suggests that the theoretical nature of the passage could be used to argue against a reference to a recent event), and we believe that this is one of the places where there is a very strong case for seeing a particular allusion behind X's generalisation.

Of course there were other occasions during the Archidamian War when the Athenians captured offshore islands and ravaged the mainland opposite. The tactic was first employed in 431, with the capture of Atalante, off the coast of Opuntian Locris, though the motive there was purely defensive, to deter pirates in the Euripus strait (Thuc. II. 32). A notable success was Nicias' capture of the island of Cythera in spring 424 (Thuc. IV. 53–7), and X may perhaps be thinking of that also here, especially since discussion of Cythera could well have begun in Athens soon after the success at Pylos. But although there is a headland opposite Cythera (Cape Malea, in the south-east corner of the Peloponnese), from which the island is separated by a short stretch of water, this is less of a 'strait' (it is a little over 5 miles / 8 km wide at its narrowest), and, more importantly, neither the headland nor the waters between the mainland and Cythera were used to advantage by the Athenians, as they were, uniquely, at Pylos and Sphacteria (Thuc. IV. 2–6, 8–23, 26–41). The Athenians fortified the headland first, then after the Spartans had entered the bay through the strait they won a naval victory in the bay, and finally they forced the surrender of the Spartan forces which had been placed on the island. After the victory, they continued to use the fortified headland as a base for damaging guerrilla raids, using disaffected helots, throughout Messenia and even into Laconia.

This campaign must surely be what X is alluding to here, beneath the generalisation. The features specified are not just topographical indicators of a locality where the rulers of the sea are at an advantage, they are each an example of how in practice that advantage can be demonstrated, through action based on a headland and an island with a strait between them. This is precisely what happened in the Pylos campaign, although the subsequent damage caused by the helot raids (attested by Thuc. IV. 41.2–3) seems not to have been as extensive as the Athenians hoped, and X's strong word λωβᾶσθαι (= 'mutilate', 'devastate') is an exaggeration.

The inevitable dating implication is that the treatise must have been written after Athens' success at Pylos in summer 425. If X's generalisation is based on more than just one example, then he may also be thinking of Nicias' capture of Cythera in spring 424, or at any rate of preliminary discussion of that. We believe that the treatise was written soon after the summer of 425, but before Brasidas' march to Thrace in the summer of 424 and the battle of Delium in the autumn of 424 (see Introduction, p. 5, and pp. 100, 106, above, 122, 129, 131–5, below).

2.14–16. In this passage X moves on to a discussion of the one strategic weakness which the Athenians as 'rulers of the sea' suffer from. Athens and Attica is not an island, and thus the country can be invaded and ravaged by its enemies. If it were an island, it would be immune from this possibility.

The hypothetical 'if they lived on an island' becomes a refrain in §§14–16: the expression in various forms occurs no fewer than five times in 14–15, and the negative of it, in a causal sense, 'since they do not live on an island', opens §16. In §15 X moves from the strategic advantages to the greater internal security which the Athenians would also enjoy if they lived on an island, and in §16 he contrasts the reality, what they do now, with the preceding hypothetical situation.

Strictly speaking, the passage 2.14–16 is a digression. It is not necessary to X's overall case in 2.2–13 (if anything, it weakens it), and it is not envisaged as something which comes from his interlocutors. Why then does he insert it? The most likely reason is that, at the time he was writing, the notion 'if only we were islanders' was a fashionable hypothesis, often to be heard in Athenian public life discussions. There is some evidence that it was. Commentators refer to, and compare, Pericles' speech in 432, on the eve of the Peloponnesian War, which contains a section where precisely this idea is expressed: 'If we were islanders (εἰ γὰρ ἦμεν νησιῶται), what people would be more impregnable? As it is we must think of ourselves as virtually islanders, abandon our land and our homes, and safeguard the sea and the city' (Thuc. I. 143.5).

It is not necessary to assume that X is directly quoting Pericles here (assuming that Pericles did indeed say what he is represented by Thucydides as saying), still less that he is following Thucydides. No doubt, after Pericles had given the idea a public airing on a famous occasion, it became a fashionable hypothesis in Athens, and was often repeated in verbal and written form.

2.14. not to have their land ravaged and not to have to face the enemy's invasions:
There is a strong implication here, and in the following sentence, that these ravaging
invasions were actually happening at the time of writing (*cf.* 'As it is', νῦν δὲ), and
that 'the enemy' (with the article: τοὺς πολεμίους occurs twice), are real enemies,
with whom the Athenians are now at war. But when? There had been a one-off,
short-lived, Spartan invasion of Attica in 446 (Thuc. I. 114.2) But the invaders
did not penetrate beyond Eleusis and the Thriasian plain, near the border with
Megara, and that can hardly be pertinent here. What X is envisaging here is surely
a strategy of repeated invasions, and that happened during the period 431–425, but
not before or after (*cf.* pp. 125–6, below). It stopped because Athens threatened
to kill the Spartan prisoners taken from Sphacteria in 425 if Attica were invaded
again (Thuc. IV. 41.4). By late 423 it must have been obvious that the invasions had
ceased indefinitely, and this passage can hardly have been written later than that (*cf.*
Introduction, section 3). J. D. Smart, arguing for a later date, saw here a reference to
ravaging which resulted from Sparta's permanent occupation of Decelea in Attica
from 413 onwards ('The Athenian Empire', *Phoen.* 31 [1977], 245–57 at 250 n. 12:
cf. Thuc. VII. 19, 27–8); but that does not fit so well with §§14–16, which seem to
envisage repeated invasions.

2.14. the farmers and the rich . . .   the* demos*: It is not absolutely clear here
whether X equates the farmers and the rich, or regards them as separate groups.
But his normal practice, when he employs class-labels in the context of a contrast
between two classes, is to use a combination of terms which all denote the same
class (*e.g.* 1.2, 4, 6, 14, 2.10). Thus almost certainly he is not making any distinction
here between 'the farmers' and 'the rich'. In any case it is clear that, for X in this
passage, the farmers of Attica are not part of the *demos,* just as the hoplites are not in
1.2. This is an absurd misconception (see Introduction, section 7). But if he were to
accept that at least some of them were part of the *demos*, it would be harder for him
to give that word the highly pejorative sense which he needs it to have. He draws the
line between his upper and his lower class in different places to suit his argument on
different occasions (*cf.* Introduction, pp. 21–2, and pp. 64, 99–100, above).

2.14. truckle to the enemy, rather: Again, μᾶλλον is used to indicate a contrast (*cf.*
1.18, 2.8), here between the farmers and the rich on the one hand, and the *demos* on
the other. The verb ὑπέρχομαι, used twice, means 'curry favour with', 'kow-tow to'
(*cf.* Ar. *Knights* 269). It implies an element of fear, as is indicated by the contrast
with ἀδεῶς ζῇ ('live without fear'), later in the sentence.

That countrymen are naturally more opposed to war and empire than townspeople
seems to have become a commonplace of conservative propaganda from the later
fifth century on (*cf.* Ar. *Ecclesiazusae* 197–8). It became linked to the idea that they
are more sympathetic to oligarchy (*cf.* Plut. *Themistocles* 19.6, attributing to the
régime of the Thirty in 404–403 and explaining the reorientation of the assembly's
meeting-place on the Pnyx to face inland). This passage in X appears to be the
earliest example of the view, though for him the reason is simply that countrymen

will suffer more. But is there any historical evidence to support X's assertion here? Was there indeed a split at Athens between the country-dwellers and the townspeople in terms of their attitudes towards the Spartans and their allies, in the years after the war began in 431? Thuc. II. 20 suggests, on the contrary, that those whose land was laid waste such as the Acharnians would be those most determined to fight. It is possible that X is alluding to the fact that in 430 there had been widespread resentment against Pericles and his strategy, and envoys had been sent to Sparta to discuss making peace, though nothing came of it. Subsequently, after a morale-boosting speech by Pericles, the Athenians broke off contacts with Sparta, and from then on pursued the war with more enthusiasm, and (in the mid 420s) more success (Thuc. II. 59–65). But Thucydides does not suggest that there was any division between the farmers and the city-dwellers on this issue. He stresses that all sections of the population were suffering through the invasions (II. 65.2), and also makes it clear that the majority of the citizens were in fact farmers (II. 14.1, 16.2).

Could it be that X is basing his assertions in §14 not on any factual examples of the phenomenon, but on the fictional presentations of comedy, in particular, Aristophanes' *Acharnians* of spring 425, and its protagonist, the disillusioned farmer, Dicaeopolis? Dicaeopolis, with his private peace treaty made with the Spartans, is the perfect example of a farmer who is a countryman longing for peace and hating the city (Ar. *Acharnians* 32–6) and who 'truckles to the enemy' (*e.g.* 514–56). Of course, in the play Dicaeopolis is an isolated figure, who is not portrayed as representative of the farmers as a whole, and he is fiercely opposed by the Acharnians, many of whom were farmers themselves. But X is an obsessive generaliser, and there are other indications that he has Athenian comedy in his mind in this part of his treatise (see 2.7, 2.18–19 and notes; also 3.4). It is certainly a possibility that his generalisation about the farmers is actually based on the portrayal of Dicaeopolis in the *Acharnians*.

2.14. know well that the enemy will not burn or cut down anything of theirs: For X's (flawed) view of the *demos* as merely the landless, urban proletariat, see Introduction, section 7.

2.14. without truckling to them: The participle (οὐχ) ὑπερχόμενος (picking up ὑπέρχονται) is parallel to the adverb ἀδεῶς, to which it is linked by καὶ.

2.15. X now turns from the strategic to the internal security advantages which the Athenians would have if they were an island, but do not in fact have as things are. Two possible concerns are envisaged: (*a*) that the city might be betrayed to the enemy by oligarchic plotters, secretly opening the gates and letting them in; and (*b*) that a civil war between classes, *stasis,* might develop, in which the anti-democratic rebels would try to bring the enemy in over the frontiers to give them military support. If they lived on an island, X claims, neither would be a concern.

The implication of X's argument is that the Athenians do now (with reason) fear these two possibilities. How does this fit with the evidence? Was there a serious danger of an oligarchic plot or of *stasis* at Athens? There was in fact no attack on the democracy there until 411, when it was encouraged by the hope that if Athens were oligarchic Persia might support Athens rather than Sparta (Thuc. VIII. 48.1, 53.2–3); and no outright civil war until 404–403, when it was provoked by the excesses of a ruling oligarchy, the Thirty, who had the backing of a Spartan garrison. Although *stasis* was prevalent elsewhere, most notably in Corcyra in 427 (Thuc. III. 69–85), there is no evidence that *stasis* was feared as a serious possibility in Athens until 415, when Thucydides reports fears (probably unjustified, but still significant) that the religious scandals of that year were a sign of an oligarchic plot (Thuc. VI. 27.3, 60.1).

Earlier, Thucydides refers to a group of oligarchs at Athens who, he asserts, had secretly negotiated with a Spartan army in Boeotia in 457 (a few years after the democratic reform of Ephialtes), 'in the hope of putting an end to the democracy and preventing the completion of the Long Walls' (Thuc. I. 107.4), though nothing came of this plot. Once this had happened, and it had become public knowledge, there may have been some fear on the part of the citizens that it might happen again. Of course, it was really only a feasible plan in a time of war, when there was an armed enemy force ready and waiting, reasonably near to the city (*cf.* Thuc. VI. 61.2, Andoc. I. *Mysteries* 45, on the year 415). It was, therefore, not something which anyone was likely to worry about during the period 446–432. But once the war, with its associated invasions, had started, then it may again have been thought of as a possibility. It does not seem that any such plot was in fact hatched at Athens during the Archidamian War, and the general message of X's treatise is that the democracy is unwelcome but very stable. However, it appears from Aristophanes that Cleon had been conjuring up fears of conspiracy and tyranny, perhaps because his opponents had accused him of being a potential tyrant (*e.g.* conspiracy in Ar. *Knights* 236, 257, 452, 476, 628, 862–3: see Rhodes, 'Oligarchs in Athens', in R. Brock and S. Hodkinson [eds], *Alternatives to Athens* [OUP, 2000], 119–36 ch. 7 at 129–31); so there may have been some contemporary worries on this score.

But it is surely more significant and relevant for X's work that just such an attempted betrayal from within had occurred at Plataea, Athens' ally, in 431, when a dissident party opened the gates to the invading Thebans (Thuc. II. 2.2). If X was writing in 425–424 (*cf.* Introduction, section 3), it may well be the thought of this attempted betrayal of Plataea which underlies his argument here. (For Plataea, see p. 129, below). Another such instance occurred in Megara in the summer of 424, when a democratic faction plotted to betray the city to Athens, but news of the plot leaked, and in the event Athens gained possession only of the harbour town of Nisaea, while the city of Megara passed into the hands of oligarchic returned exiles (Thuc. IV. 66–74). If we were to date X's treatise as late as possible before Brasidas' march through Thrace, in summer 424, we could then see an allusion to that episode here; but in view of the instance of Plataea it cannot be maintained that this passage would not make sense unless the work were dated so late (*cf.* Introduction, p. 5).

2.15. they would be free of another fear as well: There is some inconsistency in the phrase 'another fear', since the previously mentioned fear, of enemy invasion (§14), is one which X claims was felt only by the farmers and not by the *demos*. Despite himself, X tacitly admits here what was no doubt in fact the case (*cf.* above), that the *demos* too were worried and fearful about the enemy invasions of Attica.

The infinitives προδοθῆναι, ἀνοιχθῆναι and ἐπεισπεσεῖν are all dependent on the idea of fearing contained in ἑτέρου δέους. Hence the series of negatives with the prefix μη-. μηδένα, a necessary correction of the manuscript reading μηδέν, provides the subject for στασιάσαι.

2.15. *by oligarchs*: ὀλίγων here has both its descriptive and its class-label sense, *i.e.* a small number of oligarchic conspirators.

2.15. *the democracy*: τῷ δήμῳ here refers to the *rule* of the *demos*, *i.e.* the existing democratic constitution. *Cf.*, *e.g.*, the reference to κατάλυσις τοῦ δήμου ('overthrow of the democracy') in [Arist.] *Ath. Pol.* 8.4.

2.15. *if there were a civil war . . . bringing them in by land*: The subject of στασιάσαιεν (which picks up στασιάσαι above) has to be understood, *i.e.* 'the rebels' (against the democracy). The point of κατὰ γῆν is that Attica, not being an island, has (crossable) land frontiers with other mainland states. For the definite article τοῖς with πολεμίοις (*i.e.* '*the* enemy') *cf.* §14.

2.15. *this too would not be a cause of concern*: καὶ ταῦτα refers to the fear specifically of *stasis*, civil war, discussed in the second part of §15. ἀδεῶς picks up ἀδεῶς at the end of §14, and ἑτέρου δέους at the beginning of §15.

2.16. X concludes this passage (2.14–16) by explaining what the Athenians in fact do to mitigate the effects of the invasions of Attica, which they have to suffer since they do not live on an island.

2.16. *So now . . . they do the following things*: This is a very significant statement. By using the present tense ποιοῦσι in conjunction with νῦν X makes it absolutely clear that what follows is not a merely hypothetical or theoretical plan of action. It is a statement of what is actually happening now. Removing their possessions (οὐσία here denotes movable property) to islands for safety, and not defending the countryside against the ravaging of invaders, is what the Athenians are now doing at the time he is writing.

This description is very similar to that of Thucydides with reference to what the Athenians did in the period 431–425 (II. 14). Thucydides says that, from the start of the invasions, the Athenians (*i.e.* the country-dwellers) transferred their livestock to the safety of 'Euboea and the other islands off the coast of Attica', and they took their domestic property with them when they abandoned their homes (*cf.* below). This policy was followed throughout the period of annual summer invasions, *i.e.* 431–425, although the country-dwellers may not all have stayed in the city throughout the year. When contrasting the effect of these invasions with that of the Spartans' continuous presence at Decelea from 413 to 404, Thucydides says that the earlier invasions were short and did not prevent the Athenians from benefiting from the land for the rest of the time (VII. 27.4). In any case, after 425 the invasions ceased, because the Athenians threatened to kill the prisoners of war whom they had captured on Sphacteria if the invasions continued (*cf.* p. 122, above)

2.16. they have not had the natural good fortune to live on an island: οὐκ ἔτυχον οἰκήσαντες νῆσον means 'it has not been granted by nature to them to live on an island'. The verb τυγχάνειν here is used in the same sense as the cognate noun τύχη at 2.2, of what is fixed by nature, as distinct from what is achievable by human effort.

2.16. they . . . allow the land of Attica to be ravaged: What X should have said here (but does not), in order to make his argument clearer and more effective, is that the Athenians are able to do all this without serious consequences because they themselves can withdraw to the protection of the fortified areas enclosed by the city walls and the Long Walls, which are not in danger of being stormed or taken by siege (*cf.* Thuc. II. 17.1–3). Thus, in the face of invasions, they are able to save some of their property (in fact, their livestock) by removing it to islands, and they are also able to save their movable possessions and their own lives by withdrawing from the countryside and taking shelter in the protected urban areas.

2.16. if they show concern for it: *I.e.* by resisting the invasions. X's point here is that, if they were to fight an infantry battle to defend their territory, they would be severely defeated, and the losses thereby sustained would have the effect of weakening their grip on their naval empire. This, of course, was precisely the view of Pericles, when he established the strategy which was followed during the invasions (Thuc. I. 142–3). But the Athenians did make some use of their cavalry to harass the invaders (Thuc. II. 22.2).

2.16. lose other, greater, benefits: *Cf.* Lys. XXXIV. *Against Overthrow of Traditional Constitution* 9: 'We thought it a good policy to look on while our land was ravaged and not think that we should fight for it: for it was worthwhile to abandon a few things and take care of many good things'. In itself ἑτέρων ἀγαθῶν is a vague phrase, but X must be alluding here to the survival of Athens itself and the empire. That this is the reference can be seen from, *e.g.*, the remarks of Pericles in 432 and 430 (Thuc. I. 143.5, II. 62.3).

2.17. The subject of this section is the alliances which Athens makes with other states, and the allegation that the Athenian *demos,* by contrast with oligarchic states, demonstrates untrustworthiness and unreliability in this area. The explicit, contrasting, reference to oligarchies at the beginning of the first sentence suggests that in this sentence X is repeating a critical view which has supposedly been propounded by his interlocutors (see Introduction, section 5). His 'reply' begins in the second sentence (ἢν δὲ μὴ ἐμμένωσι . . .). As usual, he does not contest the factual accuracy of the critics. Rather, he enlightens the critics on the greater ease with which it is possible to get away with such untrustworthiness and unreliability in a democracy, and the way in which such behaviour works to the partisan advantage of the *demos.*

The transition from the preceding section is very abrupt. X is now no longer dealing with the advantages enjoyed by Athens as the ruler of the sea. Rather, he has reverted to the sort of arguments expounded in chapter 1 – the advantages the *demos* gets from democracy – and it is this which becomes the prevailing motif for the rest of chapter 2 (§§17–20). At first sight it seems that in the opening words, 'Further, with regard to alliances', X is referring right back to 1.14–20, which dealt with the relations between Athens and her Aegean allies, and, therefore, that we are meant to think of the whole of 2.1–16, on the superiority enjoyed by Athens as the ruler of the sea, as a sort of excursus. In fact, however, the allies envisaged in 2.17, with whom Athens allegedly makes and then ignores sworn agreements, seem to be independent allies rather than subject allies. But the theme of alliances is what chiefly makes the connexion here, albeit with a much earlier passage (for an alternative possibility, Athens' failure to commit hoplites to support Plataea in 427, see pp. 129–30, below).

Central to X's argument in §17 is the contrast between the decision-making methods of the Athenian democracy and those of an oligarchy. He argues that, where only a few people are responsible for a decision, everybody knows who they are, their names are well known, and therefore they cannot escape their obligations and responsibilities. But in a democracy, where far more men are involved, it is easy for anyone to disclaim responsibility and get away with it.

How valid is this argument, and do recorded events lend it any support? X's argument about names is misleading. When Athens made treaties and alliances with other states, those who swore the oaths did have their names officially recorded, *e.g.* at the making of the Peace of Nicias in 421 (Thuc.V. 19.2). The names of the chairman and secretary at the time and of the proposer of the decree giving effect to the treaty were recorded also in inscriptions (though they are not included in Thucydides' text of the Peace of Nicias: for an example of these details see pp. 128–9, below). It is true that the names of those voting in the assembly were not individually recorded: that would have been impractical because of the numbers involved, and because the votes were taken by a show of hands without a precise count. But the decision itself and the names of the men responsible were recorded, and in the case of inter-state documents often inscribed on a stone *stele* to serve as a publicly accessible record. The contrast which X makes with oligarchies is also rather misleading. Certainly at Sparta decisions on whether to go to war to support allies were made not by a small group, but by a mass vote of the assembly of Spartiate citizens – through shouting, which made it even harder to assign responsibility to individual voters (*cf.* Thuc. I. 87.1–2). And in fact, while Thucydides' text of the Peace of Nicias lists those who swore on the Spartan side as well as those who swore on the Athenian side, inscribed decrees from Peloponnesian states tend not to identify the proposers as inscribed decrees from Athens regularly do (P. J. Rhodes with D. M. Lewis, *The Decrees of the Greek States* [OUP, 1997], 492). It was suggested by M. Pope, 'Thucydides and Democracy', *Hist.* 37 (1988), 276–96, that Athens was an 'acephalous' city to the extent that separate decisions were separately taken by the assembly and nobody was in overall control of policy; see in reply Rhodes, 'The "Acephalous" *Polis*?' *Hist.* 44 (1995), 153–67.

As for the charge of breaking agreements, Athens may sometimes have been guilty of reneging on a sworn agreement with another state (for the example of Plataea see p. 129, below), but there is no evidence that it was more prone to do this than other, oligarchic, states.

There are a number of textual problems in the first part of §17, which affect the detailed interpretation of the argument, though the overall sense is clear enough:

(*a*) With Bowersock, we have accepted Frisch's correction ὑπό του ἀδικῇ for the impossible ὑφ' ὅτου ἀδικεῖ of the manuscripts. The introduction of the second person singular ('or if you are wronged by someone'), is rather abrupt, but not impossible in view of 1.8, 9 and 11.

(*b*) In ὀνόματα ἀπὸ τῶν ὀλίγων we have to understand the verb ἐστί with ὀνόματα (= 'the names exist, are recorded'). But the preposition ἀπὸ is unwanted, and this word may indicate more serious textual corruption. Frisch, 275, suggests ἁπτὰ <τὰ> for ἀπὸ: this would give the sense '(are) tangible'. However, ἁπτός is a rare word, first attested in Plato, and it does not quite give the required sense. We therefore read γραπτὰ (= 'are written down'), and we supply the definite article with ὀνόματα: the sense required is '*the* names'.

(*c*) ἀνατιθέντι is dative in agreement with αὐτῷ (*i.e.* τῷ δήμῳ). But it is awkwardly placed after ἑνὶ, a quite separate dative, which is syntactically dependent on ἀνατιθέντι τὴν αἰτίαν, and with which τῷ λέγοντι and τῷ ἐπιψηφίσαντι agree.

(*d*) The plural τοῖς ἄλλοις seems to replace the singular αὐτῷ (after ἔξεστιν) as the subject of the infinitive ἀρνεῖσθαι. This gives reasonable sense – the proposer and the chairman take the blame while the others can deny responsibility – but it is poor grammar, and we should expect τοῖς ἄλλοις to come before, not after, ἀρνεῖσθαι.

(*e*) ἐμοί γε is Kirchhoff's emendation of οἵ γε (AM) or εἴ γε (BC). This gives the sense 'nor do I approve of it', the first person repeating the first person οὐ παρῆν (= 'I was not present'), with ὅτι being followed, not by indirect, but by a (brief) direct quotation – a characteristic touch of liveliness.

(*f*) If we retain πυνθάνονται (obelised by Bowersock), we must follow Müller and emend τὰ to ἃ (= 'things which they are told were agreed'): *cf.* O'Sullivan, 193–4.

2.17. *alliances and the oaths*: The definite article τοὺς is inserted with ὅρκους because X is referring to the traditional, well known, accompanying oaths which were invariably sworn when alliances were concluded.

2.17. *the one man who proposed the motion and the one who put it to the vote*: X is correct on the point of detail. The proposer of a motion in the assembly, and the chairman (*epistates*) who formally put it to the vote, were different men, as is clear from the preambles of inscribed decrees (*e.g.* Cleonymus' decree of 426, where the names of the proposer, Cleonymus, and the *epistates*, Onasus, are each recorded: ML 68 = *IG* i³ 68, trans. Fornara 133, lines 4–5), and from, *e.g.*, the 'entrenchment clause' quoted in Thuc. II. 24.1. X's point here is the contrast between the conspicuous individual (whether proposer of the motion or chairman of the assembly) and the undifferentiated and allegedly irresponsible mass of voters in the assembly.

2.17. agreed in a full assembly-meeting: The word *demos* is used here not, as normally by X, as a class label but in its technical sense, and means 'people in assembly' (*cf.* LSJ *s.v.* δῆμος, III. 3: 'common people', in Osborne's translation, is wrong). Some early texts refer to the δῆμος πληθύων = 'people assembled *en masse*', which is probably just an emphatic way of denoting 'the people in assembly' (*cf.* Rhodes, *The Athenian Boule* [OUP, 1972], 196–8, *cf.* 191–2), and πλήρει here suits X's rhetoric: the more crowded a meeting of the assembly was, the more difficult it became to identify individually anyone who was or was not there. Thus, X argues, it was easy subsequently to claim that one had not been present at a meeting where a decision was taken to make an alliance with another state. One could then go on to assert that one did not in fact approve of that decision, and, in a subsequent meeting, vote against taking any action in accordance with the alliance previously agreed.

2.17. that these agreements should come into force: ταῦτα refers back to ἄσσα . . . συνθῆται and τὰ συγκείμενα. X is still concerned with alliances here, and the *demos*' alleged ability to back out of their obligations.

2.17. they have discovered innumerable excuses: This is a rare example in the work of the use of the past tense for an apparent generalisation. There certainly seems to be an implication that what is under discussion, *i.e.* a failure by Athens to act in accordance with an alliance, has happened, and that the prevarication has lasted over a period of time. Does X have any particular alliance in mind here?

Probably he does not, but if we were to look for a particular instance the most likely would be Plataea. Plataea had been an ally of Athens for 93 years when it was forced to capitulate to the besieging Spartans and Thebans in 427, after a two-year siege (*cf.* Thuc. II. 2–7, 9, 71–8, III. 52–68 for the full story). Thucydides records that fulsome Athenian assurances were given to the Plataeans when the siege began in 429 (II. 73.3), assurances which in fact proved almost worthless. Only 80 Athenian defenders were placed in Plataea when the siege began, and only 25 were still there when it ended. Had the Plataeans appealed in vain for more support? It seems very likely that they had. An anti-Athenian, or even a conservative Athenian of the old school, might well have argued that Plataea had been callously left to its fate by its ally Athens, in ruthless adherence to the Periclean strategy of no hoplite deployment (*cf.* p. 123, above), despite its status as Athens' oldest and most loyal friend. If the failure or refusal to send armed force to confront the Peloponnesians and Thebans besieging Plataea is to some extent in X's mind here, that would provide a thematic link with §16 after all, *i.e.* the Periclean strategy of not deploying hoplites resulted in abandoning Attica to the invasions (§16), and also in abandoning Plataea to its fate (§17).

2. 17. if anything bad results from the demos' policies: X moves on to a slightly different point here. Having dealt with the alleged untrustworthiness of the *demos* after making agreements in the assembly, he now highlights their political irresponsibility. Whenever one of their decisions works out badly (the context is still foreign affairs, relations with other states), he asserts, they make scapegoats out of a few individuals who, they claim, have deliberately sabotaged the policy; but, if it works out well, they claim the credit for themselves. This assertion is not made by way of criticism on X's part (nor, apparently, does it come from his assumed interlocutors). Rather, he presents the practice as (yet another) advantage enjoyed by the *demos*, derived from their way of making decisions, *i.e.* through mass meetings and mass votes in the place of assembly. The point has been suggested by his earlier reference to their policy of putting the responsibility on someone else, and his contrast between the few, who can be individually identified and held responsible for decisions (note ὀλίγοι ἄνθρωποι here, deliberately picking up ὀλίγων in the second sentence), and the masses, who cannot.

There is some evidence that this type of political reaction did sometimes occur in late fifth century Athens, when something had gone wrong, and it may have been a standard oligarchic complaint that the *demos* claimed the credit for successes but did not accept the blame for failures. It happened to Pericles in 430 (Thuc. II. 59.1–2, 65.1–3), and the assembly is criticised for it by Diodotus in the Mytilene debate in 427 (Thuc. III. 43.4–5), and by Thucydides himself in his account of public reactions to the news of the disaster in Sicily (Thuc. VIII. 1.1). It was to some extent a consequence of the high degree of suspicion of office-holders, and of the lack of party policies and party discipline, which so characterised the assembly-based democracy at Athens. On the other hand, we should bear in mind that incompetence and negligence by officials and military commanders does occur, and, when it does, it can fatally damage a well-planned foreign policy.

Does X have any recent examples of this tendency in mind here? He may just be thinking of Pericles, but, if his work can be dated as late as summer 424 (see Introduction, section 3: that date is perhaps just possible), it may then be that he has a contrast in mind. There was the delight felt at the success of the Pylos operation in 425 (see pp. 120–1, above), where the assembly's vote for Cleon's extraordinary command proved a resounding success (Thuc. IV. 39), and, on the other hand, the hostile public reaction to the decision, in early summer 424, of the three generals in command of the expeditionary force in Sicily to accept a locally-agreed settlement of the war between the various cities, and to withdraw the Athenian forces from Sicily. The original decision to send a force had been taken by the assembly in 427 (Thuc. III. 86.1–4), in response to an appeal for help by Leontini and others. When the generals got back to Athens after acquiescing in the agreement (which they could hardly have refused to do), they were prosecuted and convicted for allegedly taking bribes to abandon the campaign, 'when it was in their power to have taken control of the island' (Thuc. IV. 65.1–3). The public reaction in this case constituted a perfect example of the view that 'a few people, working against them, ruined their plans', which X here attributes to the *demos*.

The actual prosecution of the generals from Sicily took place late in the year 424, when they had returned home, but the criticisms and accusations were no doubt flying around in public as soon as the unpopular news of the peace agreement got back to Athens, *i.e.* in the summer of that year. If there is an allusion in §17 to the public reaction to the generals' decision to withdraw from Sicily, that will provide a slightly later *terminus post quem* for X's work than the allusions to Pylos (425) in 2. 13 and possibly Aristophanes' *Knights* (early 424) in 2.18 (see pp. 132–5, below).

For a recent occasion when Thucydides represents citizens as denying responsibility for a decision (interestingly, made not by a democratic assembly but by an oligarchic clique), see the speech attributed to the Thebans in the debate on the fate of Plataea in 427 (Thuc. III. 62.3–4).

2.17. they assign the credit to themselves: This is what σφίσιν αὐτοῖς τὴν αἰτίαν ἀνατιθέασι must mean here. αἰτία can denote responsibility in a favourable sense, 'credit', but usually it denotes responsibility in an unfavourable sense, 'blame': earlier in this section the same expression has been used in that sense ('refer the blame to'), and in the sentence immediately before this the verb αἰτιᾶν means 'blame'. The use of the same word or words in different senses in the same or adjoining sections is characteristic of X (*cf.* 2.19–20).

2.18. The subject of this section is Athenian political comedy (so-called Old Comedy), a public comic drama distinguished by its fierce personal invective and satire. X argues, firstly, that the *demos* as a class is not a permissible target of comic abuse, but only individuals may be targeted. Secondly, he asserts that, usually, the individuals satirised in comedy are not members of the *demos,* but of the opposing class. Thirdly, he refers to, and explains, an apparent exception to this rule.

The transition here seems exceptionally abrupt. There are some indications (see 2.7, 14 and notes) that X may have comedy in the back of his mind in this part of the treatise, and the argument in §17 about the *demos*' ability in the assembly to avoid responsibility, and put the blame for mistakes on others, may have suggested the idea of the censure (*psogos)* which was a key element of comedy. But the connexion between 2.18 and what precedes remains harsh and forced.

A further (note αὖ, 'again') criticism from X's interlocutors is indicated obliquely in the opening sentence. This criticism is directed against the existence of what was a distinctive, if not unique, feature of Athenian public life, *i.e.* political comedy. It was a particularly striking example of the *parrhesia* which so distinguished democratic Athens (*cf.* p. 79, above). This is, naturally, an objectionable feature to X's assumed interlocutors. Public mockery and abuse of one's fellow-citizens would have been anathema particularly to a Spartan, in whose state derisive public laughter was used only against outsiders like the helots, to dehumanise them, and to promote the sense of superiority of the Equals, the Spartiate citizens, at the expense of lesser, non-citizen groups (see E. David, 'Laughter in Spartan Society', in A. Powell (ed.), *Classical Sparta: Techniques Behind her Success* [London: Routledge, 1989], 1–25).

In the first sentence of §18 X starts as he did in §17, by directly repeating the imagined criticism, here in the first six words ('when it comes to comic mockery and abuse'), which denote an objectionable feature of Athenian public life. No subject is supplied, and before completing the thought grammatically X proceeds to answer the criticism, starting in the same sentence, at τὸν μὲν δῆμον: 'Yes, they have public mockery, but they use it to the advantage of the *demos*'. A similar type of opening can be found at 1.13; and at 1.14 and 2.1 the reply also begins in the same sentence, though in these two cases the interlocutors' criticism is cited indirectly, not repeated directly, as here.

2.18. they do not allow this to be directed against the demos: Some commentators have taken the view that this refers to a legal ban on comedy, and have gone on to suggest a date for the treatise during a period when legal restrictions were imposed. The legal status of comedy, with its remarkable freedom of expression and uninhibited language, has been disputed. There was apparently a decree 'about not comedying', in force from 440/39 to 437/6; some have believed in another *c.* 415/4 (*cf.* A. H. Sommerstein, 'Comedy and the Unspeakable', in *Law, Rhetoric and Comedy in Classical Athens* . . . *D. M. MacDowell* [Swansea: Classical Press of Wales, 2004], 205–22, doubting the second; for the evidence see scholiast on Ar. *Acharnians* 67, Ar. *Birds* 1297 with scholiast). Otherwise, it seems that comedy was neither specially privileged nor restricted but was subject to the same laws as defamation in other contexts; and on neither of those two occasions does the evidence suggest that any legal distinction was made between collective abuse (banned) and individual abuse (allowed), though that is clearly X's principal point in the first two sentences. Hence οὐκ ἐῶσιν here cannot refer to a legal ban, but rather to a convention, which perhaps someone had recently made a public fuss about: it means 'do not allow', 'do not put up with'.

There is a noticeably close similarity of language between the first sentence of §18 and some passages in Aristophanes' *Acharnians*, which refer to an attack on Aristophanes by Cleon, and perhaps a prosecution of him, made in the council (*Acharnians* 377–82). Cleon attacked him for 'slandering the city (or *demos*)' in his now lost play the *Babylonians*, produced at the Dionysia of 426. Two passages are worth quoting (note the italicised words):

οὐ γάρ με νῦν γε διαβαλεῖ Κλέων ὅτι
ξένων παρόντων *τὴν πόλιν κακῶς λέγω*

('For Cleon will not now slander me, saying that *I abuse the city* in the presence of foreigners') (*Acharnians* 502–3)

διαβαλλόμενος δ' ὑπὸ τῶν ἐχθρῶν ἐν Ἀθηναίοις ταχυβούλοις
ὡς κωμῳδεῖ τὴν πόλιν ἡμῶν καὶ τὸν δῆμον καθυβρίζει

('Being slandered by his enemies before the hastily-deciding Athenians, saying that *he mocks our city and insults the demos*') (*Acharnians* 630–1)

The very similar language strongly suggests that what X is thinking of in §18 is Cleon's attack on (and prosecution of?) Aristophanes before the council in summer 426, for abusing or insulting the state or the Athenian people (discussed by Sommerstein, *op. cit.* 206, 209–10). Aristophanes' own references back to this affair suggest that it became notorious as, probably, a unique attempt to punish and gag a comic poet by taking official action against him.

In fact, Cleon's attack, though it upset Aristophanes (*Acharnians* 380–2), did not succeed in damaging him in any significant way. If there was a trial in the council (*cf.* 3.5 for the council's judicial powers, through the procedure known as *eisangelia*), Aristophanes must have been acquitted, since he was free to write and stage the *Acharnians* in 425, and then, in 424, to gain his revenge on Cleon in the vitriolic *Knights* (in which personified Demos is a character, represented as well-meaning but easily fooled by flattering speakers like Paphlagon / Cleon until at the end of the play he is enabled to assert himself). But the lack of any punitive action would not have deterred X from writing as he does here ('they do not allow'). The important point is that some official action had been taken against Aristophanes, because of his alleged mockery of the state or the *demos* (in its collective and inclusive sense). That example of pressure would have been enough for X's somewhat exaggerated generalisation here. The implication of §18 seems to be that this was something which had happened recently, *i.e.* that X's treatise was written fairly soon after Cleon's attack on Aristophanes in 426, and Aristophanes' references to it in *Acharnians* in early 425.

In the nineteenth century W. Roscher thought X must have been writing before the representation of Demos in the *Knights*; but A. Kirchhoff in reply insisted that in that play Demos is not represented in a fundamentally hostile way (*cf.* Introduction, p. 31). The key point here is κακῶς λέγειν (= 'verbally abuse', 'vilify'): although Demos is presented as gullible and simple-minded in the play (except at lines 1121–50), he is not abused or vilified in it. It is essentially the element of abuse in comedy which X is concerned with here, and we agree with Kirchhoff. For the possibility that the treatise actually reflects *Knights* see below, pp. 134–5.

2.18. *in order that they may not have to hear themselves being abused:* The verb ἀκούειν can be used as the passive of λέγειν, in the sense 'be spoken of'. This is how X uses it here, but, in addition, there is a strong emphasis on αὐτοί. The point is that the comedies were publicly performed in the theatre of Dionysus, before an audience of thousands of citizens. No doubt many members of the Athenian upper-classes were also amongst the audience, but X chooses to regard the theatre audience as essentially the *demos* (in his restricted sense of the word), and so he here asserts that the *demos* does not wish to hear itself abused while it is sitting there *en masse*, watching the play. That is too much for it to accept.

2.18. But in the case of individuals: ἰδίᾳ here is emphatic. X draws a contrast between collective and individual targets of comic abuse. The latter are permissible because, he goes on to argue, the individual satirised is usually not a member of the *demos* but of the class of the 'rich or well born or influential'. The understood subject of ἐῶσιν and κελεύουσιν must be 'the *demos*' (this is entailed by αὐτοί), the understood object is 'anyone', hence εἴ τίς. We also have to understand κωμῳδεῖν καὶ κακῶς λέγειν with βούλεται.

2.18. they encourage: This must be the sense of κελεύουσιν here. The Athenians encouraged it, in particular, through the prizes which were awarded to the winning comic playwrights (see, *e.g.*, D. M. MacDowell, *Aristophanes and Athens* [OUP, 1995], 8–9, for details).

2.18. the person mocked is not, for the most part, from the demos *or the masses*, but one of the rich or well born or influential: X asserts that it is the *oligoi* (see Introduction, section 8, and Appendix 4) who are the prime targets of Athenian comedy. This is an interesting claim. Earlier interpreters regarded Aristophanes as opposed to democracy or at any rate to the newer kind of democracy associated with Cleon; after a period in which it was claimed that Aristophanes had no detectable political sympathies, it has been maintained by G. E. M. de Ste. Croix (*The Origins of the Peloponnesian War* [London: Duckworth, 1972], 359–62) and demonstrated in detail by A. H. Sommerstein ('How to Avoid Being a *Komodoumenos*', *CQ* n.s. 46 [1996], 327–56) that Aristophanes deals more gently with men from the traditional upper class than with such politicians as Cleon. That does not tally with X's assertion here. We should, however, bear in mind that X was familiar with the works of Aristophanes' comic rivals, and it may be that Aristophanes' preference for leaders from a traditional background was not shared by all of them. We know that Pericles was assailed by comic writers in his day, including Aristophanes (*e.g.* Ar. *Acharnians* 530–4, *Peace* 605–9; and, for other comedians, Plut. *Pericles* 13.8, 10, 24.7), and Cimon was mocked at least posthumously by Eupolis (quoted at Plut. *Cimon* 15.4). On Aristophanes and Cleon see below.

2.18. or influential: It is clear from the context that the participle δυνάμενος is being used as a class label here (= 'man of influence'): see Introduction, section 8. For combinations of such terms, see p. 63, above. No distinctions are intended: the rich *are* noble and influential.

2.18. Only a few . . . because of their meddlesomeness: This note of exception is interesting. Given his taste for broad generalisations, it seems unlikely that X would have bothered to insert this qualification to his preceding generalisation, unless there had been a recent, memorable, example of the phenomenon (*cf.* 3. 5 for a similar passage, in which a recent exception is implied). Aristophanes' portrayal of 'Paphlagon' (= Cleon) in his *Knights*, produced at the Lenaea early in 424, may well be relevant here. 'Because of their meddlesomeness and their attempts to get the better of the *demos*' is a perfect description of the behaviour and character of Paphlagon / Cleon in his relationship with his master, the personified Demos, throughout the *Knights* (*cf.*, *e.g.*, *Knights* 258–60, 801–9, 823–32, 864–70, 1207–25), There is a distinct possibility that X is thinking of the *Knights* here, and thus that he is writing soon after its performance.

The fact that, in reality, the politician Cleon was not poor but rich, does not, of course, invalidate the suggestion that X is thinking of Cleon here, since that is precisely how Paphlagon is portrayed throughout the play, *i.e.* as the lowest of the low, and there can be no doubt that Paphlagon in the *Knights* represents Cleon. Doubtless X shared the snobbish disdain shown by Aristophanes and by Thucydides (III. 36.6, IV. 28.5) towards Cleon, who was not of aristocratic birth, and whose wealth came not from land, but from his father's tannery business (*cf.* p. 65, above).

According to Aristophanes (*Clouds* 545–59), his *Knights* was soon followed by a flurry of comedies imitating the *Knights* and attacking politicians such as Cleon and Hyperbolus. These included Eupolis' *Marikas*, which was produced, probably, in 421 (for the date, see I. Storey, 'Dating and Re-dating Eupolis', *Phoen.* 44 [1990], 1–30). By that date comedies of this sort could not have been regarded as exceptions, and X could hardly have made this claim if he were writing then.

2.18. because of their meddlesomeness: The word πολυπραγμοσύνη and its cognates invariably have a pejorative sense like the English 'busybody' (*cf.*, *e.g.*, Ar. *Ach.* 833, Hdt. III. 15.2). συκοφαντία (see pp. 86–7, above) was perceived as πολυπραγμοσύνη in the particular area of initiating prosecutions. Interestingly, the characteristic was applied to Athens as a state by those who disliked its interventionism. For them the opposite, ἀπραγμοσύνη, 'minding one's own business', was the ideal (*cf.*, *e.g.*, Thuc. VI. 87.3–4 – but Thuc. II. 40.2, *cf.* 63, 64.4, represents Pericles as saying that the *apragmones* are in fact ἀχρεῖοι, 'useless'). P. Harding, 'In search of a Polypragmatist', in *Classical Contributions* . . . *M. F. McGregor* (Locust Valley, NY: Augustin, 1981), 41–50, argues that nearly all Athenians, of all classes, supported the democracy and the empire.

2.18. they are not upset at seeing such people, also, mocked in comedy: In fact the *Knights* was awarded the first prize by the judges, a decision which very probably indicated that it was the play best received in terms of audience approval and applause. The implication of οὐδὲ here is 'even though such people are members of the *demos*, like themselves'.

2.19. In yet another apparently abrupt transition, X in this section strongly rejects (note the emphatic φημὶ as first word, followed by ἔγωγε, the strong form of the first person pronoun, indicating authorial reply) the implicit suggestion that the Athenian *demos* is ignorant about the character of its would-be political leaders, that it chooses which politicians to follow through ignorance of who are the valuable and the worthless. This is a rather different point from that made at 1.7, where he has claimed that the *demos* realises that the instinctive class loyalty to it on the part of its individual members, when they are proposing policies in the assembly, overrides their natural political ignorance and inexperience. Here, in direct opposition to what seems to have been the traditional anti-democratic view, as expounded, *e.g.*, by Megabyxus in the constitutional debate in Herodotus (III. 81.1–2: see Introduction, p. 18), X asserts that the *demos* do know what they are doing in their choice of politicians to follow: they know these men's true colours, and, despite their moral failings, they use them to their class advantage.

The suggestion (we are probably to think of it as coming from X's assumed interlocutors) that the *demos* is foolish and gullible, hence easily deceived by politicians who are *poneroi*, recurs constantly throughout Aristophanes' *Knights* (except in one passage, 1121–50, where the character Demos abruptly asserts the contrary). It was argued in discussion of the previous section, 2.18, that X may well have this play in his mind at this point of the treatise, and, if he has, that would provide the link and explain the transition from §18 to §19. In reply, X vehemently rejects this view of the *demos*, and aligns himself to a large extent with the very different sentiments expressed by Demos at *Knights* 1121–50.

2.19. know ... despite this knowledge: Throughout the treatise X insists that the *demos* know what they are doing politically (*cf.* pp. 65, 66, 70, above). The participle γιγνώσκοντες here is probably best taken in a concessive sense.

2.19. even if they are worthless; as for the valuable ones, they hate them rather: The second πονηροὶ here is used primarily in its moral sense, though earlier in the sentence it has its class-label sense. Similarly with χρηστοὺς and the preceding χρηστοί (see Introduction, section 8). It is common ground between X and his interlocutors here that the class and moral senses of these terms coincide: that indeed the members of the upper classes are morally valuable and the members of the lower are morally worthless. So why do the *demos* not cherish the *chrestoi*? X replies that despite knowing their moral worthlessness the *demos* regard politicians who are *poneroi* as 'convenient and useful to themselves'. They are right to hate the *chrestoi* because, if they get a chance to exercise their *arete* ('innate excellence': *cf.* below), it will inevitably result in policies which are harmful to the *demos* (*cf.* 1.9).

2.19. they hate them rather: X is fond of this, probably colloquial, use of μᾶλλον (*cf.* 1.18, 2.8, 14). It indicates an explicit or implicit contrast, here between the *poneroi* and the *chrestoi*.

2.19. the innate excellence of such men: For X the *arete* of the *chrestoi* is inborn, hence the use of πεφυκέναι rather than εἶναι. It is transmitted automatically by birth (*cf.* 1.7), and thus it is the exclusive possession of one class (his own); it is not attainable by the *demos*. Political affiliation therefore is, or should be, totally determined by birth. Hence, for X, it is all the more reprehensible in the few cases where it is not, where *chrestoi* 'are actually on the side of the *demos*', thus rejecting their innate *arete*.

2.19. not ... to bring about their good but, rather, to bring about their harm:
The prepositions πρὸς and ἐπὶ, both with the dative, are obviously being used in the
same sense here (= 'with a view to', 'to bring about'). This is an unusual use of πρὸς
(not recognised in LSJ *s.v.*: sense B. 2 is nearest), but it is softened by the pairing
with ἐπὶ, which is often used in this way (LSJ *s.v.*, B. III. 2).

2.19. Conversely, there are some men ... take the side of the people ... not by
nature commoners: Although the accusative of respect τὴν φύσιν here is suggested
by, and refers back to, πεφυκέναι in the previous sentence, this sentence is actually
the beginning of the final section of chapter 2. It coheres with the thought and
argument of §20, and the section division should be made here rather than at the
beginning of the next sentence. The connexion of thought is through the contrast
signalled by τοὐναντίον γε τούτου (= 'conversely', indicating an exception), *i.e.* the
demos are right in thinking that most *chrestoi* use their natural *arete* to damage the
interests of the *demos*, but, on the other hand, there are some *chrestoi* who do not,
who actually take the *demos*' side.

This sentence, on our interpretation (*cf.* next note), introduces us to the subject of
§20, those members of X's class, *chrestoi* by birth, who do not show class solidarity,
who embrace the democratic constitution and pursue public careers within it. X
launches a scathing attack on such men: for him they are class traitors and would-be
criminals.

2.19. who actually take the side of the people: ὡς ἀληθῶς implies that what is
asserted is somewhat surprising. This phrase has been variously interpreted. Most
recently, Osborne translates: 'Those who are in fact of the common people are
not sympathetic to the common people by nature.' However, we believe that the
meaning is the opposite to that. The fact that this follows and makes a contrast with
a sentence stating that the *chrestoi* work for the harm of the *demos*, and the clear
antithesis (ὄντες is concessive) between τὴν φύσιν οὐ δημοτικοί, echoing πεφυκέναι,
and ὄντες ... τοῦ δήμου, suggest that here X means that certain men, although
they were born into the upper classes, and thus are not by nature commoners, pay
allegiance to the democracy / common people , and are 'of the *demos*' in that sense,
i.e. 'on the side of' the *demos*.

The difficulty is caused by the fact that, when X returns to talk of such men,
and to criticise them, in the third sentence of §20, he there uses the very similar
expression, μὴ ὢν τοῦ δήμου, to mean 'not being by nature, birth, a member of the
demos' (which is uncontroversially its meaning in that context). In other words,
within the space of three sentences, two quite different, indeed opposite, senses are
given to an almost identical expression. This is a particularly striking example of
X's addiction to close verbal repetition, even when the words repeated are used in a
different sense (*cf.* 1.10, 19–20, 2.17, 3.1), to the detriment of clarity of argument.

2.20. I forgive the demos themselves for their democracy: The highly personal,
almost egotistical, element in X's work and approach is particularly evident here, in

the use of the emphatic personal pronoun ἐγὼ and the choice of verb, συγγιγνώσκω, which is then reinforced by deliberate repetition through the cognate noun συγγνώμη. The tone is one of condescending superiority.

2.20. one has to forgive anyone for looking after himself: If we take παντὶ to refer strictly to 'every individual man', then X actually undermines his own argument here. Men of aristocratic origin who adopted a democratic stance and pursued a career under the democracy, such as Pericles or (in parts of his career) Alcibiades, could justifiably have claimed that looking after themselves was precisely what they were doing, by achieving a successful and rewarding political career under the democratic constitution, and that they should therefore be 'forgiven' by X! In fact such men are denounced in the second sentence of this section. But X is thinking exclusively in class terms here. What he means in this sentence is that, since it is pardonable for anyone to look after himself, it is pardonable for the members of the *demos* collectively to favour a régime which looks after their interests.

The generalisation, as he expresses it, reads like a maxim taken from sophistic moral theory, which X has introduced into his text here, even though it does not properly fit the rest of his argument in §§19–20 (*cf.* 1.14 for a similar misapplication of apparently imported sophistic theory). For this view, that men naturally prefer a régime conducive to their own interests, see Introduction, section 6.

The repeated μὲν . . . μὲν in the first two clauses of §20 indicates that X is arguing concessively: 'I can accept that the members of the *demos* will themselves support democracy; naturally it is in their own interests as a class to do so, *but* . . . ' (the following δὲ after ὅστις is strongly emphatic).

2.20. But whoever . . . has chosen to have a political life in a democratic city: X now (resuming, we believe, the subject begun in the last sentence of §19) proceeds to excoriate those members of his own class, the *chrestoi,* who have chosen to οἰκεῖν in a city with a democratic rather than an oligarchic constitution. But what is X's basic point here, and what is the correct translation of οἰκεῖν? There are three possible interpretations of the relative clause introduced by ὅστις δὲ:

(*a*) If the infinitive οἰκεῖν is used in the sense 'live', 'reside', (as it is, *e.g.,* in 2.14–16) and the emphasis is placed on this, he is implying that, given the present constitution, all the *chrestoi* should physically remove themselves from Athens, and go into voluntary exile in an oligarchic state abroad. This is the interpretation of, *e.g.,* Frisch, 91. Indeed, Frisch concludes from this passage that X himself is writing in exile; and D. M. Lewis writes, 'Unless he is confessing himself a crook, he is outside Athens' (review of Bowersock 1968: *CR* n.s. 19 [1969], 45–7 at 46). However, this cannot be X's meaning here. He cannot be implicitly recommending a mass emigration of the Athenian *chrestoi,* since it is a firm assumption throughout the rest of the treatise that there are, and always will be, *chrestoi* in Athens and Attica.

(*b*) If the emphasis is being placed on the participles δημοκρατουμένῃ and ὀλιγαρχουμένῃ, used here as characterising adjectives, then X is suggesting that the Athenian *chrestoi* should not accept the democratic constitution under any circumstances. Rather, they should undertake a revolution against the rule of the *demos*, in an attempt to change the democratic constitution into an oligarchic one. However, nowhere else in the treatise is there any suggestion that the Athenian *chrestoi* could or should do this. On the contrary, X's thesis throughout is that the democracy is extremely well-entrenched, and is being preserved and promoted in the most effective way. Indeed, at 3.12–13 he asserts that a violent attack on the constitution would need a large number of men to have any hope of succeeding, and there simply are not enough discontented and resentful men for such an attack to be viable. X surely cannot here be suggesting an action which he assumes elsewhere in the treatise would be, in effect, suicidal.

(*c*) The third possibility, recently championed by Osborne, is that οἰκεῖν is being used here not in the sense of 'live', 'reside', but rather with reference to political life, *i.e.* with the sense, 'manage affairs', 'be politically active'. We agree. Both οἰκεῖν and the compound διοικεῖν (*cf.* 1.16) are well attested in this political sense when they are used transitively (*e.g.* Thuc. III. 37.3, Eur. *Hippolytus* 486; and there may be a suggestion of this sense at 2.9), and οἰκεῖν can also have this sense when it is used intransitively, as here (Thuc. II. 37.1, Pl. *Republic* VIII. 557a). Here, intransitive οἰκεῖν is both preceded and followed by the preposition ἐν, which might suggest that it must mean just 'live in'. The context, however, is the crucial factor, and this shows that X must be using οἰκεῖν in its political sense here. His argument from τοὐναντίον γε τούτου in §19 to the end of §20 is one of strong criticism of those *chrestoi* who have chosen to pursue political careers by holding important offices under the democratic constitution. It is through and in the course of their holding of office, not through mere residence, that they are able, allegedly, to commit acts of injustice and get away with it. What X objects to is not the continuing presence of the *chrestoi* in Athens and Attica, but any active involvement in democratic politics on their part. They must remain totally aloof from public life; any 'collaboration' with the system is class treachery.

Does he have anyone particular in mind here? His use of the aorist tense εἵλετο (= 'has chosen') in §20 suggests that he does, that it has happened. But whom? One thinks immediately of Alcibiades, and his disingenuous defence of himself at Sparta in winter 415/4, that democracy at Athens had to be accepted, but he had tried to moderate its excesses (Thuc. VI. 89: *cf.* below). But Alcibiades had not yet become a really prominent political figure in the mid 420s (the probable date of the treatise). It is much more likely that X is alluding to the life and career of Pericles. With his aristocratic background, as son of Xanthippus and the Alcmaeonid Agariste, and his democratic politics, Pericles was the classic example of the phenomenon castigated here by X. Of particular interest is the comment made by Plutarch in his *Life of Pericles* (7.3), that 'he devoted himself to the *demos*, choosing (ἑλόμενος) the cause of the many and the poor (τῶν πολλῶν καὶ πενήτων) as against the rich and the few (ἀντὶ τῶν πλουσίων καὶ ὀλίγων), contrary to his own nature, which was anything but common (παρὰ τὴν αὐτοῦ φύσιν ἥκιστα δημοτικὴν οὖσαν)'. The close similarity of language (as well as thought) between this passage and §§19–20 of X's treatise suggests either that Plutarch's comment ultimately goes back, probably indirectly rather than directly, to X's treatise, or that they are drawing on a common source. X's scathing evaluation, of course, represents a very different view of Pericles from that taken by Thucydides (himself no great admirer of Athenian democracy), and by Plutarch, and it is, for that very reason, particularly interesting.

2.20. has chosen: For X an Athenian *chrestos* should typically be like Antiphon (son of Sophilus, of the deme Rhamnous), a man who, before the oligarchic takeover in 411, chose not to hold office or speak in the assembly (Thuc. VIII. 68.1), despite being the most brilliant speech-writer and adviser of his day. He took a leading role in the planning and execution of the oligarchic revolution of 411, was an extremist member of the oligarchy of the Four Hundred, and, when democracy was restored in 410, he was tried, convicted and executed for that role (Thuc. VIII. 68.2, 90.1, [Plut.] *Lives of the Ten Orators* 832f–834b). His self-defence speech at his trial was much admired by Thucydides, who seems to have been dazzled by Antiphon's intellectual and forensic talents.

Three single speeches and three 'tetralogies' (sets of four sample speeches, on both sides of homicide cases) have been preserved as speeches by Antiphon. It is accepted that the single speeches are by the Antiphon of Thucydides, and the tetralogies may be by the same man, though there are problems with that attribution. Ancient writers refer also to 'Antiphon the sophist' (Xen. *Mem.* I. 6), whose writings (fragments at no. 87 DK) included a treatise entitled *On Truth*, which explored consequences of the contrast between *physis*, 'nature', and *nomos*, 'human convention' (*cf.* Introduction, pp. 16–17). There has been much argument as to whether Antiphon the speech-writer and Antiphon the sophist were one man or two (they are considered to be one man by M. Gagarin, *Antiphon the Athenian* [Austin: U. of Texas P., 2002], to be two different men by G. J. Pendrick, *Antiphon, of Athens* [CUP, 2002]). But there can be little doubt that Antiphon the speech-writer had pupils whom he taught forensic and political rhetoric: the *Tetralogies*, if they are by him, would make that clear, and Plato says so explicitly (*Menexenus* 236a). X seems to be still a pupil, influenced by the thinking of a man of this kind, and it is a possibility that X was in fact a pupil of this Antiphon. Certainly the chronology fits (Antiphon the speech-writer was born about 480), as does the similar political, social and moral outlook, and there may perhaps be an indirect reference to Antiphon and his speeches in defence of subject-allies at 1.14 (see pp. 87–8, above).

2.20. act unjustly ... a man who is wicked: At 1.5 X has asserted that 'within the best men there is the least amount of licentiousness and injustice'. But the comment here is not really a contradiction of that view. It is only when a *chrestos* cooperates with the democracy, by pursuing a political career within it, that he 'has set himself to act unjustly' – and X slides from the idea of someone's cooperating in that way, which he regards as unjust (ἀδικεῖν), to that of his being morally wicked (which must be the sense of κακῷ here: X does not use κακός as a class label). X appears to assume that this was exceptional, though in fact it had happened regularly until the 420s (after which the leading politicians continued, like Cleon, to be rich men, but were rarely from the established families which had dominated Athenian politics until then).

Of course, X's allegation, that the only motive of such *chrestoi* for pursuing their political careers within a democracy must be a desire to get away with criminal activities, is absurdly unfair. Even if there were no ideological commitment to democracy by any of them (and it is hard to believe that, *e.g.*, Pericles did not sincerely subscribe to the principles of democracy), that is no reason to assume that they were all motivated by immoral considerations, rather than by a desire to achieve (perfectly legally and honestly) that public honour, *time,* which was a characteristic Greek preoccupation throughout antiquity.

Nevertheless, there is some evidence that politically active *chrestoi* at Athens were viewed with some suspicion by Athens' oligarchic enemies abroad, and perhaps that is the reason for X's outburst here, *i.e.* he is adopting the prejudices of his imagined interlocutors. It is significant that, when Alcibiades sought political asylum in Sparta in the winter of 415/4, he felt it necessary first to defend his previous apparent embracing of democracy. This part of his speech, as reported by Thucydides (VI. 89), employs many of the key political expressions and concepts which are to be found in X's treatise, with which it should be closely compared. Naturally, Alcibiades argues that he never had any commitment to the principles of democracy (*cf.* above). Given his audience, and his parlous position, that is only to be expected, though it may have been true in fact. Rather, he claims in his defence that he and others like him exercised a moderating and restraining influence on the *demos,* countering the extreme proposals of the *poneroi,* the men responsible for his flight from Athens; and that he had accepted the existing democratic constitution simply because it was the one under which Athens was most strong and independent as a *polis.* On this latter point, at least, Alcibiades and X are in complete agreement (*cf.* 1.1–2, 2.2–12, 3.12–13).

2.20. easier … to escape notice in a democratically governed city: The implication here must be that the volume of public business, and the scale of political involvement and activity, are so great in a democracy like Athens (*cf.* the argument of 3.1–9) that criminal behaviour on the part of individual office-holders and politicians will 'get lost in the crowd' (*cf.* the argument at 2.17). A similar, though not quite the same, point is made by Thucydides, with reference to Cleon and his alleged motive for wanting to prolong the war (if Athens was at peace, and by implication less busy, his misdeeds would be more likely to be detected: V. 16.1), and by Aristophanes in his simile of the eels (*Knights* 864–7), referring to the political confusion allegedly created deliberately by Paphlagon / Cleon in order to exploit it.

As a matter of fact, the claim has little or no justification. There was a rigorous and comprehensive system of formal checks and restrictions on all office-holders at

Athens, which X himself refers to, and to some extent discusses, at 3.2, 4, 6 and 7. Even a man as influential as Pericles had been prosecuted, convicted and removed from office for a time (Thuc. II. 59–65.4; removed from office Diod. Sic. XII. 45.4, Plut. *Pericles* 35.3–5).

3.1. This section opens with a programmatic summation, two sentences which at first sight appear to constitute a closing statement, rounding off X's case and concluding his thesis. As an instance of 'ring composition', by which the concluding words of a section echo the opening words, the words used here deliberately pick up, and refer back to, those used in his programmatic opening, 1.1, especially περὶ τῆς Ἀθηναίων πολιτείας τὸν μὲν τρόπον οὐκ ἐπαινῶ, εὖ . . . διασῴζεσθαι τὴν δημοκρατίαν and ἐπέδειξα here, and περὶ δὲ τῆς Ἀθηναίων πολιτείας . . . τὸν τρόπον . . . οὐκ ἐπαινῶ, εὖ διασῴζονται τὴν πολιτείαν and ἀποδείξω at 1.1.

However, we then find that, starting at ἔτι δὲ καὶ τάδε, there follows a further chapter. Structurally this third chapter is similar to the rest of the work, in that the arguments are constructed on the basis of imagined opponents' criticisms, all clearly indicated (at 3.1, 3, 7, 10 and 12), to which the author replies (a marked feature of chapter 1; less evident, though still present, in chapter 2: see Introduction, section 5). There can be no doubt that X intended chapter 3 (at any rate up to and including §9) to be part of the original whole. What then is its connexion with what precedes? Closer examination shows that the subject matter of chapter 3 (at least in §§1–8) corresponds to a second programmatic intention announced in 1.1, viz. the conduct of public business, the administrative effectiveness of the system; and that the summarising sentences at the beginning of §1 refer only to the first programmatic intention announced there (see pp. 59–60, above).

Throughout §§1–8 X is concerned to respond to the criticism that at Athens it takes too long to get one's public business dealt with, there is too much delay in the system. In essence, X's answer is that at Athens there just is a great deal of public business to get through each year (he goes into some detail on its nature), and so such delays are inevitable. Interestingly, X does not argue in this passage that this is a conscious policy, that the *demos* deliberately arrange things so as to cause these delays, in order to gain some partisan economic or political advantage for themselves as a class (as he argues for practices discussed in chapter 1, and to some extent in chapter 2). Rather, for X, these delays are a natural and inevitable consequence of the great mass of public business at Athens, which needs to be dealt with by the appropriate administrative bodies. This mass of business itself is a natural consequence of Athens' having a democratic constitution and also a very large population (3.6).

The detailed account in this chapter of the various types of administrative business which have to be dealt with is therefore mostly matter-of-fact, with some sensible comments, and largely free from the attribution to the *demos* of selfish motivation, which was so characteristic a feature of chapter 1 and some parts of chapter 2. Indeed, X does not use the word *demos* at all in its party political or class label sense until §§10 and following, in a passage which reads like a later addition, not properly worked into the rest of the treatise (see p. 161, below). However, the mode of expression is sometimes awkward and elliptical, and it is not always obvious exactly what procedure X is referring to.

3.1. But, since: The manuscripts, apart from C, have ἐπειδήπερ here. However, a contrasting 'but' is clearly required by the context. C has ἐπειδὴ δ': this is probably a copyist's correction, but it does give the required sense and may well be what X wrote.

3.1. by adopting the practices which I have explained: Note the emphatic first person pronoun ἐγώ, characteristic of an assertive, argumentative approach. It is used frequently in the treatise (*cf.* 1.10, 2.12, 19, 3.3, 8, 12). The verb which X uses here, ἐπέδειξα, has connotations of an orator's proving a point (see Introduction, section 5). It deliberately refers back to ἀποδείξω ('I shall demonstrate') in the programmatic introduction (1.1). There is no need to emend in either place to obtain the same verb: X's slight variation of compound form is deliberate.

The double use of τρόπος in different senses in this section is an example of careless writing on X's part (*cf.* 2.19). In the first sentence (τὸν μὲν τρόπον) the sense is 'form' or 'type of constitution', *i.e.* democracy, whereas in the second sentence (τούτῳ τῷ τρόπῳ) it means something like 'manner of politics', *i.e.* policies and practices deliberately designed to maximise the economic and political self-interest of the *demos*.

3.1. I see that some people blame the Athenians: This is the first imagined criticism in this chapter, and is clearly indicated as such. The phrasing again indicates (as in chs. 1 and 2) that X's unspecified interlocutors (τινὰς) are to be thought of as non-Athenians, but that does not imply that X himself is writing or speaking outside Athens (*cf.* Introduction, section 5, and p. 63, above). Correspondingly, the expression 'I see' does not (*pace* Frisch, 290) imply that X is replying to what he has read in some written pamphlets. He soon reverts to the language of discussion ('some people say', at the beginning of §3); and here 'I see' is just a stylistic variation, which indicates only that his opponents are imagined as being visibly present before him (see Introduction, section 5, on the assumed agonal background of the treatise). It suggests a performance context. In a similar fashion, the regular expression for the audience at the theatre was οἱ θεώμενοι = 'the spectators' (Ar. *Clouds* 518, *Frogs* 2).

3.1. for the council or the assembly to do business with a person: The verb χρηματίζειν is used to mean 'transact business' in §§1–3, in the active voice of the body which deals with the business and in the middle voice of the person who gets his business dealt with. Thus here χρηματίσαι is used with τῇ βουλῃ οὐδὲ τῷ δήμῳ as subject and καθημένῳ ἀνθρώπῳ as indirect object (*pace* LSJ *s.v.*, I. 2. b), and in the following sentence the subject with which χρηματίσαντες agrees is οἱ Ἀθηναῖοι, extrapolated from Ἀθήνησι (*cf.* Frisch, 291).

3.1. the council or the assembly: Here and in 3.3 *demos* means not the lower classes but the 'people in assembly' (*cf.* 2.17), and in his use of this expression X is alluding to the probouleutic system, *i.e.* the constitutional requirement that all matters to be decided by the assembly must have been previously put on the agenda by the council, though the council itself had no power to pass decrees of its own, except of a minor kind ([Arist.] *Ath. Pol.* 45.4; *cf.* Rhodes, *The Athenian Boule* [OUP, 1972], 82–7).

3.1. sometimes . . . even though he sits waiting for a whole year: Despite its position at the beginning of the clause, ἐνίοτε here belongs in sense primarily with ἐνιαυτὸν καθημένῳ. The insertion of 'sometimes' thus does not weaken the imagined criticism as much as Frisch, 290–1 suggests: X's interlocutors claim that there are always delays, and sometimes they last a whole year. The point underlying the expression (*cf.* Frisch, 293) is that all offices at Athens were annual, and so any business uncompleted at the end of the year lapsed, since the cycle had to start all over again in the new official year (which ran from midsummer to midsummer).

3.1. This happens: καὶ is awkward here, because τοῦτο Ἀθήνησι γίγνεται οὐδὲν δι' ἄλλο ἢ clearly signals the beginning of X's reply, not a continuation of the criticism. We should expect, and perhaps ought to correct to, . . . ἀνθρώπῳ. τοῦτο <δ'> Ἀθήνησι … Alternatively, καὶ perhaps implies 'I can answer this too'. O'Sullivan, 194, points out that if we place a colon after πραγμάτων there is no need for Kirchhoff's insertion of διότι, and we punctuate accordingly.

3.1. sending them away: The word ἀποπέμπειν suggests that, for the benefit of his interlocutors, X here has in mind not Athenian citizens but foreigners, those who had to come to Athens to transact public business with 'the authorities'. An indication of what was likely to happen in such cases is given by Athens' decree of 446/5 for Chalcis (ML 52 = *IG* i[3] 40, trans. Fornara 103, lines 12–14), where the Athenians promise that 'when an embassy arrives, I shall bring it before the council and the *demos* within ten days'. In this case a speedy hearing is promised for official visitors; but the need for such a promise implies that without it official visitors and, even more, private individuals coming to Athens could usually expect a much longer wait before they were granted access to the relevant official bodies.

3.2. more festivals than any of the Greek states: *I.e.* more than any one of the other Greek states. In §8 X will say that 'they actually hold twice as many festivals as the others do'. *Cf.* Pericles' funeral speech, Thuc. II. 38.1 (also Ar. *Clouds* 299–313, Sophocles *Oedipus at Colonus* 1006–7, Pl. *Alcibiades ii.* 148e). There are nearly 150 festival dates in the year attested for the *polis* of Athens, and we must allow, in addition, for festivals whose dates we do not know and festivals concerning not the whole *polis* but a deme or other body within the *polis* (see J. D. Mikalson, *The Sacred and Civil Calendar of the Athenian Year* [Princeton UP, 1975], 201).

3.2. even less possibility: We have to understand 'even' with ἧττόν. At 3.8 X says explicitly that the lawcourts did not meet on festival days: this is confirmed by Ar.

Knights 1316–17, *Clouds* 620. The council did not meet on 'days of exemption' ([Arist.] *Ath. Pol.* 43. 3), which appears to mean annual (but not monthly) festival days, of which there were about sixty in the year (see Rhodes *ad loc.*, Mikalson, *The Sacred and Civil Calendar*, 196–7 with 198).

3.2. first of all ... secondly ... and then: The references here are to (*a*) festivals, (*b*) lawsuits, and (*c*) the *boule*, the council of five hundred. This introductory order of topics is reversed (no doubt a deliberate attempt by X to use the stylistic feature known as chiasmus) in the more detailed treatment which follows, *i.e.* council §§2–3; lawsuits (though with the council still involved in some of the processes referred to) §§4–7; festivals §8.

3.2. any of the state's business can be transacted: διαπράττεσθαι is a key word for understanding the structural connexions of thought of the treatise. After its appearance here in §2 it is repeated three times in §3, and these frequent usages in §§2–3 deliberately pick up διαπράττονται in 1.1. The indefinite τινα here is neuter plural, going with τῶν τῆς πόλεως.

3.2. conduct private and public lawsuits: *Dike* can be used as a generic term for lawsuits of any kind, but here X follows the Athenians' technical distinction between *dikai* as 'private' suits, which could be initiated only by the injured party or by his or her family, and *graphai* as 'public' suits, which could be initiated by any citizen (the appointment of public prosecutors was very rare): see, *e.g.*, D. M. MacDowell, *The Law in Classical Athens* (London: Thames and Hudson / Cornell UP, 1978), 57–62). The infinitives ἐκδικάζειν here and βουλεύεσθαι below are, like ἑορτάσαι, dependent on δεῖ above.

3.2. examinations of officials: All Athenian officials had to undergo a formal examination at the end of their year of office. In the fourth century this comprised a financial examination (*logos*, but the term *euthynai* can be used of both parts of the process: [Arist.] *Ath. Pol.* 54.2) and a general examination (*euthynai*: [Arist.] *Ath. Pol.* 48.3–4): the *euthynoi* responsible for the general examination were appointed from the council, the *logistai* responsible for the financial examination from the citizen body at large; if a case of wrongdoing was established *prima facie*, the individual was sent for trial before a lawcourt.

3.2. in greater numbers than the whole of mankind: Again, as in the first point about festivals, we have to understand 'other', 'rest of'. This is no doubt an exaggeration. However, the Athenians had a reputation for being addicted to litigation (*cf.* Thuc. I. 77.1; Ar. *Wasps*, also *Clouds* 208, *Birds* 39–41, 109–11), and Athens had a far larger population (*cf.* 3.6), and, particularly in the time of the Delian League, was the site of far more political and commercial activity, than any other Greek state.

3.2. the council has to deliberate a great deal: Instead of a very brief summary, as has been given with regard to the scope of the lawcourts (just four key words), X proceeds to specify in some detail the various areas of responsibility of the council (down to νεωρίων ἐπιμεληθῆναι καὶ ἱερῶν). For the rather awkward arrangement of material in §§2–4, see pp. 148–9, below.

X stresses the enormous work-load of the council (note the emphatic quintuple repetition of πολλά, 'many things'). The areas of its responsibility which are specified here are: (*a*) war, (*b*) state revenues, (*c*) law-making, (*d*) day-to-day internal public business, (*e*) allies, (*f*) receipt of tribute, (*g*) care of dockyards and temples. For similar lists of business to be dealt with see Xen. *Mem.* III. 6.1–13; Arist. *Pol.* IV. 1298a 3–7 *cf.* 1299a 1–2, *Rhet.* I. 1359b 21–3 *cf.* 1360a 6–7. Let us examine X's items one by one.

3.2. the war: 'The war', with the definite article, might be seen as another indication that Athens was at war when X was writing (*cf.* pp. 122, 125–6, above), but that is not a necessary implication: the article is used in the reference to the games celebrating 'those who have died in the war' in [Arist.] *Ath. Pol.* 58.1, written when Athens was not at war (*cf.* the heading of an Athenian casualty list, ML 33 = *IG* i³ 1147, 2, for which the translation of Fornara 78 gives 'in the war' with a footnote, 'Or, "fighting" '; also vases cited by Rhodes, 651). In the texts cited at the end of the previous note, Xenophon writes of war without the article (III. 6.10), Aristotle of 'war and peace' without the article; but perhaps there were official texts which used the article and X is here echoing them.

In what way was war the sphere of the council? It did not, of course, have the power to declare war, but it did have a responsibility to ensure that all the necessary equipment for a war was available, especially the ships (see [Arist.] *Ath. Pol.* 46.1, with Rhodes *ad loc.*, and in *The Athenian Boule*, [OUP, 1972], 115).

3.2. provision of finances: See [Arist.] *Ath. Pol.* 47–8, Rhodes *The Athenian Boule*, 91–102. The council oversaw the various boards involved with receiving and spending Athens' revenue, and it is connected with the raising of revenue in Ar. *Knights* 774–6. X is thinking of internally raised and monitored revenues here, as his separate references later to allies and tribute show.

3.2. the framing of legislation: What exactly does περὶ νόμων θέσεως mean, and what is its reference to? The Athenian council had no sovereign power to enact legislation or pass major decrees (see p. 144, above). Nor is it credible (*pace* Frisch, 302) that the expression has anything to do with the council's responsibility for appointing *nomothetai* (lawgivers), in a complicated procedure necessary for the enactment of laws, since *nomothetai* appointed by the council are attested only for the revision of the laws in 403/2 (decree quoted in Andoc. I. *Mysteries* 83–4), and it was only in and after that revision that the Athenians distinguished between decrees (*psephismata*) of the assembly and laws (*nomoi*). J. D. Smart, arguing for a late date for this work, in fact saw here an allusion to the revision of the laws which was begun in 410 when the democracy had been restored after Athens' first bout of oligarchy ('The Athenian Empire', *Phoen.* 31 [1977], 245–57 at 250 n. 12); but such a late date for the treatise is incompatible with many other passages (see Introduction, section 3).

Before the end of the fifth century laws could be enacted only by decree of the assembly, and they could be referred to either as decrees, to emphasise the mode of enactment, or as laws, to emphasise their status as part of the body of Athenian law. X must surely here be referring to the probouleutic function of the council in drawing up the agenda for the assembly, preparatory to the assembly's passing of decrees (in placing an item on the agenda the council sometimes, but not always, made a recommendation which it hoped the assembly would ratify: Rhodes, *The Athenian Boule*, 52–81). To refer to the council's *probouleusis* as 'the framing of legislation' is a loose use of language, but it is the only activity of the fifth-century council to which X could plausibly be referring here, and otherwise, in this detailed list in §§2–5, there would be no reference at all to what was the original and a fundamental function of the Athenian council.

3.2. day-to-day domestic matters: κατὰ πόλιν means 'domestic', 'internal'. What is being referred to here? The expression is very vague. X may intend it to refer to anything domestic not covered so far in *a–c*, but the principal reason for the expression is to set up a contrast, and pave the way for his transition to the council's responsibilities in relation to the allies. *Cf.* the distinction in [Arist.] *Ath. Pol.* 24.3 between ἀρχαὶ ἔνδημοι and ὑπερόριοι ('domestic' and 'overseas officials').

3.2. also with regard to the allies: The isolated dative τοῖς συμμάχοις (like the previous items introduced by περὶ, dependent on βουλεύεσθαι) is harsh; but varying the grammatical structure in this way is also a feature of X's older contemporary Thucydides (*cf.* K. J. Dover's small editions of Thucydides VI / VII [OUP, 1965], p. xvi / xv): so there is no need to follow Schneider in reading <περὶ τῶν ἐν> τοῖς συμμάχοις. καὶ before τοῖς συμμάχοις indicates that X intends a correspondence and contrast with the preceding expression, *i.e.* day-to-day domestic business *and* day-to-day business 'with regard to' the allies. But what is the business 'with regard to the allies'? The phrase cannot refer to receipt of tribute, since that is mentioned separately afterwards, or to assessment of tribute (to be mentioned in §5). Probably X is making the easy contrast between domestic and imperial matters without asking himself what day-to-day imperial matters other than tribute there may be.

3.2. it has to take receipt of tribute: This is explicit enough, and is an indication that the work was written before the tribute was replaced with a harbour tax in 413 (*cf.* Introduction, p. 5, and p. 101, above). For the council's responsibilities in the matter of the annual receipt of tribute see particularly the decree of Cleinias (ML 46 = *IG* i³ 34, trans. Fornara 98), probably now to be dated shortly after Thudippus' assessment decree of 425 (*IG* i³ 71; decree and extracts from assessment list ML 69, trans. Fornara 136). *Cf.* Rhodes, *The Athenian Boule*, 89–91, and, for the date of Cleinias' decree, Rhodes, *A History of the Classical Greek World, 478–323 B.C.* (Blackwell, 2005, dated 2006), 50, 92–3.

3.2. look after the dockyards and sanctuaries: For these areas see [Arist.] *Ath. Pol.* 46. 1 (the council's responsibility for ships and dockyards) and 46.2 (the council's general responsibility for public works); in 50.1 a board of ten *hieron episkeuastai*, 'repairers of sanctuaries', is the first of many boards listed after [Arist.] *Ath. Pol.*'s section on the council. *Cf.* Rhodes, *The Athenian Boule*, 113–22, 122–7.

3.2. when they have so much existing business: ὑπαρχόντων indicates regular items of public business, unavoidable matters.

3.2. to deal with all mankind: Frisch, 304, following Gelzer, persuasively argues that ἀνθρώποις χρηματίσαι here, like χρηματίσαι . . . ἀνθρώπῳ in §1, refers to the authorities' dealings with an individual (what he calls 'private affairs'), which had always to be relegated to the background, in comparison with public matters. It may well be that X has particularly in mind *foreign* individuals trying to deal with the Athenian authorities (*cf.* p. 144, above).

3.3. some people say . . . with money . . . I would agree . . . But . . . I am quite sure of: The structure of imagined criticism and authorial reply is very clear here. As usual, X accepts the factual accuracy of the criticism. It is important to be clear exactly what this is. Neither X nor his assumed interlocutors are critical of the taking of bribes *per se*. They do not take a moral line at all, and X claims in a matter-of-fact way that there is actually scope for more bribery. Rather his opponents cite the existence of the practice as evidence that there is, after all, time to spare for public bodies at Athens to deal with an individual's business. In reply, X argues in effect that all that can be gained thereby is occasional queue-jumping. He reiterates that there just is so much regular public business to get through that it is simply not possible for all individual petitioners to be dealt with in the time available, however much money is offered in bribes.

X writes of approaching the council or the assembly with money. How does the allegation of bribery in this area square with the facts? There is an interesting passage in Ar. *Peace* 905–8 (of 421), where Trygaeus 'returns' the beautiful Theoria to the council. The *prytanis* (presiding official) takes her willingly (no doubt anticipating her sexual favours), but Trygaeus comments sourly that he would not have shown such eagerness if he had had to introduce an item of Trygaeus' business for no reward (προῖκα), but rather would have held his hand out, *i.e.* for a bribe (*cf.* also Ar. *Thesm.* 936–8, again of a *prytanis*). These passages suggest that a certain amount of small bribe-taking ('tips') by the presiding officials, to introduce an individual's business to the council, was routine. It happens not to be attested that the members of the council swore not to take bribes, as it is for the archons and jurors, but it is still likely that that was included in the councillors' oath. This kind of bribery is what we might expect, and is to be distinguished from the bribing of juries (a notorious instance, allegedly the first, in 410 or 409 according to [Arist.] *Ath. Pol.* 27.5), or the massive bribe-taking allegedly indulged in by politicians, to advocate particular policies in the assembly: such allegations are frequent in comedy, and may or may not have been justified. But X does not have either of those sorts of bribe-taking in mind here. See F. D. Harvey, '*Dona Ferentes*: Some Aspects of Bribery in Greek Politics', in *Crux . . . Presented to G. E. M. de Ste. Croix* (*History of Political Thought* 6 and Exeter: Imprint Academic, 1985), 76–117.

The argument about bribe-taking interrupts the natural transition from the business of the council to that of the lawcourts (starting at §4), a topic already signalled in §2. A neater and clearer arrangement of material would have been produced if X had not gone into such detailed explanation of the business of the council in §2, but had just briefly summarised it (as he has done with the lawcourts' business in §2 – just four key words), and then had gone into more details about the council after §3, just as in §§4–7 he reverts to, and examines in more detail, the business of the lawcourts.

3.3. the council or assembly: For the pairing *cf.* §1; but in fact between that mention and this X has written only of the council. This must be because the assembly was not where the delays were. The bottleneck was the council; but, because formally business had to pass through the council before reaching the the assembly, X mentions both bodies here (and in §1).

3.3. money ... money ... gold and silver: We have translated ἀργύριον as 'money' in the first two sentences here, but as 'silver' in the last sentence (where it is coupled with gold, χρυσίον). Attic coins were made only of silver down to *c.* 406, when in their financial emergency in the last years of the Peloponnesian War the Athenians started to coin both gold and silver-plated copper (*cf.* Ar. *Frogs* 718–26). But there were foreign coins in circulation at Athens earlier (*e.g.* Cyzicene staters or Persian darics), some of gold or of the alloy of gold and silver known as electrum. After the Peloponnesian War the Athenians reverted to silver coinage.

3.3. the state is simply not capable: Interestingly, X here speaks of the state (*polis*), rather than the *demos*. Indeed, there is no use of the word *demos* in its partisan political sense in chapter 3 until §§10–13.

3.4. X now moves on to matters of public administration where a judicial decision is required. This becomes the theme of §§4–7. No grammatical subject is provided for (δεῖ) διαδικάζειν: we have to understand the vague 'they', *i.e.* the Athenians. καὶ (= 'also') is used to link the next sub-category of business to be dealt with, judicial, to the decision-making business of the council and assembly. The *dikasteria* are not specified directly until §7, and some of the judicial items to be mentioned involve the council, but not all. However, it would not be safe to infer simply from X's text that the council was involved with matters with which its involvement is not otherwise attested: essentially X is listing categories of business without worrying too much about which bodies handle them.

3.4. They also have to judge: X is fond of the word διαδικάζειν, and uses it at least eight times in §§4–6. The word can have a quasi-technical sense, 'make a legal decision as between two or more claimants'. It seems to bear this sense twice in §4 (with χορηγοῖς and τοῖς βουλομένοις). But it can also mean simply 'judge', and that seems to be how X mostly uses it here (see §6, where δικάζειν and διαδικάζειν are used interchangeably).

3.4. a man does not repair his ship: The reference is to trierarchs (*cf.* 1.13 with p. 82, above), mentioned specifically two sentences further on. The trierarchs were responsible for returning their ships in good repair at the end of the year, and the records published by the *epimeletai ton neorion* (curators of the dockyards) in the fourth century show that it was commonly the council (but sometimes the assembly) which took such decisions as were needed about ships and equipment (*cf.* Rhodes, *The Athenian Boule*, 117–20).

3.4. builds something on public land: In the later fourth century there were public officials called *astynomoi*, chosen by lot, who were responsible among other things for preventing private buildings from encroaching on the public roads (*cf.* [Arist.] *Ath. Pol.* 50.2). We do not know when they were instituted.

3.4. adjudicate . . . the appointment of choregoi: For the *choregia* and liturgies in general see 1.13. The word διαδικάσαι is used in its technical sense here (*cf.* above). The procedure was that the archon appointed three *choregoi* for the tragedies and (in X's day) five for the comedies ([Arist.] *Ath. Pol.* 56.3). If there was a protest on the part of the selected person, *i.e.* a claim to exemption (*skepsis*), or to replacement by another, wealthier citizen, the archon was responsible for referring the matter to a lawcourt. In the latter instance, the man selected would challenge another either to perform the liturgy in his place or, if that second man denied that he was richer, to exchange property with him (*antidosis*). We do not know how often this happened, but, when it did, it obviously took up valuable lawcourt time.

3.4. at the Dionysia, Thargelia, Panathenaea, Promethia and Hephaestia: These annual Athenian festivals seem to be named in the order in which they occurred in the seasonal (rather than the official) year. We do not know when the last two were celebrated, but the Dionysia was in Elaphebolion (month ix), about March, the Thargelia in Thargelion (xi), about May, and the Panathenaea in Hecatombaeon (i), about July (whereas the official year began in Hecatombaeon). They are listed in the same order (without the Panathenaea) in *IG* i³ 1138, of shortly after 403/2. This is a clear indication of close familiarity with Athenian public life on X's part. On all these festivals see H. W. Parke, *Festivals of the Athenians* (London: Thames and Hudson / Cornell UP, 1977). Dithyrambic choral performances at the Dionysia and Thargelia are attested by [Arist.] *Ath. Pol.* 56.3, and at the Panathenaea by [Arist.] *Ath. Pol.* 60.1. The Panathenaea also involved games and a horse race. The Prometheia and Hephaistia both involved torch races, and may have involved choral performances as well (perhaps supported by the fragmentary *IG* i³ 82, 14, *cf.* R. Parker, *Athenian Religion: A History* [OUP, 1996], 154 n. 7; but see J. K. Davies, 'Demosthenes on Liturgies: A Note' *JHS* 87 (1967), 33–40 at 35–6, against). It was actually gymnasiarchs who performed for the torch races the function which *choregoi* performed for choral contests, but X may simply have conflated the two categories.

It is slightly odd that X does not mention here the Lenaea (in Gamelion [vii], about January), which certainly had dramatic contests. But the Lenaea was also a festival of Dionysus, and it may be that it is subsumed within the one word 'Dionysia'.

The inscription *IG* i³ 82, concerned with the Hephaestia, is dated 421/0. Mattingly, 353–4, argues that the inscription records the original institution of the festival, and that X's work must therefore be later than 421/0; but most scholars consider that it provides for the reorganisation of an existing festival through a major celebration every four years (*e.g.* Parke, *Festivals*, 172, Parker, *Athenian Religion*, 154).

3.4. four hundred trierarchs: For this liturgy *cf.* 1.13. X turns to this subject as a natural development after his reference to *choregoi* in the previous sentence. Although καὶ τριήραρχοι begins a new sentence, with διαδικάσαι we must again understand δεῖ from the beginning of the section. τοῖς βουλομένοις is indirect object: 'for those who wish' to challenge their selection by means of a *skepsis* or *antidosis* ([Arist.] *Ath. Pol.* 61.1) – and X may also be thinking of legal claims, likewise referred to as *skepseis* or *diadikasiai*, which might arise out of their performance of their duties. We do not know who in the late fifth century was responsible for selecting trierarchs and assigning them to ships, or for bringing their cases to court; but in the 'decree of Themistocles', supposedly of 480, trierarchs are selected and ships assigned by the generals (ML 23, trans. Fornara 55, lines 18–23: we cannot tell whether this detail is authentic or later reconstruction), and in the later fourth century this was the responsibility of the one out of the ten generals who by then was in charge of the naval organisation ([Arist.] *Ath. Pol.* 61.1, *cf. IG* ii² 1629 = RO 100, 204–17).

τετρακόσιοι ('four hundred') is the reading of all the manuscripts, and the text should not be emended (as Bowersock considered doing). It is wrong in principle to emend a text simply because it says something unexpected, without strong reason to believe that the author cannot have written what the text states. However, there has been much dispute over the accuracy of this figure. Assuming that there were the same number of triremes as trierarchs, the total number of ships implied here, four hundred, is much greater than the figure given by our other sources for the size of the Athenian fleet in this period, viz. three hundred (*cf.* Pericles in 431, reported by Thuc. II. 13.8, and Ar. *Acharnians* 544–5 [425]). It is true that the figure four hundred is given by the manuscripts of Andocides III. *Peace* 9 (in a passage which is historically unreliable, and in any case refers to the period after 421), but that figure is regularly emended to three hundred, since the text of Aeschin. II. *Embassy* 175, in a passage which seems to be taken directly from Andocides' speech, has three hundred. There are two other relevant but difficult passages in Thucydides. II. 24.2 refers to an Athenian decision taken in 431 to keep in reserve each year a special force of the hundred best triremes, together with their trierarchs: it is hard to believe that the Athenians would in fact keep their best ships out of service, but the hundred seem to be envisaged as taken from the three hundred, not additional to it. III. 17.1–2 seems to say that in 428 some 250 ships were all on active service, which if combined with the other passage would imply an overall total of 350: what is said in that chapter seems easier to believe of the beginning of the war than of 428, but probably the chapter is an interpolation and should not be believed at all. At any rate, the evidence seems to show that, whatever the exact total number of

Athenian triremes was during the Archidamian War, there were never as many as four hundred.

There are two serious possibilities. Either X is exaggerating, or there were more trierarchs selected annually than there were triremes. Given X's predilection for exaggeration, the former may be thought to be more likely. But his exaggerations tend to be made through generalisations, rather than in the use of definite, checkable, figures. It may therefore be the case that a number of 'reserve' trierarchs were selected annually, in addition to those who were allocated to specific vessels, though there is no evidence to support this. That would produce a total in excess of three hundred, and would perhaps explain X's figure of four hundred, which is obviously a round number. The suggestion of Frisch, 311–2, that trierarchs were allocated to vessels other than triremes, for which again there is no evidence, is less likely.

3.4. to approve and judge officials: Again we must understand δεῖ. Here δοκιμάσαι refers clearly to the compulsory preliminary vetting (*dokimasia*) of all incoming officials, at the start of their year of office ([Arist.] *Ath. Pol.* 45.3, 55.2–4, 59.4). In the fifth century, certainly after 462/1, the *dokimasiai* of the archons and councillors were conducted by the retiring council, which may at that time have had the final authority in the matter (but by the later fourth century the council performed the first stage and there was then automatic reference to a lawcourt); *dokimasiai* of other officials were conducted by a lawcourt. As far as we know, officials were appointed from candidates who volunteered, and there was no scope for *diadikasiai* concerning their appointment as there was in the case of men selected for liturgies. It is therefore not evident what X is referring to with διαδικάσαι here, but, immediately after δοκιμάσαι, he must surely be thinking, at least in part, of the *euthynai*, the examinations of officials' conduct at the end of their term of office (*cf.* p. 145, above), for which the council provided the *euthynoi* responsible for the general, non-financial examination. διαδικάσαι must therefore be used here in its non-technical sense, to mean simply 'judge' (see p. 149, above). Frisch, 313–4, takes διαδικάσαι here to refer to the second stage of the preliminary *dokimasia, i.e.* when there was referral from the council to a lawcourt. But this seems mistaken, since (*a*) there was a two-stage *dokimasia* only for archons and councillors (and it is not certain whether even that was in two stages in X's day), and (*b*) in that case X would make no further reference to the *euthynai* of officials. But this was such an important area of Athens' administrative processes that it is hard to think that he would omit it here, especially after the introductory appearance of *euthynai* in §2.

3.4. to approve orphans and appoint guards for prisoners: The infinitives are still dependent on δεῖ, with the unspecified 'they' as subject. The same rather surprising combination, of orphans and guards for prisoners, is found at [Arist.] *Ath. Pol.* 24.3, at the end of a list of men allegedly paid for from the tribute of the Delian League, and it is possible that a common source lies behind X and [Arist.] *Ath. Pol.* here (Rhodes, 301–2, 309; for the theme in comedy *cf.* Ar. *Wasps* 655–724).

The Greek word ὀρφανός means, particularly, 'fatherless', and the reference here is not to all such orphans, but specifically to those sons whose fathers had been killed in war. State support for these is well attested (*e.g.* Pericles' funeral speech, Thuc. II. 46.1; Diog. Laert. I. 55 attributed the institution to Solon, but according to Arist. *Pol.* II. 1268a 8–11 Hippodamus claimed to be creating something unprecedented when he instituted this in Miletus, perhaps in the second quarter of the fifth century). These inspections may well have been a responsibility of the council. We do not have any direct evidence, but [Arist.] *Ath. Pol.* 49.4 attests that it was the council which inspected cripples, and approved the state allowance paid to them (*cf.* also Lysias XXIV. *Invalid*), and it is reasonable to assume the same authority in the case of war-orphans.

X says here that these inspections take place every year. This may give some support to the view that there is a war on at the time he is writing, thus causing children to be made fatherless on a regular, ongoing, basis; but the Athenians did some fighting, and could have suffered some deaths in battle, in most years.

3.4. appoint guards for prisoners*:* The regular officials in charge of the Athenian state prison were called the Eleven, and in the later fourth century they were chosen by lot ([Arist.] *Ath. Pol.* 52.1). It may be that there was a change of procedure in the intervening years, but, even so, it is hard to see how making these routine appointments could have been the time-consuming chore that X implies it to be here. It may therefore be that he is referring to guards other than the Eleven.

A period of time in prison was only rarely imposed as a legal punishment in Athens (and some have denied that it was ever used as a punishment). There was only one public prison-building, and imprisonment was used mainly for those awaiting trial or the death penalty, and men with outstanding fines and other debts to the state (see Rhodes, 580). The only significant group of people who might have to spend a long time, maybe several years, under guard were prisoners of war. This is perhaps what X is thinking of here, not Athenians or others in prison awaiting trial or execution after trial.

In the summer of 425 no fewer than 292 prisoners of war (120 of them Spartiates) were captured on the island of Sphacteria, opposite Pylos, and taken back to Athens (Thuc. IV. 38). There they were 'guarded in chains' (IV. 41.1), perhaps initially in the state prison, and used as hostages to deter further Spartan invasions of Attica. They were returned home some 3½ years later, under the terms of the Peace of Nicias in 421 (Thuc. V. 18.7, 24.2). It is not clear what arrangements were made for the long-term guarding of these prisoners. Were they all housed in the state prison throughout that period? Given its restricted size, that seems unlikely. It would certainly have been uncomfortable for the inmates, yet we are told that Alcibiades, acting as the Spartans' *proxenos* at Athens, had 'looked after' the men captured at Pylos (Thuc. VI. 89.2, Plut. *Alcibiades* 14.1), and there is no suggestion that any of them ever suffered any great discomfort while they were in captivity at Athens. It is a distinct possibility that, after a time, these (and other) prisoners of war were on occasions moved out of the state prison and based, probably in small groups, in private quarters, and that the Athenian owners of the properties to which they were confined were officially designated during that period as their guards and guarantors. The implication of what X says here (through the link he makes with war-orphans) is that he has in mind such 'guards', whose properties needed to be vetted in advance. If the arrangements were as we have suggested, that would have been necessary for obvious security and financial reasons. This might well have been a time-consuming business (as X implies here), much more so than the routine appointment of the Eleven.

It should be noted that it was not until late 425 that the question of what to do with prisoners of war became a serious issue at Athens, and, if X had drawn up this list of business himself and if we take δεσμωτῶν in this sense, we might here see confirmation that he is writing after the success at Pylos / Sphacteria in summer 425. On the other hand, the corresponding passage in [Arist.] *Ath. Pol.* 24 begins with the heyday of the Delian League and indeed with its first organiser, Aristides; it adds men paid for 'when the Athenians subsequently organised their military affairs', apparently referring to peace-time quotas before the Peloponnesian War (*cf.* Rhodes, 305–6); and <meals in> the *prytaneion*, orphans and guards for prisoners are tacked on at the end. *Cf.* p. 152, above, for the suggestion that X and [Arist.] *Ath. Pol.* derive this material from a common source, which they could unthinkingly have applied to their different contexts.

3.4. All these things have to happen every year: There is heavy repetition for emphasis here, the phrase ὅσα ἔτη occurring three times and ἑκάστου ἐνιαυτοῦ once in §4. The point is that all the matters mentioned by X in §4 are annual standing items of public business These are now contrasted with other sorts of public business, which come up διὰ χρόνου ('intermittently'), *i.e.* not on a recurrent annual basis, and some of these items are specified in the next section.

3.5. The three activities mentioned in the first part of §5 were all legal offences. They are cases of (*a*) *astrateia*, avoidance of military service; (*b*) *hybris*, violent arrogance, and (*c*) *asebeia*, impiety. These are all characterised as 'sudden', 'unusual' offences (ἐξαπιναῖον, ἄηθες). Again no subject is specified with δεῖ (we must understand the vague 'they'), and διαδικάσαι is here used in its non-technical sense (= 'judge cases of').

It is not clear why X should single out these three offences here. As usual, he supplies no illustrative details, but it is tempting to think that he has in mind some recent high-profile cases involving important individuals. The word ἐξαπιναῖον suggests something more substantial than routine cases.

3.5. avoidance of military service: The emendation to ἀστρατείας of the manuscript reading στρατια(ς) is generally accepted: the word means 'avoidance of military service', not 'desertion' from the ranks after joining them (which is *lipotaxia* or *lipotaxion*: see S. C. Todd, *The Shape of Athenian Law* [OUP, 1993], 183). *Astrateia* was an offence against the law (note X's word ἀδίκημα), and these *graphai* (prosecutions which could be initiated by any citizen) and other charges of military offences were normally tried by juries of fellow-soldiers under the presidency of a general (A. R. W. Harrison, *The Law of Athens*, ii [OUP, 1971], 32). We do not know of any case in the mid 420s which could reasonably have been prosecuted as *astrateia*. R. Brock and M. Heath, 'Two Passages in Pseudo-Xenophon', *CQ* n.s. 45 (1995), 564–6 at 565–6, thinking a more serious charge more appropriate here, prefer Lipsius' στρατηγικὰς, or else στρατηγικὰς <δίκας>, and note that charges against generals and charges of outrageous impiety (they seem to take ὑβρίζωσί and ἀσεβήσωσι as a hendiadys) might both be tried by *eisangelia*. However, that reading is much further from στρατια(ς).

3.5. commit an . . . act of arrogance: Like *astrateia*, *hybris* (violent arrogance) was a prosecutable offence in fifth- and fourth-century Athens (see N. R. E. Fisher, *Hybris* [Warminster: Aris and Phillips, 1992]; also D. M. MacDowell, *The Law in Classical Athens* [London: Thames and Hudson / Cornell UP, 1978], 129–32, and his *Demosthenes Against Meidias* [OUP, 1990]). Normally a *graphe* of *hybris* would go directly to a lawcourt (Dem. XXI. *Meidias* 47, quoting the law of *hybris*). Again we do not know of any case about this time.

3.5. or (an act) of impiety: For the legal procedure in cases of *asebeia*, impiety, see MacDowell, *The Law in Classical Athens*, 197–200. There was a *graphe* for *asebeia*; but one of the most notorious examples of this offence was the parodying of the Mysteries and the mutilation of the Hermae in 415, and on that occasion the procedure employed was *eisangelia* (Plut. *Alcibiades* 22.4), on one occasion to the assembly, but otherwise always to the council (Andoc. I. *Mysteries* 15, 17, 27, 37–43, 61–5). Indeed the council set up a commission of inquiry (Andoc. I. 36, 43–5), and took general control of the investigation (Andoc. I. 36, 43–5, 65–6). Andocides' account suggests very strongly that the council was centrally involved in dealing with the *asebeia* of 415, but that was perhaps because the affair was perceived as political (*cf.* Thuc. VI. 27.3). Some scholars have believed that the mention of *asebeia* here is a reference to those acts of sacrilege, and that the treatise is therefore to be dated to the period soon after that (*e.g.* Mattingly, 352–7). But there are no other indications of such a late date for the work, whereas there are a large number of indications which point to a date during the Archidamian War. It is thus preferable simply to say here too that X may well have in mind here some recent high-profile case of *asebeia*, but, if so, we do not know who it involved or what it was about. There had certainly been earlier accusations of, and perhaps prosecutions for, *asebeia*: against Pericles' mistress Aspasia (Plut. *Pericles* 32.1: perhaps just an attack in a comedy), and against his intellectual friend Anaxagoras (Plut. *Pericles* 32.2, Diog. Laert. II. 12: possibly prosecuted in 437/6, as argued by J. Mansfeld, 'The Chronology of Anaxagoras' Athenian Period and the Date of His Trial', *Mnemosyne* 4th series 32 [1979], 39–69 + 33 [1980], 17–95).

3.5. apart from the assessments of tribute: This detail reads like an afterthought, tacked on as it is at the end of X's list (see next note). Receipt of tribute has been mentioned in §2; for the implication that Athens was collecting tribute from the allies at the time when this work was written, *cf.* Introduction, p. 5, and p. 101, above.

3.5. *This usually takes place every four years:* The evidence bears X out on this. After the transfer of the Delian League treasury to Athens in 454/3 the tribute assessments were normally reviewed every four years. But the insertion of 'usually' here seems to indicate that there had been at least one exception before X wrote his treatise. The traditional view is that there were exceptional assessments in 443/2 (instead of 442/1), and again in 428/7 and 425/4 (but not 426/5). This is contested by Mattingly, 352–3, who argues that there were not exceptional assessments in 443/2 and 428/7 but, rather, regular assessments in 442/1 and 426/5; however, there was certainly an extraordinary and major reassessment of tribute, involving large increases, in 425/4. The procedures involved are detailed in the decree of Thudippus (*IG* i^3 71; decree and extracts from assessment list ML 69, trans. Fornara 136), and the requirement that future assessments are to be made in the years of the Great Panathenaea (lines 26–33) confirms that there has been a departure from that pattern. It is clear that, although the decree itself was as always passed by the assembly, the overall responsibility and much of the detailed work involved in the reassessment was assigned to the council (*cf.* lines 7–10, 17–25, 45–6, 58–60). The decree enjoins a tight timetable and a full work load on the council. Disputes about, and appeals against, assessment, were heard in the lawcourts (*cf.* the tribute decree of Cleonymus, of 426 (ML 68 = *IG* i^3 68, trans. Fornara 133).

Was this exceptional and obviously time-consuming reassessment in 425/4 a recent, perhaps very recent, event at the time X was writing? If it was, it would explain why he decided to tack on a reference to tribute assessment at the end of the detailed list of administrative public business in §§2–5. Why otherwise would he have regarded something which normally was done only once every four years as one of the state's 'most important', *i.e.* time-consuming, activities?

3.6. *Well then . . . Let someone say:* This lively interjection (note the repeated φέρε δή here and at the beginning of §7) is a sudden change of style after the rather tedious detail of §§2–5. X issues a rhetorical challenge to the imagined opposition, in a language and tone characteristic of a speech in the lawcourts. The implication is that X's interlocutors are present, listening to his arguments (*cf.* p. 143, above). The assumed setting is clearly an agonal one of some sort, in our view probably a student debate or discussion group (see Introduction, section 5).

Wachsmuth's insertion of χρή before χρῆναι (producing οἴεσθαι <χρή>, as in §8, below: accepted by Bowersock and other editors) is one way to restore grammar and sense to the first sentence of §6. Alternatively, one might read the second person plural οἴεσθε (= 'do you think') instead of the infinitive οἴεσθαι. That would suit the lively tone of this section.

3.6. *they ought to judge them all:* From this point X seems to focus exclusively on the lawcourts, *dikasteria*, and their vital importance within the Athenian political system. Hence in §§6–7 he uses διαδικάζειν three times (in its non-technical sense), δικάζειν four times, δικαστήριον twice, and δικασταί and δικαίως once each. His point in §6 is that the number of cases to be judged by the courts cannot be fewer, that nothing can be dropped.

3.6. throughout the year: The repeated δι' ἐνιαυτοῦ shows that here this expression means 'throughout the year', not 'within the year' (which Frisch takes to be the meaning in the first instance). There is so much business that the courts need to sit on nearly every available day (M. H. Hansen reckons that the courts could have met on about 240 days in the year and actually did meet on 175–225 days: 'How Often Did the Athenian *Dicasteria* Meet?' *GRBS* 20 [1979], 243–6).

3.6. are they in a position to stop: ὑπάρχουσιν followed by ὥστε and the infinitive is an unusual usage, but all the manuscripts have these words, and this is what the context requires them to mean.

3.6. because of the large size of the population: ὑπὸ τοῦ πλήθους τῶν ἀνθρώπων here refers to the total citizen population of Athens, not (*pace* Bowersock) to the number of wrong-doers there (τοὺς ἀδικοῦντας). The very much larger population of Athens in comparison to other states (a well attested fact), and, consequently, the much greater amount of public business, is a key point in X's argument here, and underlies everything he says in §§2–8.

3.7. All right, but someone will say . . . that fewer people ought to do the judging: This is a new (imagined) objection, clearly signalled. Logically, after what has preceded, the point ought to be that, if juries for each case were smaller, more courts could sit at the same time, and business could therefore be dealt with more quickly; but X's reply shows that the objection which he is postulating is different, viz. that Athens uses too many men *in total* as jurors (and therefore has to provide payment and to resort to the lower classes in order to recruit them). But this point does not have a logical connexion with the complaint which underlies §§1–6, viz. the delays involved in getting one's business dealt with by the authorities at Athens, and X's reply to it, that there just is inevitably a great deal of regular public business to get through, none of which can be dropped. Using fewer jurors in total would have no effect on that problem, since, as far as we know, there were no difficulties or delays involved in recruiting the annual panel of 6000 registered jurors (*cf.* [Arist.] *Ath. Pol.* 24.3, Ar. *Wasps* 662, with pp. 91, 94, above), or in selecting particular juries from it. Indeed, as X points out by implication, if fewer jurors overall led to fewer courts' being in session at any one time (ἐὰν μὴ ὀλίγα ποιῶνται δικαστήρια), the delays within the system would become even worse. Probably X has, in the manner of which he is all too capable, simply allowed his mention of the lawcourts in §6 to prompt another objection to the legal system.

It is not clear why a critic should be imagined as being concerned simply about the overall numbers of jurymen; but what X has in mind here may be something which was later to become a standard anti-democratic complaint (*cf. e.g.* Plato

Gorgias 515e, Plutarch *Pericles* 9.2–3), not about the large number of jurymen *per se*, but about the amount and effects of the money which the state spent on jurymen's fees (*misthos*), at the rate of three obols a day each by the mid-420s. (*cf.* [Arist.] *Ath. Pol.* 27.4–5, 62.2, Ar. *Knights* 255). However, the complaint as presented by X here does not specifically mention payment, and if that is point of the criticism it is not spelled out. This is an example of excessive compression of argument, almost to the point of incoherence, on X's part.

In his reply, starting at ἀνάγκη τοίνυν, X first points out that a smaller total number of jurymen would mean either fewer courts in session (which would worsen the delays complained of), or smaller juries for individual cases. But that too, he argues, would not be desirable, since smaller juries are easier to bribe into giving a corrupt verdict. This is a rare example of a sensible and justified argument on X's part (for the point, one may compare [Arist.] *Ath. Pol.* 41.2, Arist. *Politics* III. 1286a 31–3). Indeed, the clear implication of X's argument here is that, with their system of large juries for individual cases, the Athenians are consciously concerned to prevent corruption and to ensure that cases are judged fairly and impartially (πολὺ ἧττον <δὲ> δικαίως δικάζειν). This is a (possibly unintended) compliment, which does not square with his jaundiced view of the *demos*' relationship with justice elsewhere (*e.g.* 1.5, 13, 14–16).

3.7. to make an arrangement: Not 'prepare all one's tricks for a trial' (LSJ *s.v.* διασκευάζω, II) but 'make a corrupt approach' to the jurors. διασκευάσθαι here has a similar sense to παρασκευάζεσθαι (LSJ *s.v.* παρασκευάζω, B. I. 2).

3.7. to bribe them . . . much less likely to judge justly: συνδεκάσαι (*cf.* δεκάζειν in [Arist.] *Ath. Pol.* 27.5) is a certain emendation of the manuscripts' reading, συνδικάσαι. With Kalinka's insertion of δὲ before δικαίως there is an abrupt change of subject for the infinitive δικάζειν: the understood subject of διασκευάσθαι and συνδικάσαι is 'the litigants', that of δικάζειν must be either 'they' (as with ποιῶνται) or 'the juries' (picking up ὀλίγοι) – *i.e.* 'and (it will be easier) for them ("they" or the juries) to judge much less justly.' Without the δὲ, δικάζειν has to be understood as explanatory, dependent on συνδεκάσαι, *i.e.* 'it will be easy to bribe them to judge much less justly'. This would be very clumsy, and is less likely.

3.8. the Athenians ought to hold festivals: *I.e.* they have to hold them, given that they are on the traditional religious calendar. It is worth noting that X does not question the need for Athens to continue holding all these religious festivals, nor does he imagine his interlocutors as questioning that need.

3.8. festivals, during which they do not have the ability to judge lawsuits: Finally, X reverts by chiasmus to the first topic (πρῶτον μὲν) mentioned (briefly) in §2. He is more explicit here that the lawcourts are closed during festivals. The large number of festivals at Athens is well attested (see pp. 144–5, above), though 'twice as many . . . as the others' is probably an exaggeration; in §2 he said merely that they have 'more . . . than any of the [other] Greek states'. The courts did not meet on assembly days, or on taboo days or annual festival days, but like the council they did meet on monthly festival days (see p. 157, above, and the article by Hansen cited there).

3.8. But I am assuming that they only hold: What is X's argument here? He seems to be qualifying his immediately prior statement, to the effect that they hold double the number of festivals held elsewhere. But why? The argument is very elliptical. First of all, he restates the point made in §2, that public business cannot be conducted during festival time and the Athenians do have many festivals – twice as many as anyone else. This is an admitted fact (ἄγουσι μὲν), but (ἀλλ'), he proceeds to argue, even if they had only a few festivals, only as many as the state having the fewest, they would still not be able to accommodate everyone's public business, or be free from delays in dealing with it. The word τίθημι is here used in the sense 'assume for argument's sake' (see LSJ *s.v.*, B. II): idiomatically, we should say, 'Let us assume'.

What then is the antithesis to ἐγὼ μὲν τίθημι, which will complete the thought? We expect it to be something like, 'even so, the situation with regard to delays in getting one's business dealt with by the authorities would not be significantly different'. This, with a balancing δὲ clause, is what we expect, but it is not there in the text as we have it. We thus have to assume either an ellipse of the conclusion (very harsh, but perhaps not impossible for this writer), or a lacuna after πόλει, where some words giving the above sense have been lost in the copying and transmission of the text.

3.8. Since these things are so: In his translation, Moore takes the expression τούτων τοίνυν τοιούτων ὄντων as linking with and providing the antithesis to ἐγὼ μὲν τίθημι, *i.e.* the genitive absolute is being used in a concessive sense, = 'even if these things were to be so', so that the expression refers to the possibility that Athens might only have a few festivals. But there are two problems with this interpretation: (*a*) what follows in the last part of §8 seems rather to be a summarising statement which refers back at least to the whole of the argument of §§2–7, if not to the whole of the treatise, not just the particular (and hypothetical) point about festivals made at the beginning of §8; (*b*) τοίνυν standing at the beginning of a concluding statement is invariably used in an inferential sense (= 'so', 'therefore') rather than an antithetical, and its use here reinforces the likelihood that the genitive absolute is being used in a causal sense = 'since these things are so', and that the reference is indeed to the whole of §§2–7 or the whole treatise (thus Frisch, 327).

3.8. except in so far as there is the ability to remove or add something just to a slight extent: What is X referring to here? In what way are 'slight' changes in the way things are done at Athens possible? A more widespread employment of bribery to expedite one's business with the authorities is the only 'change' which X has envisaged as a possibility in §§2–7: is that what he is referring to in this vague expression? It is possible, but it is more likely that X begins his overall summary here. He then repeats the point for emphasis in §9. From τούτων τοίνυν τοιούτων ὄντων X seems to move away from the administrative details of the previous sections of chapter 3, and on to the main argument of the treatise. X does not bother to specify what the 'minor' changes are which in his view would be possible. His emphasis is on his interlocutors' suggested major changes, which in his view are not possible without undermining the democracy itself.

3.9. This section must cohere with §8, because of the deliberate reference back to the previous point, 'as I have just said' (ὅπερ ἄρτι εἶπον). The wording κατὰ μικρόν τι προσθέντα ἢ ἀφελόντα obviously harks back to, and picks up, τὸ μὲν ἀφελεῖν, τὸ δὲ προσθεῖναι at the end of §8. It seems to restate more emphatically the conclusion X has begun to draw, and to refer back to what was said in chapters 1 and 2 as well as the earlier part of 3, since the 'many ways' by which one can 'make the constitution better' are most naturally taken as a reference to the various explicit and implicit suggestions of his imagined interlocutors in chapters 1 and 2, which were not simply directed to matters of administration and public business (the subject of 3.1–8). In other words, this passage seems on the face of it to be a concluding paragraph, summarising chapter 3 in particular and the treatise as a whole up to this point.

3.9. It is possible to devise many ways to make the constitution a better one; but . . . : X's overall point in this sentence, down to οὐ ῥᾴδιον, is clear enough: it is possible to discover ways by which the Athenian constitution might be improved, but such improvements will change its nature, it will no longer be a democracy. What he tries to say, through a deliberate contrast (ὥστε μέντοι . . . οὐ ῥᾴδιον following ὥστε μὲν . . . πολλὰ ἐξευρεῖν), is, 'but it is not easy to discover ways by which the constitution may be improved whilst still allowing it to remain a democracy'. But X's syntax is very awkward. He starts off with ὥστε μέντοι, signalling an antithesis with the preceding ὥστε μὲν, but then he immediately attempts to divide this antithetical assertion itself into two contrasting parts, ὑπάρχειν μὲν . . . ἀρκούντως δὲ (= 'the democracy will continue in existence, yet with sufficient change to result in their having a better constitution'). The second ἐξευρεῖν is awkwardly placed between τοῦτο and ὅπως; it would be better before or after οὐ ῥᾴδιον. The construction of ἐξευρεῖν with ὥστε and infinitive (used twice) is jettisoned, and instead we have τοῦτο as a direct object, followed by ὅπως with the future indicative. The adverb ἀρκούντως ('sufficiently') seems to be in the wrong place before τοῦτο: in sense it must be taken with the following ὅπως (= 'sufficient to result in'). X can be a clumsy writer, but it may be that the text needs emendation here. ABM have δὲ after ὅπως, which certainly cannot be right: C omits it, in what is no doubt a copyist's correction; Bowersock emends to δὴ ('in fact', 'definitely').

3.10–13. The treatise appears to come to a formal conclusion at the end of §9. However, the manuscripts contain four further sections of text, in which X replies to two further imagined criticisms (10–11 and 12–13). See Kalinka, 301–2, Frisch, 330–1, and Marr (1983), 51. Neither of these points has been properly worked into the text so as to cohere in any way with what precedes. They may be additional notes, which X for some reason did not, or could not, properly incorporate into the first version of this treatise, or they may have been omitted from their original place in the body of the work by an early copyist, and subsequently tacked on at the end, when the omission was noticed. The theme of §§10–11, Athenian involvement in the affairs of other Greek states, is not dissimilar to that of 2. 17, Athens' foreign alliances, and the Athenian *demos'* alleged lack of reliability in adhering to them, and it is possible that the original position of §§10–11 was between 2. 17 and 2. 18. It is, however, harder to find a suitable place anywhere within the treatise for §§12–13. See further pp. 165, 168, below.

It is worth noting that only at this point in chapter 3 (four times in §§10–11, once in §13), is the word *demos* used in its partisan political sense, so common in chapters 1 and 2. This supports the view that §§10–13 do not naturally cohere with what precedes.

3.10–11. This passage is concerned with Athenian intervention in the civil war, *stasis*, of other states, where (it is alleged by X's interlocutors) the Athenians mistakenly (οὐκ ὀρθῶς) take the side of the lower classes. As usual, X does not contest the factual accuracy of the imagined allegation. Rather, he first explains why the practice is absolutely necessary, then provides a justification based on historical examples.

The argument put forward by X in §10 is similar to that found at 1.14, that there is a universal natural antipathy between the two classes, the *demos* and the *oligoi*, and, conversely, an attachment to and loyalty between the same classes in different states; this instinctive class loyalty is international and crosses national frontiers. In 1.14 this thesis is proffered to explain why the Athenians discriminate against the upper classes in the subject states within their *arche* (where it is taken for granted that the upper classes would naturally rule, if they were not prevented from doing so by the power of the Athenian *demos*). Here the application of the thesis is first broadened to apply to all Athens' interventions in the affairs of other states (not just those in their *arche*), and then it is turned into a purely general political theory: 'like is well disposed to like'.

In the following section (§11) X produces a different sort of argument, of a type not found elsewhere in the treatise. He adduces some (negative) historical examples to show that, when in the past Athens has acted in a different way, supporting the upper classes in *stasis* abroad, it has always turned out badly for them. Hence they no longer act in this way.

3.10. are thought to have a mistaken policy: The manuscripts' μοι after τοῦτο must be deleted (as was done long ago by Morus; other editors suggested emendations). The criticism expressed in the first sentence is not proffered by X, but by his interlocutors. Indeed, he answers it with οἱ δὲ τοῦτο γνώμῃ ποιοῦσιν and what follows. The first word, δοκοῦσι, as often, serves to indicate a supposed objection;

οἱ δὲ signals the start of the reply. There is a very similar formula at the beginning of 1.16, without the μοι (δοκεῖ . . . κακῶς βουλεύεσθαι). See Introduction, section 5, and Marr (1983), 49.

3.10. they take the side of the inferior classes in states which are involved in a civil war: Does X have any recent historical events in mind here? The repeated use of the verb αἱρεῖσθαι ('choose') in §§10–11 makes it clear he is thinking of active intervention by Athens in other states' civil wars, not just the taking of a favourable attitude towards the *demos* elsewhere. Such intervention did happen often during the Peloponnesian War (Ar. *Politics* V. 1307b 19–24 is explicit), most strikingly when Athens actively supported the democrats of Corcyra (not a subject-ally) in their brutal civil war against the oligarchs in 427–425 (Thuc. III. 69–85, IV. 46–48.5). This action may well be what X has in mind beneath the generalisation and theory of §10. If so, this is yet another indication of a date about the mid 420s for the treatise.

3.10. For in no state is the best element well disposed to the demos: Is X referring here to the *demos* within the particular foreign state, or to the Athenian *demos*? If the former (as translators generally assume), then he is reiterating a point made explicitly at 1.5; if the latter, he is broadening the point made implicitly at 1.14. That he means the latter here (though without making it clear) is suggested by 'do not have the same views as themselves' before this sentence and 'the side which is related to themselves' after it.

3.10. the best element . . . the worst element: For X's theory of universal bi-polar class opposition, and his use of loaded class labels, see Introduction, sections 7 and 8.

3.10. the Athenians choose to support the side which is related to themselves: The word προσήκοντα is used of 'belonging', in the sense of having kindred ties, and emphasises the close connexion allegedly felt between *demoi* everywhere in the Greek world. For X, they are like a family.

3.11. Whenever they have attempted to take the side of the best men, it has not worked out well for them: In this section, for the only time in his treatise, X refers explicitly to some particular decisions and events in Athenian history, which he cites as (negative) examples which prove his point. The examples are introduced very suddenly (after the preceding generalisations) in the sentence beginning ἀλλ' ἐντὸς ὀλίγου χρόνου, a phrase which then becomes a refrain throughout the section. The events themselves can all be dated to within the period 462–443 and, consequently, the treatise must have been written later than 443. No example is cited from a period subsequent to 443, and in particular there is no reference to the revolt of Samos in 440–439: this is the basis for the early date championed by Bowersock and some others. However, the lack of reference to later events proves nothing at all about the *terminus ante quem* of the treatise (see Marr (1983), 46–7, and Introduction, section 3, and p. 165, below).

The three examples given are not meant to be exhaustive, of course, but they are deliberately chosen to give a comprehensive illustration of X's point. However, X's language in this section is obscure and elliptical, and this has led to some uncertainty about what precisely he is referring to. What he gives are examples of (*a*) Athenian intervention abroad to further their land power; (*b*) Athenian intervention abroad to further their Aegean power; (*c*) Athenian intervention abroad to support Sparta. Because of his view that 'like is well disposed to like' (§10), he puts his emphasis on the unfortunate fate of the *demos* in each case; but, in addition, there was a more direct bad consequence for the Athenians, viz. revolts against them in Boeotia and Miletus, and war with Sparta.

3.11. within a short time, the demos *in Boeotia were enslaved:* The verb ἐδούλευσεν is obviously being used in a metaphorical sense here, to denote loss of political independence rather than actual enslavement (*cf.* 1.8–9).

X provides no indication of date here, but the comment must refer to events some time after Athens' victory at the battle of Oenophyta *c.* 457, as a result of which the Athenians were able to dominate most of Boeotia until their defeat at Coronea in 447 or 446 (Thuc. I. 108, 113). It has sometimes been thought, on the basis of Thucydides' references to Boeotian exiles, that Athens set up democracies in the towns of Boeotia and exiled the oligarchs – except in Thebes, which Thucydides does not directly mention at I. 108 and 113, and which perhaps remained independent and oligarchic during this period (*cf.* also Diod. Sic. XI. 83.1; Thuc. III. 62.5, IV. 92.6, does not make clear what happened in particular cities), and that these oligarchic exiles were able to regain control of their cities after defeating the Athenians at Coronea in 447. But, given these facts, how could the Athenians be said, as here, to have 'chosen the side of' the upper classes in Boeotia? A passage of Aristotle (*Pol.* V. 1302b 29–31) may shed light on the problem. According to this, 'Thebes was badly governed after the battle of Oenophyta, and so the democracy was overthrown.' If we accept this as historical, it may be that there was a spontaneous democratic revolution at Thebes in the immediate aftermath of Oenophyta, but that some time later this was replaced by a moderate oligarchy, which the Athenians decided to 'support', *i.e.* not take action against by backing the ousted democrats, in the hope of securing its non-intervention elsewhere in Boeotia. However, this policy eventually failed when the Thebans supported the exiled Boeotian oligarchs at Coronea, as a result of which Athens lost control of all Boeotia, and the democracies there were overthrown (*cf.*, *e.g.*, A. W. Gomme, *Historical Commentary on Thucydides*, i [OUP, 1945], 318). If Gomme's reconstruction is correct, then 'within a short time' would not be such an exaggeration as if it referred to the period of nearly nine years between Oenophyta and Coronea.

3.11. Miletus . . . they had revolted and massacred the demos *there:* The main verb, κατέκοψαν ('cut down'), is a strong one, but the participle ἀποστάντες carries equal emphasis. The reference must be to an anti-Athenian revolt, by an oligarchic régime at Miletus (which had previously been accepted by Athens), resulting in a more extreme oligarchy, which also took violent, punitive action against the Milesian *demos*. Developments in Miletus between the 450s and the 430s are not entirely certain. From Miletus itself a decree of uncertain date (ML 43, trans. Fornara 66) outlaws certain men and their descendants; a decree probably of 434/3 (published by P. Herrmann, 'Zu den Beziehungen zwischen Athen und Milet im 5. Jahrhundert', *Klio* 52 [1970], 163–73, dating it 437/6; for 434/3 see Rhodes, 'Milesian *Stephanephoroi*: Applying Cavaignac Correctly', *ZPE* 157 [2006], 116) displays constitutional machinery on the Athenian model. The tribute record makes it likely that Miletus was in revolt *c.* 450; there may have been a second revolt later; the democratic constitution may have been imposed either *c.* 450 or somewhat later. In 440–439 Athens supported Miletus in a dispute with Samos (*cf.* p. 165, below): clearly a loyal régime had been re-established by then.

3.11. the Spartans had subdued the Messenians, and were at war with the Athenians: The reference here is clearly to the Athenian decision (made at the urging of Cimon) probably in 462/1, to support the Spartans in dealing with a serious revolt of the helots and *perioikoi* in Messenia. An Athenian expeditionary force was dispatched. However, this force was humiliatingly sent back home by the Spartans, as a result of which the Athenians in reaction adopted a much more anti-Spartan foreign policy (Thuc. I. 102). This involved them in military action against some of Sparta's allies, and eventually a pitched battle against the Spartans themselves, at Tanagra *c.* 457, in which they were defeated. X probably has this battle in particular in mind here.

However, this is not such a well chosen example on X's part. The Spartan victory at Tanagra had no serious consequences for Athens, but was followed shortly afterwards by the Athenian victory at Oenophyta and conquest of central Greece mentioned above; and the souring of relations between Athens and Sparta was the result of Sparta's unexpected rebuff of Cimon's expeditionary force and Athens' reaction to that, rather than of Athens' original decision to send it. Furthermore, 'subdued' is a considerable exaggeration. It was not until slightly later, *c.* 456, that those rebels who were still undefeated were finally allowed a safe passage away from Laconia and Messenia, and were settled by the Athenians at Naupactus, on the north side of the Corinthian Gulf (Thuc. I. 103.1–3).

It is interesting to note that the Messenian revolt of the mid fifth century is presented here by X as an example of *stasis*, civil war, with the helots in the role of the *demos*. It would be much more accurate to see it as a nationalist revolt by a suppressed people against an occupying power. But X here naturally adopts the point of view of his imagined interlocutors, who seem to be envisaged primarily as Spartans (see Introduction, section 5, and 1.9, 10–11, 13, with notes): they naturally would not recognise the Messenians as having a distinct national identity.

3.11. Boeotia . . . Miletus . . . Spartans: It must obviously have been difficult for X (or indeed for anyone) to find many historical examples by which he could prove his thesis here, viz. that 'whenever they have attempted to take the side the best men' in another state's civil war (note ἐν ταῖς πόλεσι ταῖς στασιαζούσαις in §10), it has not worked out well for them. In the nature of things, this was something which did not happen very often in Athens' fifth-century history, and perhaps not at all after the 30 Years Peace of 446/5. The revolt of Samos in 440–439 was not an example of this phenomenon, so could not be used by X here. It is true that Samos was an oligarchy before 440, but the revolt occurred because of prior Athenian intervention *against* the oligarchic government there, in support of the Milesians (who had the backing of some Samian democrats), over the territory of Priene to which both cities laid claim (Thuc. I. 115–7).

So the fact that the three illustrative examples which X provides here do not include the revolt of Samos, and are all taken from the period before that revolt, cannot (*pace* Bowersock [1966], 37–8) be used as evidence for an 'early' date for the treatise, before 440 or before the Peloponnesian War, given the rarity of the phenomenon before 445, and its probable non-existence afterwards. See Marr (1983), 45–7.

3.12–13. This is the final point of the treatise. Again, like §10–11, this passage does not seem to have been properly integrated into the rest of the work. It has little connection with what immediately precedes, the only tenuous link being the idea of *stasis*, civil war (abroad in §10–11, an unlikely possibility at Athens in §§12–13). As it stands, with this as its final passage, X's treatise ends abruptly and rather lamely, without any attempt at a summarising conclusion (see p. 168, below).

The subject of this passage is the Athenian *atimoi*, the disfranchised: those Athenians who either temporarily or indefinitely have lost some or all of their political rights, and the threat which they may or may not pose to the stability of the democratic constitution. Such men were not required to leave Athens, but they may sometimes have decided that it was better to do so than to live as *atimoi* in Athens. The most illuminating source for Athenian *atimoi* in the later fifth century is Andoc. I. *Mysteries* 73–80, citing and commenting on the decree of Patroclides in 405, a decree which restored rights to various categories of *atimoi*; interestingly, at a time when it was felt important to restore political unity.

3.12. *Someone might object:* The section starts with an imagined direct question from an opponent. In the first sentence all the words after ὡς should be placed within inverted commas with a question mark at the end (see Marr [1983], 50–2): 'Has no one then been unjustly disfranchised at Athens?' The question is ironic; it is equivalent to an assertion, 'Surely there have been such cases'. The implication of the comment is that such a group will be disgruntled, resentful at their treatment, and will thus constitute a serious threat to the stability of the democracy. They will wish to overthrow it (*cf.* τῶν ἐπιθησομένων below). Thus, it might be alleged by an opponent, despite X's claims, the democracy does not preserve itself so well after all.

3.12. *I reply:* In his reply, with a characteristic assertive use of the first person pronoun ἐγώ, X starts off by claiming that, though there are some, there are not many unjustly disfranchised Athenians, and thus there is no threat here to the democracy, because a revolution against it by the disgruntled would need to involve a large number of people to have any chance of succeeding. He then attempts to provide an argument in support of his assertion that there are only a few unjustly disfranchised at Athens (starting at the last sentence of §12).

3.12. some . . . unjustly disfranchised, but only a few: Who are these 'few' who X agrees have been unjustly (on this point *cf.* below) disfranchised? These must be mostly, if not all, members of his own class, *i.e.* not the *demos*. How can that be? Despite his assertion in §13 that 'it is the *demos* who hold the offices', he has admitted in 1.3 that some offices at Athens are not held by the *demos* (in particular, military offices, *e.g.* the *strategia* and the *hipparchia*).

In fact, we know of a number of instances of generals' being prosecuted and convicted for offences committed in office in the 420s. But the penalties we hear of are exile (often the result of condemnation in absence to death) and fines, not *atimia* (Pericles fined, Thuc. II. 65.3; two generals exiled and one fined, IV. 65.3; Thucydides himself exiled, V. 26.5); and prominent men who were fined were usually rich enough to pay their fines, and so would not become long-standing *atimoi* at Athens. It is the presence either inside or outside the state of a group of permanently or indefinitely disfranchised citizens, with a legitimate grievance, large enough to be able to achieve a violent overthrow of the constitution, which is the nub of the issue in §§12–13. X is adamant that there is no chance of that's happening, since the number of people in this category is very small.

Again one thinks of the contrasting situation in Sparta and Laconia, where citizens could be, and were, demoted to the lesser status of Inferiors (*hypomeiones*), not for unlawful conduct, but for economic or military failings. We do not know how early this practice began or on what scale it occurred; but the bitter resentment felt by this group surfaced in the conspiracy of Cinadon *c.* 400, when they and other lower status groups were involved in a revolutionary plot (Xen. *Hell.* III. 3.4–11; *cf.* P. A. Cartledge, *Sparta and Lakonia* [Routledge, ²2002], 234–5, 267–70). X does not explicitly mention Sparta in §§12–13, but in view of passages such as 1.8–9, 10–12, 13, 2.1, 7, it would not be too fanciful to see an implicit allusion here too to the contrasting situation at Sparta, where the phenomenon of demoted and resentful former citizens may have been familiar to his interlocutors.

3.12. one must not count those . . . justly disfranchised: X insists on making a distinction between those justly and those unjustly disfranchised. Only the latter, he claims, will feel resentment and hostility towards the democracy. He goes on in §13 to argue (perhaps surprisingly) that most of the *atimoi* at Athens have in fact been justly disfranchised.

As the text stands there is an incoherence in ἐπεί τοι καὶ οὕτως ἔχει. This is clearly inferential, 'since this is indeed the case'; but what does it refer to? One would expect it to refer to the assertion, in the immediately preceding sentence, that 'one needs more than a few to make an attack on the democracy'. But the following statement, that 'one must not count those people who have been justly disfranchised, but only those who have been so unjustly', does not have any very logical connection with that assertion.

The manuscripts read οὐδὲν before ἐνθυμεῖσθαι (οὐ δεῖ is an emendation of H. Fränkel), and there may be a lacuna here, something having been lost either before or after ἐπεί τοι καὶ οὕτως ἔχει. Keeping οὐδὲν, we might insert after it δεινὸν τῇ δημοκρατίᾳ τῇ Ἀθήνησιν (= 'there is no danger to the Athenian democracy'), the words having been lost through the similarity of sentence ending. The phrase would then provide a logical conclusion to the whole argument of §12 up to this point. We should then need something like οὐ γὰρ δεῖ before ἐνθυμεῖσθαι.

3.13. the majority of people: The argument so far, based on numbers, requires τοὺς πολλοὺς to have its descriptive sense (= 'the majority') here. But this expression can function in X as a class-label word, = 'the masses' (*cf.* 1.20), and this political sense is probably also present here, since it seems to trigger X's transition to his further point: 'it is the *demos* who hold the political offices' at Athens.

3.13. where it is the demos who hold the political offices: Why does X introduce this point about its being the *demos* who hold the political offices at Athens? He could have argued simply that those who have been disfranchised (whoever they are) at Athens have become so because they acted unjustly when in office. Therefore they are justly disfranchised, and should not feel resentment against the democracy.

His point seems to be that, since a large majority of the disfranchised are members of the *demos*, by misbehaving in office or in other ways they have *ipso facto* damaged the collective self-interest of the *demos*. He also needs to rebut the objection that someone who has been disfranchised for behaving unjustly in office, and therefore can be said to be 'justly *atimos*', might nevertheless not accept his punishment meekly, but might feel resentment and hostility to the democracy. Hence there seems also to be an implication here that, since such a person is invariably a member of the *demos*, he will not wish to overthrow the democratic constitution from which his class gains so many benefits, and to which he has such instinctive class-loyalty. He will accept that his disfranchisement, imposed by the fellow members of his class, is just, and will remain quiet.

3.13. or (from failing) to say or do what is just: Why add this to 'failing to hold office justly', which in itself would have been enough for X's argument? As an Athenian, X is aware that by no means all Athenian *atimoi* were so as a consequence of unjust activities as office-holders. Andoc. I. *Mysteries* 73–9 provides what seems to be a comprehensive list of *atimoi* at the time of the decree of Patroclides in 405. This passage shows that many *atimoi* were indeed disfranchised as a result of offences committed when holding public office, either directly so (those convicted of theft or accepting bribes), or indirectly (those unable to pay fines imposed for offences committed when holding office). However, some *atimoi* in Andocides' list were so as a result of quite different activities, *e.g.* those unable to pay fines imposed by the courts for offences committed in a non-official capacity, defaulting tax-farmers or bail-sureties, those found guilty of offences connected with military service, or of maltreating their parents, or of misdemeanours such as giving false evidence, or of acting as false summons-witnesses. These offences, all mentioned in Andocides' list, also carried the penalty of *atimia*.

3.13. one has to conclude that there is nothing to fear: Whether or not one agrees with X's peculiar argument about the effects of 'unjust' as against 'just' disfranchisement, it seems that the facts support his basic political point in §§12–13 (*cf.* also 2. 15). Before the disaster in Sicily in 413, all the evidence suggests that there was no group of people at Athens or in exile large enough and resentful enough to pose a serious threat to the democratic constitution (the earliest sign of fear that there might be a serious threat to the constitution is seen in the Athenians' reaction to the religious scandals in 415: *cf.* p. 124, above). The implication here and throughout the treatise is that, at the time of writing, the Athenian democracy is in its heyday – successful, popular, well-entrenched, and unchallengeable. X does not like this, and he offers an often flawed, sometimes perceptive, analysis of why it should be so. But he does appreciate this basic fact far better than his assumed interlocutors.

3.13. at Athens: The final word of the treatise (Ἀθήνησιν) occurs no fewer than five times in §§12–13, too often for effective emphasis, and the work itself ends very abruptly, after the addition of the two further, unintegrated, points argued in §§10–13. This is careless writing as well as poor composition, and it is hard to believe, even accepting X's manifest stylistic limitations, that the original version of the treatise could have ended as baldly as this. There is a possible explanation. It may be that the points made in §§10–13 were (hastily) tacked on to the text of the treatise (which appears to come to a formal end at 3.9) after X had originally completed it, in the light of some subsequent discussion and debate, or in response to his tutor's comments (see Introduction, section 5).

APPENDIXES

Appendix 1. The imagined criticisms answered in the work

Sometimes these criticisms are very clearly indicated in the treatise, by means of an introductory tag such as 'someone might say that', or 'if anyone is surprised at the fact that', followed by either an indirect or direct quotation. Examples of this type are 1.4, 6, 11, 3.1, 7 (indirect), and 1.7, 15, 3.3, 12 (direct). Occasionally a direct quotation occurs without any introductory tag, *e.g.* at 1.10, and probably 1.11 (though this is less obvious). In all these case the author clearly signals the beginning of his reply in the immediately following sentence.

Sometimes δοκοῦσι or δοκεῖ ('they seem . . . ' or 'it seems . . . ' = 'it is thought that they . . . ') is used as a signpost to signal an imagined criticism, *e.g.* at 1.14, 16, 2.1 and 3.10. Sometimes the criticism is introduced and the author's reply given, or at least started, in the same sentence, *e.g.* at 1.13, 14, and 2.1.

Sometimes the criticism is indicated more obliquely, by implication rather than directly, *e.g.* at 1.2 (possibly), 2.17, 19, and (probably) 2.18, where both features seem to occur, *i.e.* oblique introduction and the reply begun in the same sentence. Finally, there is a vaguer example of imagined criticism at 1.8–9, the point about lack of *eunomia* at Athens.

X thus demonstrates a certain amount of skill in the variety of expressions and methods he employs to introduce what is a constantly repeated feature of the treatise. In all, we calculate that there at least twenty examples of the phenomenon: eleven or twelve in chapter 1 (at 1.2 [?], 4, 6, 7, 8–9, 10, 11 [twice], 13, 14, 15, 16), four in chapter 2 (at 2.1, 17, 18, 19), and five in chapter 3 (at 3.1, 3, 7, 10, 12). There may be some uncertainty about one or two of these instances, but there can be no doubt that this is a primary thematic and structural feature of the treatise, which simply cannot be understood or interpreted without a full appreciation of it (see D. M. Lewis, *CR* n.s. 19 [1969], 46–7).

The full details are as follows:

1.2? (*cf.* 2.19, below)	πρῶτον μὲν οὖν τοῦτο ἐρῶ, ὅτι δίκαιοι
1.4	ἔπειτα δὲ ὃ ἔνιοι θαυμάζουσιν ὅτι
1.6	εἴποι δ' ἄν τις ὡς
1.7	εἴποι τις ἄν, τί ἂν οὖν γνοίη
1.8–9	ὃ γὰρ σὺ νομίζεις οὐκ εὐνομεῖσθαι . . . εἰ δ' εὐνομίαν ζητεῖς
1.10	"τῶν δούλων δ' αὖ . . . σοι ὁ δοῦλος"
1.11	εἰ δέ τις καὶ τοῦτο θαυμάζει ὅτι
1.11 (*cf.* 1.10)	"ἐν δὲ τῇ Λακεδαίμονι ὁ ἐμὸς δοῦλός σε δέδοικεν"
1.13	τοὺς δὲ γυμναζομένους αὐτόθι . . . καταλέλυκεν ὁ δῆμος

1.14	περὶ δὲ τῶν συμμάχων . . . καὶ μισοῦσι τοὺς χρηστούς
1.15	εἴποι δέ τις ἂν
1.16	δοκεῖ δὲ ὁ δῆμος . . . καὶ ἐν τῷδε κακῶς βουλεύεσθαι ὅτι
2.1	τὸ δὲ ὁπλιτικὸν αὐτοῖς, ὃ ἥκιστα δοκεῖ εὖ ἔχειν Ἀθήνησιν
2.17	ἔτι δὲ συμμαχίας . . . ταῖς μὲν ὀλιγαρχουμέναις πόλεσιν ἀνάγκη ἐμπεδοῦν
2.18	κωμῳδεῖν δ' αὖ καὶ κακῶς λέγειν
2.19	φημὶ μὲν ἔγωγε τὸν δῆμον . . . γιγνώσκειν . . . καὶ οἵτινες πονηροί

In 2.17, 18 and 19 the criticism is indicated only by implication (see commentary *ad locc.*).

3.1	ἔτι δὲ καὶ τάδε τινὰς ὁρῶ μεμφομένους
3.3	λέγουσι δέ τινες· "ἤν τις . . . προσίῃ . . . χρηματιεῖται"
3.7	φέρε δή, ἀλλὰ φήσει τις
3.10	δοκοῦσι δὲ . . . καὶ τοῦτο οὐκ ὀρθῶς βουλεύεσθαι, ὅτι
3.12	ὑπολάβοι δέ τις ἂν ὡς

Appendix 2. Occurrences of the words demos / demotikoi / demokratia

Demos

(*a*) as political label: 1.2 (×2), 3 (×4), 5, 7, 8 (×2), 9, 10, 13 (×4), 14, 16 (×4), 17, 18 (×3), 2.9 (×2), 10, 14, 17 (×3), 18 (×3), 19 (×2), 20 (×2), 3.10 (×2), 11 (×2), 13.
(*b*) = 'people in sovereign assembly': 2.17 (×1), 3.1, 3.
(*c*) = 'democracy': 2.15.
Demotikoi (virtually a synonym for *demos*): 1.4 (×3), 6, 15, 2.18, 19.
Demokratia / verb *demokrateisthai*: 1.4 (×2), 5, 8, 2.20 (×3), 3.1 (×2), 9 (×2), 12.

Appendix 3. Qualities and characteristics ascribed to the demos and the oligoi

Demos

ἀκολασία	1.5 (implied)	licentiousness
ἀδικία	1.5 (implied)	injustice
ἀμαθία	1.5 (×2), 7	ignorance
ἀταξία	1.5	disorder
πονηρία	1.5, 7	worthlessness
πενία	1.5	poverty
ἀπαιδευσία	1.5	lack of education

ἔνδεια χρημάτων	1.5	lack of money
κακονομία	1.8	being governed badly

Oligoi

ἀκρίβεια . . . εἰς τὰ χρηστά	1.5	scrupulousness over what is valuable
ἀρετή	1.7, 2.19	excellence
σοφία	1.7	wisdom
εὐνομία	1.8, 9	being governed well

Appendix 4. Class designations and class labels

(i) List of words, with suggested translations

In the following list A are descriptive terms / class labels, B are socially evaluative, C1 are morally evaluative, C2 are both morally and socially evaluative. (Although X uses the comparatives βελτίων and χείρων and the superlatives ἄριστος / βέλτιστος and κάκιστος as class labels, he does not use the positive forms ἀγαθός and κακός in this way.) The italicised words are our chosen translations.

	APPROVAL			DISAPPROVAL	
A	οἱ πλούσιοι	the *rich*		οἱ πένητες	the *poor*
A	οἱ ὀλίγοι	the *few*		οἱ πολλοί	the *many*
A				τὸ πλῆθος	the *populace* / the *masses*
A	οἱ δεξιώτατοι	the *cleverest*		μαινόμενοι	*wild persons*
B	ὁ δυνάμενος	the capable / able / powerful / *influential*		ὁ δῆμος	the common people / (untranslated as) the demos
B	οἱ ἰσχυροί	the powerful / *strong*		οἱ δημοτικοί	the *common people*
B	οἱ εὐδαίμονες	the prosperous / *well-to-do*		ὁ ὄχλος	the throng / the *mob*
C1	οἱ βελτίους	the upper class / *better classes*		οἱ χείρους	the lower class / *inferior classes*
C1	οἱ βέλτιστοι / τὸ βέλτιστον	the *best men* / *element*		τὸ κάκιστον	the *worst element*
C1	οἱ ἄριστοι	the *best men*			
C2	οἱ χρηστοί	the useful / effective / good / worthy / *valuable*		οἱ πονηροί	the toiling / suffering / in a bad way / bad / *worthless*
C2	οἱ γενναῖοι	the nobility / noble / *well born*			

(ii) Occurrences in the text

APPROVAL

A	οἱ πλούσιοι / πλούσιος	1. 2, 4, 13 (×3), 14, 2. 10, 14, 18
A	οἱ ὀλίγοι	2. 10, 15, 17
A	οἱ δεξιώτατοι	1. 6, 9
B	ὁ δυνάμενος	2.18
B	οἱ ἰσχυροί	1.14
B	οἱ εὐδαίμονες	2.10
C1	οἱ βελτίους	3.10
C1	οἱ βέλτιστοι / τὸ βέλτιστον	1.5 (×2), 14, 3.10, 11 (×2)
C1	οἱ ἄριστοι	1.6
C2	οἱ χρηστοί / χρηστός	1.2, 4 (×2), 6, 7, 9 (×2), 14 (×5), 2.19 (×2)
C2	οἱ γενναῖοι / γενναῖος	1.2 (×2), 2.18

DISAPPROVAL

A	οἱ πένητες	1.2, 4 (×2), 2.9, 18
A	οἱ πολλοί	1.20 [but (without article) = 'numerous' at 1.4; = 'the majority' at 3.13]
A	τὸ πλῆθος	2.18
A	μαινόμενοι	1.9
B	ὁ δῆμος	1.2 (×2), 3 (×4), 5, 7, 8 (×2), 9, 10, 13 (×4), 14, 16 (×4), 17, 18 (×3), 2.9 (×2), 10, 14, 17 (×3), 18 (×3), 19 (×2), 20 (×2), 3.10 (×2), 11 (×2), 13 [but = 'democracy' at 2.15; = 'the assembly' at 2.17 (×1), 3.1, 3]
B	οἱ δημοτικοί	1.4 (×3), 6, 15, 2.18, 19
B	ὁ ὄχλος	2.10
C1	οἱ χείρους	1.4, 3. 10
C1	τὸ κάκιστον	3.10
C2	οἱ πονηροί / πονηρός	1.4, 6 (×2), 9, 14, 2.19 (×2)

Appendix 5. Characteristic vocabulary

(* with verbs denotes with the *demos* as subject)

(*a*)   1ST PERSON VERBS (singular unless indicated; : 1.1 (×3), 2, 10, 11 (plural), 12 (plural ×2), 2.12, 19, 3.1 (×3), 3 (×2), 5, 8 (×2), 9, 12.

(*b*)   1ST PERSON PRONOUNS / ADJECTIVES (ἐγώ, ἔγωγε, ἐμέ, μοι / ἡμῖν / ἐμός): 1. 10, 11 (×3), 2.11, 12 (×2), 19, 3.1 (×2), 3, 8, 12.

(*c*)   'KNOW' (γιγνώσκειν, γνώμη / οἶδα): 1.3*, 7* (×2), 11* (γνώμη), 13*, 14* (×1* + ×1), 18, 2.9*, 14* (εἰδώς), 16*, 18* (εἰδώς), 19* (×2), 20, 3.3 (οἶδα), 10* (×2).

X constantly reiterates throughout the treatise that the Athenian *demos*, despite their innate ignorance (ἀμαθία 1.5, 7), know what they are doing politically, and are thereby very successful in preserving their democracy.

(*d*) 'SEEM, THINK, DECIDE' (δοκεῖ, δοκοῦσι, ἔδοξε): 1.1 (×2), 2, 14, 15, 16, 2.1, 17, 3.1, 10.

(*e*) 'CHOOSE' (αἱρεῖσθαι): 1.1* (×3), 2.20, 3.10* (×4), 11* (×3).

(*f*) 'NECESSARY' (ἀνάγκη, ἀναγκάζειν): 1.11, 14, 16, 18 (×2), 19, 2.17, 3.6, 7.

(*g*) 'NEED' (δέομαι): 1.3*, 12, 2.3, 3.3.

(*h*) 'MUST' (δεῖ, χρή): 1.3, 6, 18, 2.7, 3.2, 4, 5, 6 (×3), 7 (×2), 8 (×2), 12 (×2), 13.

(*i*) 'ABLE' (οἷόν τ᾿ ἐστι, οἷοί τ᾿ εἰσι): 1.20, 2.2 (×2), 4, 5 (×2), 9, 11, 3.1, 2 (×2), 8 (×4), 9.

(*j*) 'POSSIBLE' (ἔξεστι): 1. 10, 2. 4, 5, 13, 17.

(*k*) 'GOOD / ILL WILL' (εὔνους, εὔνοια / κακόνοια): 1.7 (×2), 3.10 (×3).

(*l*) 'JUST, JUSTIFIED / UNJUST' (δίκαιος, δίκαιον, δικαίως / ἄδικος, ἀδίκως, ἀδικεῖν): 1.2 (×2), 13, 2.17, 20, 3.5, 6, 7, 12 (×4), 13 (×3).

(*m*) 'PRIVATE, INDIVIDUAL' (ἰδίᾳ): 2.8, 10 (×2), 18.

(*n*) 'RATHER' (μᾶλλον), usually indicating a comparison: 1.5, 18, 2.8, 14, 19.

(*o*) 'SOME, SOMETIMES' (ἔνιοι, ἐνιότε): 1.5, 11, 2.4, 10, 19, 3.1.

(*p*) 'STRONG' (ἰσχύς, ἰσχυρός, ἰσχύειν): 1.4, 14 (×2, once as class label), 15.

(*q*) 'HAVE / ASSIGN MORE' (πλέον ἔχειν, ἀπολαύειν / νέμειν): 1.2*, 4, 2.10*, 18.

(*r*) 'DO WELL, BETTER' (εὖ, ἄμεινον πράττειν): 1.1, 4 (×2), 17 (×2).

(*s*) 'GOOD THING/S' (neuter) (ἀγαθόν, ἀγαθά):1.6 (×3), 7, 9, 14, 15, 16, 2.17, 19 (in the last two passages contrasted with 'bad', κακόν).

(*t*) 'BENEFIT / ADVANTAGE' (ὠφελεῖν, ὠφελία / λυσιτελεῖ / σύμφερον): 1.3* (×2), 7, 11, 13.

(*u*) 'THERE' (αὐτόθι): 1.2, 10 (×2), 11, 13, 3.1, 6 (always of Athens).

(*v*) 'AT ATHENS' (Ἀθήνησι): 1.10, 14, 16, 2.1, 19, 3.1, 3, 8, 12 (×2), 13 (×3).

Appendix 6. Examples of verbal repetition

1.1 οὐκ ἐπαινῶ . . . οὐκ ἐπαινῶ.

1.2 τῶν γενναίων . . . οἱ γενναῖοι.

1.2–3 μετεῖναι ἔν τε τῷ κλήρῳ . . . (3) κλήρῳ . . . μετεῖναι.

1.3 ὁ δῆμος . . . αὐτὸς ἄρχειν . . . ἄρχειν . . . ὁ δῆμος ἄρχειν.

1.5 τὸ βέλτιστον . . . τοῖς βελτίστοις.

1.6 βουλεύειν . . . βουλεύονται . . . ἐβούλευον.

1.6–7 οὐκ ἀγαθά . . . τὸ ἀγαθὸν . . . (7) ἀγαθὸν.

1.8–9 εὐνομουμένης . . . εὐνομεῖσθαι . . . (9) εὐνομίαν.

1.10–12 τῶν δούλων δ᾿ αὖ καὶ τῶν μετοίκων . . . ὁ δοῦλος . . . τὸν δοῦλον . . . ἢ τὸν μέτοικον . . . δοῦλον . . . οἱ δοῦλοι καὶ οἱ μέτοικοι . . . (11) τοὺς δούλους . . . δοῦλοι . . . τὸν ἐμὸν δοῦλον . . . ὁ ἐμὸς δοῦλος . . . ὁ σὸς δοῦλος . . . (12) καὶ τοῖς δούλοις . . . καὶ τοῖς μετοίκοις . . . μετοίκων . . . καὶ τοῖς μετοίκοις.

1.13 ἐπιτηδεύοντας . . . ἐπιτηδεύειν.
1.13 ταῖς χορηγίαις . . . χορηγοῦσι . . . χορηγεῖται.
1.14 μισοῦσι . . . μισεῖσθαι.
1.14 σῴζουσι . . . σῴζειν.
1.14–16 τῶν συμμάχων . . . ταῖς συμμαχίσι πόλεσι . . . (15) οἱ σύμμαχοι . . . τῶν συμμάχων . . . (16) τοὺς συμμάχους . . . τὰς πόλεις τὰς συμμαχίδας.
1.19 ἐν τοῖς ὑπερορίοις . . . τὴν ὑπερορίαν.
1.19 τῇ κώπῃ . . . κώπην.
1.20 μελέτην . . . ἐμελέτησαν . . . προμεμελετηκότες.
2.1 τὸ δὲ ὁπλιτικὸν . . . τὸ ὁπλιτικόν.
2.2–7 τοῖς δὲ κατὰ θάλατταν ἀρχομένοις . . . οἱ δὲ κρατοῦντες θαλασσοκράτορές εἰσιν . . . (3) τῶν ἀρχόντων τῆς θαλάττης . . . (4) τοῖς ἄρχουσι τῆς θαλάττης . . . (5) τοῖς μὲν κατὰ θάλατταν ἄρχουσιν . . . (6) οἱ δὲ κατὰ θάλατταν preceded by κράτιστοι . . . (7) διὰ τὴν ἀρχὴν τῆς θαλάττης . . . διὰ τὴν ἀρχὴν τῆς θαλάττης.
2.9 θυσίας . . . θύειν . . . θύουσιν.
2.9 εὐωχεῖσθαι . . . εὐωχούμενος.
2.11 πλοῦτον . . . εἰ γάρ τις πόλις πλουτεῖ . . . εἴ τις . . . πλουτεῖ πόλις.
2.11 ποῖ διαθήσεται, ἐὰν μὴ πείσῃ τὸν ἄρχοντα τῆς θαλάττης . . . ποῖ διαθήσεται, ἐὰν μὴ πείσῃ τὸν ἄρχοντα τῆς θαλάττης.
2.13 ἤπειρον . . . ἤπειρον.
2.14 ὑπέρχονται . . . ὑπερχομένους.
2.14–16 εἰ γὰρ νῆσον οἰκοῦντες . . . (15) εἰ νῆσον ᾤκουν . . . νῆσον οἰκούντων . . . εἰ νῆσον ᾤκουν . . . εἰ δὲ νῆσον ᾤκουν . . . (16) οἰκήσαντες νῆσον.
2.15 στασιάσαι . . . εἰ στασιάσαιεν . . . στασιάσειαν.
2.17 τὴν αἰτίαν . . . αἰτιᾶται . . . τὴν αἰτίαν.
2.18 κωμῳδεῖν . . . ὁ κωμῳδούμενος . . . κωμῳδοῦνται . . . κωμῳδουμένους.
2.19–20 γιγνώσκειν . . . γιγνώσκοντες . . . (20) ἔγνω.
2.19–20 ὄντες . . . τοῦ δήμου . . . (20) ὢν τοῦ δήμου.
2.20 συγγιγνώσκω . . . συγγνώμη.
3.1 τὸν μὲν τρόπον . . . τῷ τρόπῳ.
3.1–3 χρηματίσαι . . . χρηματίσαντες . . . (2) χρηματίσαι . . . (3) χρηματιεῖται.
3.2–3 διαπράττεσθαι . . . (3) διαπράττεσθαι . . . διαπράττεσθαι . . . διαπρᾶξαι.
3.3 ἀργύριον . . . ἀργύριον . . . ἀργύριον.
3.4 ὅσα ἔτη . . . ὅσα ἔτη . . . ὅσα ἔτη.
3.4–6 διαδικάζειν / διαδικάσαι / διαδικάζεσθαι × 8.
3.5 ὑβρίζωσί . . . ὕβρισμα.
3.6 δι' ἐνιαυτοῦ . . . δι' ἐνιαυτοῦ.
3.6–7 ἀνάγκη . . . (7) ἀνάγκη.

3.7 δικάζειν . . . δικάζειν . . . δικαστήρια . . . τῷ δικαστηρίῳ . . . δικαστὰς
. . . δικαίως δικάζειν.
3.8 ἑορτὰς . . . ἑορτὰς.
3.8–9 πλὴν εἰ κατὰ μικρόν τι οἷόν τε τὸ μὲν ἀφελεῖν τὸ δὲ προσθεῖναι . . . (9)
πλὴν . . . κατὰ μικρόν τι προσθέντα ἢ ἀφέλοντα.
3.9 ἐξευρεῖν . . . ἐξευρεῖν.
3.10–11 αἱροῦνται . . . ᾑροῦντο . . . ᾑροῦντ᾽ . . . αἱροῦνται . . . (11) αἱρεῖσθαι . . .
εἵλοντο . . . εἵλοντο.
3.10 εὔνουν ἐστὶ τῷ δήμῳ . . . εὔνουν τῷ δήμῳ . . . εὐνοοί.
3.11 ἐντὸς ὀλίγου χρόνου ×3.
3.12–13 ἀδίκως ἠτίμωται . . . ἀδίκως ἠτίμωνται . . . δικαίως ἠτίμωνται . . .
ἀδίκως . . . (13) ἀδίκως . . . ἠτιμῶσθαι . . . δικαίως . . . τὰ δίκαια . . .
ἄτιμοί . . . τῶν ἀτίμων.
3.12–13 Ἀθήνησιν ×5.

Appendix 7. Generalisations

1 Present tense generalisations ('they do') about (a) the *demos* or 'they', (b) the
Athenians / Athens / the city, (c) others:
   1.2 a, 3 a, 4 a + a, 5 c + a, 6 a + c, 7 a + a, 8 a + a, 10 c + a, 11 a + c, 13 a, 14
   a + a + c, 15 a, 16 a + a, 19 a, 20 a.
   2.1 a, 2 c, 3 c, 5 c, 8 b + c, 9 b + a, 10 c + a, 11 a, 12 c, 13 c, 14 c + a, 15 a + b
   + a, 17 c + a + a, 18 a + c + c, 19 a + a, 20 c + c.
   3.1 c + a, 2 a + a + a, 5 c, 6 a, 8 a, 9 c, 10 b, 12 c, 13 a + a.

2 Past tense generalisations ('they have done'):
   1.13 a.
   2.7 a, 8 a, 9 a, 17 a.
   3.11 a.

3. Conditional generalisations ('if they do' / did') with (d) future or (e) present
implications:
   1.4 e, 6 e, 9 d, 14 d, 16 e.
   2.2 d, 11 d, 12 d.
   3.3 d + e, 7 d, 10 d.

4. Theoretical generalisations, (f) political, (g) military / strategic:
   1.5 f, 14 f.
   2.2 g, 4 g, 5 g + g, 6 g (all about 'the rulers of the sea').
   2.20 f.
   3.10 f.

INDEX

(References are to pages of the Introduction, Commentary and Appendixes)